DATE DUE			

GAYLORD M-2

Twayne's United States Authors Series

Sylvia E. Bowman, *Editor*

INDIANA UNIVERSITY

Eudora Welty

EUDORA WELTY

by RUTH M. VANDE KIEFT

Queens College

 15

Twayne Publishers, Inc.   ::   New York

To My Friend and Mentor
Austin Warren

Preface

FOR THE PAST THREE DECADES it has become increasingly apparent that some of the most vital American literary expression has been coming from the South. Among southern writers, the name and achievement of William Faulkner looms largest. He has taken what he calls his "postage stamp" of native Mississippi soil, given it a name (Yoknapatawpha County), populated it, and become its "Sole Owner & Proprietor." But as surely as the piece of country he has taken is created by his vision, and is therefore completely his own, so surely, in the domain of art, is that or any other country free for the taking of any artist who has the insight and vision to make it his own.

Eudora Welty has made no secret of her admiration for Faulkner's achievement. "People ask me about Faulkner," she says. "It's a big fact. Like living near a mountain." The remark shows a characteristic modesty and an equally characteristic independence and detachment. Faulkner's monumental achievement is a fact she recognizes with respect and pleasure, but it is essentially irrelevant to her own artistic aims and performance. She has staked out her own claim in that Mississippi country; and because of the strength and originality of her creative imagination, she has also made that country uniquely her own: attached it to her Mississippi "place" and its times, past and present, and as securely placed it in the timeless and universal realm of art.

For twenty-five years Miss Welty's fiction has delighted and puzzled her readers. A number of critical articles and reviews have been devoted to one or more of her volumes, and many explications have been written of individual stories. But the variety and significance of her work demand a more comprehensive treatment, which it is the purpose of this critical study of her fiction to supply.

Eudora Welty attempts to convey the inner life of Miss Welty's stories, and to show both their variety in form and content, and the patterns of their relationship to each other. The first chapter is an account of her literary career, and of the importance of "place" to her artistic creed and practice. The central themes of Miss Welty's fiction are discussed in the next two chapters: her emphasis on the mysteries of the universe, of personal identity, of human relationships; the methods she uses to convey these mysteries; and the varying and complex attitudes shown in their presentation. In the following two chapters Miss Welty's use of comedy and its related modes, and her projection of the world of dream and fantasy, are discussed. These four chapters are concerned primarily with the stories in the first two collections: *A Curtain of Green* and *The Wide Net*. Interpretations of Miss Welty's next two volumes, *Delta Wedding* and *The Golden Apples,* are followed by a study of the most recent collection of her stories, *The Bride of the Innisfallen,* and a tracing of the development of her technique and artistic vision. The final chapter seeks to clarify Miss Welty's position in relation to southern and other contemporary writers of fiction, and to provide a general appraisal of her achievement.

Because of their richness and complexity, Miss Welty's stories require the kind of patient and loving scrutiny we apply to poems. Hence the critical method of this present volume is largely that of detailed explication, with the free use of quotation. To treat the stories with dispatch would be to strip away tone and feeling, to leave only a skeletal idea or concept which could not be faithful to their total meaning. The stories go beautifully fleshed out in their language and their details; in showing the reader so much of these (though so little in comparison with what the stories contain), it is my hope that he will find himself led to where a discerning and sympathetic reading can place him: firmly and happily in their heart.

RUTH M. VANDE KIEFT

Acknowledgments

I am greatly indebted to the American Association of University Women Educational Foundation, which granted me the Minnie Cumnock Blodgett Fellowship, 1960-1961, for the purpose of writing this book, and to the Corporation of Yaddo for the privilege of working at Yaddo during the first two months of 1961. For her discerning and thorough critical reading of my manuscript and her salutary comments and suggestions, I am deeply indebted to Miss Virginia Prettyman; for similar kindly offices of friendship and criticism performed at various stages of my work, I should like to thank Professors Austin Warren and Joe Lee Davis, Miss Sylvia Berkman, Miss Virginia Rock, Robert Garis, Caesar Blake, Galway Kinnell, and Leonard Greenbaum. To Miss Sylvia Bowman I am obliged for her thoughtful editing. My greatest debt is to the gentle lady who wrote the stories, chiefly for writing them, but also for her kindness and generosity in granting me much valuable information through interviews and correspondence, and for giving me full permission to quote from her work.

I wish to make further acknowledgments to the following:

To Harcourt, Brace & World, Inc. for permission to quote from *A Curtain of Green*, copyright, 1936, 1937, 1938, 1939, 1941, by Eudora Welty; *The Robber Bridegroom*, copyright, 1942, by Eudora Welty; *The Wide Net*, copyright, 1943, by Eudora Welty; *Delta Wedding*, copyright, 1945, 1946, by Eudora Welty; *The Golden Apples*, copyright, 1947, 1948, 1949, by Eudora Welty; *The Ponder Heart*, copyright, 1953, 1954, by Eudora Welty; *The Bride of the Innisfallen*, copyright, 1949, 1951, 1952, 1954, 1955, by Eudora Welty.

To Russell & Volkening, Inc., 551 Fifth Ave., New York, for permission to quote from *Short Stories*, copyright, 1949, by Eudora Welty, and "Ida M'Toy," which first appeared in *Accent*, the Summer, 1942, issue.

To the Duke University Press for permission to quote from "Place in Fiction," by Eudora Welty, which first appeared in *South Atlantic Quarterly*, in the January, 1956, issue.

To *The Virginia Quarterly Review* for permission to quote

from "How I Write," by Eudora Welty, which first appeared in the Spring, 1955, issue.

To *The Hudson Review* for permission to quote from "In Yoknapatawpha," by Eudora Welty, copyright, 1948, by The Hudson Review, Inc., Vol. I, No. 4, Winter, 1949.

To *Harper's Bazaar* and Russell & Volkening, Inc. for permission to quote from "Some Notes on River Country," by Eudora Welty, which appeared in the February, 1944, issue; and "The Abode of Summer," by Eudora Welty, which appeared in the June, 1952, issue.

To The Condé Nast Publications Inc. and Russell & Volkening, Inc., for permission to quote from "Literature and the Lens," by Eudora Welty, which appeared in *Vogue* in the August 1, 1944, issue, copyright (c) 1944 by The Condé Nast Publications Inc.

To *The New York Times Book Review* and Robert Van Gelder for permission to quote from his article on Eudora Welty, which first appeared in the *Book Review* of June 14, 1942.

To the Johns Hopkins Press and Louis J. Rubin, Jr. and Robert D. Jacobs, eds., for permission to quote from *Southern Renascence*.

To The Macmillan Company for permission to quote "The Song of the Wandering Aengus," by W. B. Yeats, copyright, 1906, renewed 1934 by W. B. Yeats, from *Collected Poems*.

To *The Georgia Review* for permission to use my article on "The Mysteries of Eudora Welty," which first appeared in the September, 1961, issue, as a substantial part of Chapter Two in this present volume.

Contents

Chronology

1909   Born, April 13, in Jackson, Mississippi, daughter of Christian Webb Welty and Mary Chestina (Andrews) Welty.

1921- Attended Central High School, Jackson, Mississippi.
1925

1925- Attended Mississippi State College for Women, Columbus, Mississippi.
1927

1927- Attended University of Wisconsin, Madison, Wisconsin.
1929   June, took B.A.

1930- Attended Columbia University School of Business, studied advertising.
1931

1931   Return to Jackson; death of father.

1931- Work for local radio station. Society correspondent for Memphis *Commercial Appeal.*
1933

1933- Publicity work for W.P.A.
1936

1936   One-man show of unposed studies of Mississippi Negroes in Lugene Gallery, New York City. "Death of a Traveling Salesman" published in June *Manuscript.*

1937   "A Memory" and "A Piece of News" published in *The Southern Review;* "Flowers for Marjorie" and "Lily Daw and the Three Ladies," in *Prairie Schooner.*

1940   Diarmuid Russell becomes Miss Welty's literary agent.

1941   "A Worn Path" and "Why I Live at the P.O." published in *The Atlantic Monthly; A Curtain of Green* published. Second prize O. Henry Memorial Contest Award for "A Worn Path."

1942   *The Robber Bridegroom* published. First prize O. Henry Memorial Contest Award for "The Wide Net."

1942- Awarded a Guggenheim Fellowship.
1943

1943   *The Wide Net* published; *A Curtain of Green* published in England. First prize O. Henry Memorial Contest Award for "Livvie is Back."

1944 $1000 award from American Academy of Arts and Letters. On staff of *New York Times Book Review* for six months.

1945 *Delta Wedding* appeared serially in *The Atlantic Monthly*.

1946 *Delta Wedding* published.

1947 Speech entitled "Some Views on the Reading and Writing of Short Stories" given at Pacific Northwest Writers' Conference, University of Washington, Seattle, Washington. Three months' residence in San Francisco.

1948 *Music from Spain* published.

1949 *The Golden Apples* published.

1949- Renewal of Guggenheim Fellowship, travel to France,
1950 Italy, England.

1950 *Short Stories* published.

1951 Second prize O. Henry Memorial Contest Award for "The Burning."

1952 Election to National Institute of Arts and Letters; recording of three stories for Caedmon Publications; trip to Europe, England and Ireland.

1953 *The Ponder Heart* published in *The New Yorker*.

1954 *The Ponder Heart* published in book form; Modern Library Edition of *A Curtain of Green* and *The Wide Net.* Honorary LL.D. from the University of Wisconsin.

1955 Trip to Europe. Address on "Place in Fiction" given at Cambridge University. Receives William Dean Howells Medal of the Academy of Arts and Letters for *The Ponder Heart. The Bride of the Innisfallen* published. Honorary LL.D. from Western College for Women.

1956 *Place in Fiction* published; *The Ponder Heart* dramatized on Broadway; Honorary LL.D., from Smith College.

1958- Lucy Donnelley Fellowship Award from Bryn Mawr
1959 College.

1958- Honorary Consultant of Library of Congress.
1961

1960 Ingram Memorial Foundation Award in Literature.

1962 William Allan Neilson Professor, Smith College.

CHAPTER 1

The Natchez Trace

THE LITERARY CAREER of Eudora Welty[1] has something in common with several of her best stories. Striking in either case is both the disarming simplicity of the external facts, the setting, basic actions, and style, and the richness and complexity of the inner reality inherent in that simplicity. "Except for what's personal, there is really so little to tell, and that little lacking in excitement and drama in the way of the world"—this is the attitude speaking from behind the blue eyes of this tall, gentle woman when she is pressed for biographical information.

And yet how refreshing is even the fact of the modesty, simplicity, and privacy of the life and public manner, in contrast with so many noisier modern literary careers which keep pulling us sharply back to the life and away from the art. The detachment of Miss Welty's artistic vision, her habit of drawing her material from the outside world, and entering and meeting it with what is universal rather than personal and particular in her own private experience, keeps our eyes clearly focused on the stories; and in them, as in the person herself, we are struck not by poverty of experience, but by all the abundance of a life richly and fully lived.

Eudora Alice Welty was born on April 13, 1909, in Jackson, Mississippi, where she has spent most of her life. Her mother, Mary Chestina Andrews Welty, from West Virginia, and her father, Christian Webb Welty, from Ohio, moved to Jackson soon after their marriage in 1904. Her mother, a Virginian by descent, is of English, Irish, Scottish and French Huguenot stock, her father, German Swiss; both families came to America before the American Revolution. The families were alike in being country people who were also often schoolteachers, preachers, and country barristers. Christian Welty was president of the Lamar Life Insurance Company, a large and prominent southern firm. Miss Welty was an only daughter, but two

sons completed the family: one of them, Edward, is an archi-
tect; the other, Walter, who died in 1959, was with the Stand-
ard Life Insurance Company in Jackson.

One surmises from her fiction that Miss Welty's childhood
was packed full of events—the small glories, excitements, or
terrors which happen largely in the child's fantasies, play, and
delighted exploration of the world of nature and books: they
are best learned of through such stories as "The Winds," "Moon
Lake," and *Delta Wedding*, though these are not autobiographical in their facts. A bright, imaginative child and an avid
reader, she devoured everything she could lay her hands on,
including fairy tales and legends, Mississippi history, and adult
fiction. Like the little girls in "June Recital" she studied the
piano; she indulged her imagination by writing romantic stories
with exotic Parisian settings, one of which began with the sentence, "Monsieur Boule deposited a delicate dagger in Made-
moiselle's left side and departed with a poised immediacy."[2]
During her teens she was also instructed in drawing and painting, locally and in college.

From 1921 to 1925 Miss Welty attended Central High School
in Jackson, and then for two years she attended Mississippi
State College for Women, in Columbus. Encouraged by her
parents, who were always sympathetic toward her varying
hopes, she transferred to the University of Wisconsin in 1927,
where she became an English major and began a more serious
and focused study of English literature under Ricardo Quintana
and other professors. During these undergraduate years she was
interested in the great Russian novelists, and also began reading
Yeats, Virginia Woolf, Faulkner, and other modern writers.

After receiving her bachelor of arts degree in 1929, Miss
Welty decided to equip herself to earn a living. She entered
the School of Business at Columbia University, studied advertising for a year, wrote and sold advertisements on the side,
attended the theater, and enjoyed a pleasantly varied social
life. She sought work in New York, but it was the Depression;
she found nothing, and returned to Jackson. During the next
eight or nine years she held a number of jobs in advertising
and publicity and did some free-lance writing. The first of
these was a part-time job with radio station WJDX—the first
in Mississippi and a venture initiated by her father's insurance
company—at which she earned $65.00 a month for writing scripts
and being generally useful at assorted tasks (among which,

she said, was cleaning the canary bird-cage). She then did free-lance work for local papers, wrote the Sunday column of Jackson society for the Memphis *Commercial Appeal,* and worked briefly for an enterprising newspaperman whose attempts at starting a paper were, however, unsuccessful.

At her next (and first full-time) job with the W.P.A. she had the official title of "Junior Publicity Agent." In this capacity she traveled by bus and car all over the state of Mississippi, writing newspaper copy and taking photographs of various "projects," such as the rebuilding of Tupelo, Mississippi, after it had been demolished by a tornado, studying juvenile delinquency, putting up booths in county fairs, interviewing "everybody from farmers to the Key Brothers who stayed up in an airplane longer than anybody else up to then." This work, she later said, "let me get about the State and gave me an honorable reason to talk to people in all sorts of jobs."[3] The job was finished in 1936—"ten seconds after the election"—and then for a year she worked for the Mississippi Advertising Commission, writing copy and taking photographs designed to attract industry and tourists to the state.

Odd jobs these—but with her habit of sensitive observation she was developing as an artist. Always attracted to the colors, shapes, textures of the world, trees, the effects of light and shade, she had early combined her youthful interest in painting with a subsequently developed interest in photography. After her return to Mississippi in 1931, she began serious writing in a solitary, intuitive way, in an attempt to capture the mysterious atmosphere of places and the elusive, revealing actions and gestures of the people she encountered. She had the stories ready for publication, but she tried first to sell her unposed photographs of rural-Negro life to New York publishing houses, "thinking or hoping if they liked my pictures (which I thought were fine) they might be inclined to take my stories (which I felt very dubious about, but I *wondered* about them —they being what I cared about), but they weren't decoyed. Once a year for three or four years I carried around the two bundles under arm on my two-weeks' trip to New York, and carried them home again—not much downcast, perhaps because all the time I simply loved writing, and was going to do it anyway."[4] In 1936 a number of her unposed studies of Mississippi Negroes were displayed for a month in a one-man show in a small New York camera shop named the Lugene Gallery (the sponsor of the show being amazed at what could be done with her "beat-up, second-hand equipment").

More important, in June of that year her first published story appeared in a small magazine called *Manuscript*. The story, which had been accepted by editor John Rood, was "Death of a Traveling Salesman." During the next two years Robert Penn Warren and Albert Erskine, editors of the *Southern Review*, published six of her stories, including "A Memory," "A Piece of News," "A Curtain of Green," and "Petrified Man." In 1940 Diarmuid Russell (son of the Irish poet George Russell —"A. E.") became her friend and literary agent, and sold such stories as "Why I Live at the P.O." and "A Worn Path" to the *Atlantic* and other nationally known magazines. With the added championship of John Woodburn, an editor of Doubleday, Doran and Company, *A Curtain of Green* was published in 1941.

Her stories were well received; and with her literary career safely launched, Miss Welty was able to give up odd jobs and devote herself more fully to writing. She spent a summer at Yaddo in Saratoga Springs, New York, where her friend Katherine Anne Porter was working at the same time. A short novel, *The Robber Bridegroom*, was published in 1942, and her second collection of short stories, *The Wide Net*, in 1943. A full-length novel, *Delta Wedding*, appeared in 1946; a collection of related stories titled *The Golden Apples* in 1949; *The Ponder Heart*, a long story which had originally appeared in *The New Yorker*, was published in 1954; and the same year saw the publication of a Modern Library edition of *A Curtain of Green* and *The Wide Net*. Her last collection of short stories, *The Bride of the Innisfallen*, appeared in 1955. She is currently working on a long, comic story laid in the northeastern hill country of Mississippi.

Miss Welty's literary achievement has been recognized by the conferring of several honorary awards. In 1942 and 1943 she received first-prize O. Henry Memorial Contest awards for "The Wide Net" and "Livvie is Back"; she also held a Guggenheim Fellowship for two years and won the William Dean Howells medal for "the most distinguished work of American fiction" of the period from 1950-1955 (for *The Ponder Heart*); she has been elected to the National Institute of Arts and Letters, and from 1958 to 1961 has been an Honorary Consultant of the Library of Congress. In 1954 she gave a lecture on "Place in Fiction" while taking part in a six weeks' Conference on American Studies held at Cambridge University. In 1956 *The Ponder Heart* was dramatized by Jerome Chodorov and Joseph Fields, and produced on Broadway; "Why I Live at the P.O." has been televised. Her stories have been widely anthologized; most of her works have appeared in one or more British editions; and there have been translations into Italian, German, French, Dutch, Swedish, Danish, Japanese, and Burmese.

II

These facts speak of a solid achievement which, though it has not made Eudora Welty a public figure, has been gratefully acknowledged by lovers of good fiction. What is the most important conclusion to be drawn from these biographical facts as they relate to Miss Welty's fiction? It is that her paradoxical relation of simultaneous attachment to and detachment from the countryside, towns, and people of Mississippi, has given her work much of its peculiar intensity and perspective.

To speak of the attachment rather than the detachment is easier because the results are everywhere apparent in her stories and because Miss Welty has stated clearly, in several different contexts, the importance of place, not only to her own creative process but to fiction generally. Traveling around Mississippi on various "assignments," she had gathered material for some of her earliest stories; but there was quite enough to write about when she settled down in Jackson. In 1942 she told an interviewer: "When I decided just to go ahead and write stories I no longer could meet as many people, but that doesn't seem to matter much. Why, just to write about what might happen along some little road like the Natchez Trace—which reaches so far into the past and has been the trail for so many kinds of people—is enough to keep you busy for life."[5] And later, in "Some Notes on River Country," she said: "Perhaps it is the sense of place that gives us the belief that passionate things, in some essence, endure. Whatever is significant and whatever is tragic in a place live as long as the place does, though they are unseen, and the new life will be built upon those things—regardless of commerce and the way of rivers and roads and other vagrancies."[6] So Miss Welty reached back into history—the pioneer days when the Natchez Trace was wilderness—for such stories as "A Still Moment" and *The Robber*

Bridegroom; but the same country, in present time, was the setting for "Livvie" and "At the Landing." She has not often strayed from the Mississippi settings of her stories: the Jackson area; the Yazoo Delta cotton country; the red clay farms and hill country in the north and northeast; the forests, the Mississippi river bottoms; and the Natchez Trace. And when she has shifted to other settings, as in "Music from Spain" or "The Bride of the Innisfallen," she has continued to use place to define the feelings conveyed.

In her small volume *Place in Fiction*[7] Miss Welty provides a gentle apologetic for her view of place. She shows how the validity of great novels depends on the inevitability of their being placed exactly where they are because of the accumulated feelings which are associated with places and because characters are made actual and credible when they are fixed and confined by and in their settings. "Imagine *Swann's Way*," she says, "laid in London, or *The Magic Mountain* in Spain, or *Green Mansions* in the Black Forest. The very notion of moving a novel brings ruder havoc to the mind and affections than would a century's alteration in time." When place is convincingly drawn, the reader is under the "pleasing illusion" that what he views is indeed the world's reality instead of the author's. When the author has a place of his own (though he need not live there to write about it), he has roots, a "base of reference." She does not imply that the writing will be merely "regional" —a term she calls an "outsider's" term—for the writer, whether Jane Austen, Cervantes, Turgenev, or Emily Brontë, is simply writing about life. "It seems plain," she concludes, "that the art that speaks most clearly, explicitly, directly, and passionately from its place of origin will remain the longest understood. It is through place that we put out roots, wherever birth, chance, fate, or our traveling selves set us down; but where those roots reach toward—whether in America, England, or Timbuktu—is the deep and running vein, eternal and consistent and everywhere purely itself—that feeds and is fed by the human understanding."

If Miss Welty's attachment to her Mississippi "place" comes from the simple fact that it has long been her home, we may see in other biographical facts some of the reasons for her detachment from it. Since neither of Miss Welty's parents came from the deep South, we might call her a "second generation" southerner, her father the northern "immigrant," her mother from a "border state." Although she once remarked humorously that she could not remember suffering as a child "except from my father's being from Ohio, a Yankee,"[8] she has also—and more seriously—spoken of the advantages of her particular parentage because of its benefits in giving her perspective. Her ancestors were not part of the landed, aristocratic South, or southern small farmers, or politicians, or anything else which might have given her that strong sense of a blood inheritance of southern tradition which is to be found in so many of her distinguished southern contemporaries.

The pattern which made for detachment and perspective was enforced by her experiences in advertising and publicity. She was neither totally immersed in this work, nor strongly rebellious against it. Her father, whom she has described as being "of the gentlest possible character," was a cautious and successful businessman; it was he who urged her to take the advertising course at Columbia. The period was mid-Depression; her flair for painting and writing, which her adventurous mother always encouraged, could be put to practical uses in the writing of publicity and advertising copy, and in commercial photography. That she should have done this work at all is amusingly ironic, considering that several of her classmates must now be among the race which flourishes on Madison Avenue, with its techniques and goals so alien to those of art. That Miss Welty made an interesting and humane occupation of publicity work is, however, apparent from a humorous little sketch called "Hello and Good-bye" (*Atlantic*, July, 1947). In it she tells of an assignment on which she had to photograph a pair of Mississippi Beauty Queens who were leaving for a trip to New York. One of the girls, a sweet shy country-girl with a lovely soft face, is obviously new to the "beauty business." She is hot, bewildered, edging on exhaustion and panic, innocent of the techniques of posing. The other Queen, her "Hostess," has the bright confidence of experience, an inoffensively cheap readiness for posing, a proud, managerial air. The picture-taking narrator is witnessing and participating in a little human comedy, to which she responds with warmth and laughter.

It is apparent from this sketch, as from stories Miss Welty has written about people encountered in her travels, that her interest must have been focused on persons as ends in themselves rather than as means to the end of her function as publicity photographer and writer. This same humane attitude is evident in her remark about why she quit advertising: "It was too much like sticking pins into people to make them buy things that they didn't need or really much want. And then, too, advertising is so filled with taboos—you are scared to say this thing and that thing; scared to use this page and that kind of type, and so on. What's the use of learning fears?"[9]

This statement is mild personal protest, not an expression of disillusionment or revulsion. Miss Welty's attitude toward her odd jobs may be taken as symptomatic of her attitude toward American culture generally. As an artist, she does not seem to have felt any deep personal alienation from her culture; she has made no strong protests about the encroachments of industrialism or the passing of the old order. If she has preferred the South, it is not that she has condemned the North for commercialism or that she might not privately condemn the South for faults of its own. She has displayed in her stories no strong partisanship with any social or political cause. She is matter-of-factly at home in her Mississippian and American culture, and just as matter-of-factly distanced from it; she is both fully engaged in the life about her ("under-foot locally," as she once said), and observing it from without.

The independence which made for detachment is visible in other phases of Miss Welty's life. During her first two college years she attended a southern women's college: the last two she spent in a midwestern university. She has been a solitary, self-taught writer, and has never been attached to any literary group such as the Nashville Fugitives or Agrarians. She met certain members of those groups, many of whom became widely known as creative writers and "new critics" after a nucleus of them had settled at the University of Louisiana in Baton Rouge and used the *Southern Review* as the vehicle for their distinguished criticism, stories, and poems. Robert Penn Warren and Cleanth Brooks were serving as editors for the review, and Katherine Anne Porter, who also lived in Baton Rouge at the time, was a frequent contributor. Most warmly, they gave Miss Welty their friendship along with their encouragement. Without doubt Miss Porter's introduction to *A Curtain of Green* and Brooks and Warren's inclusion of "A Piece of News" and "Old Mr. Marblehall" in the first edition (1943) of their influential critical anthology, *Understanding Fiction*, did much to stimulate interest in Miss Welty's fiction among discerning readers. But before meeting any important literary friends, she had developed independently as a writer; she has never consciously been a member of any literary, political, or philosophical "school."

III

In happy possession of a supple, clear, and sympathetic mind and sensibility, Miss Welty has found the germs of her fiction in the living world around her. The inspiration of a story, she has said in an essay called "How I Write,"[10] is like a "pull on the line, . . . the outside signal that has startled or moved the creative mind to complicity and brought the story to active being: the irresistible, the magnetic, the alarming (pleasurable or disturbing), the overwhelming person, place, or thing." The pull of "Powerhouse" on the line of her imagination must have been strong and insistent, for she wrote that story rapidly just after going to a dance where the Negro jazz musician, Fats Waller, played with his band. Sometimes a vivid impression was made on her mind and heart by a few words and gestures of a person, and out of this simple human encounter the story was developed. For example, one day Miss Welty took a book and went along for company on a little excursion to the country with a painter friend. While the two were quietly engaged, an ancient Negress with a bright, weathered face chanced along. She asked Miss Welty to tie her shoes, a few words were exchanged, and the old woman, when asked about her age, said, "I was old at the Surrender." She became, of course, Old Phoenix, caught, fully rendered, on the worn path of her Natchez countryside "place," in serene and timeless ceremonial.

The stories which Miss Welty writes "by ear," as she puts it, are most easily set down. In these stories she surrenders to the sound of her characters' speaking voices: she is all along consciously selecting and shaping what they will say, and she rewrites extensively—as she does with all her stories—with the sense of being an auditor. "Petrified Man" is one of these stories, and she has an interesting tale to tell about it. She had sent it to "every editor in the alphabetical list" without success; when even her old friends at the *Southern Review* rejected the manuscript, she assumed the story to be a failure and threw it out. Somewhat later Robert Penn Warren, reversing his decision, wrote and asked her for it. She sat down and quickly rewrote the story "by ear." When years later she met Mr. Warren, the first thing she did was confess this, and he told her what had never occurred to her: she hadn't practiced duplicity, she'd revised!

Her stories "hang around" in her mind for a long time, and in the writing undergo countless and continuous revisions.[11] In the account of "How I Write" she describes a process of transformation in the creation of a story eventually titled "No Place for You, My Love." A change in the setting of the story produced drastic changes in characters and action: what was preserved was the subject itself, "exposure, and the shock of the world." The central predicament of the story had come to life for her in a scene altogether removed from that in which it had originally presented itself.

Because the creative process has worked in such widely differing ways for Miss Welty, she finds it difficult to generalize about how she writes her stories, except to say that she works harder the more she knows about writing. "I don't believe they are written in any typical, predictable, logically developing, or even chronological way." But she feels that all stories spring from one source within a writer, the "lyrical impulse of his mind—the impulse to praise, to love, to call up, to prophesy." What is praised, loved, and evoked in her stories is the life around her that presents itself as real, as irresistible.

To an interviewer she said, several years ago, "When you see yourself in proportion—as you're bound to do when you get some sense—then you see how much greater what is real is than anything you can put down";[12] and more recently, she remarked: "life keeps a jump ahead of art." Such a philosophy as Miss Welty's bestows a solid and scrupulous artistic integrity and preserves the writer from any inflation of ego. It has clearly relieved Miss Welty from undue concern for the fortunes of her stories. She is pleased and gratified when readers understand and enjoy her fiction, but seems to take quietly, on the whole, notices of failure. She is pleased too by the success of other writers; she is eager to praise their work, and she has frequently done so publicly in reviews and critical essays,[13] and privately, in conversation. Our principal concern is not, however, with the life or opinions of this modest author, but with her fiction.

CHAPTER 2

The Mysteries of Eudora Welty

I

ONE CANNOT undertake to write about the stories of Eudora Welty without feelings of trepidation and of hope because she has provided her readers and critics both with ominous warnings and with delightful allurements. It is as if the welcome mat were clearly out before her door while the sign on the gate post read "Keep Out," or as if she had given us a map to reach her but had not promised it wouldn't turn out to be the sketch of a labyrinth in which we would get hopelessly lost. The allurements are chiefly in the stories themselves. The warnings have been posted (quite unofficially) in a small volume on *Short Stories* (1950)[1] and in the essay called "How I Write" (1955). Following are some of the warnings:

> I have been baffled by analysis and criticism of some of my stories. When I see these analyses—most usually, "reduced to elements"—sometimes I think, "This is none of me". . . . Not that I am too proud to like being reduced, especially—but that I could not remember *starting* with those elements—with anything that I could so label.

> . . . .

> Beauty may be missed or forgotten sometimes by the analyzers because it is not a means, not a way of getting the story along, or furthering a thing in the world.

> . . . .

> It's hard for me to think that a writer's stories are a unified whole in any respect except perhaps their lyrical quality.

> . . . .

> The analyst, should the story come under his eye, may miss this gentle shock and this pleasure too, for he's picked up the story at once by its heels (as if it had swallowed a button) and is examining the writing as his own process in reverse, as though a story (or any system of feeling) could be more

accessible to understanding for being upside down. "Sweet Analytics, 'tis thou hast ravish'd me!"

. . . .

It's a mistake to think you can stalk back a story by analysis's footprints and even· dream that's the original coming through the woods. Besides the difference in the direction of the two, there's the difference in speeds, when one has fury; but the main difference is in world-surround. One surround is a vision and the other is a pattern for good visions (which—who knows! —fashion may have tweaked a little) or the nicest, carefullest black-and-white tracing that a breath of life would do for.[2]

We have to admit some pertinence to these complaints and warnings when we read some of the criticism of Miss Welty's fiction. But from another point of view, we can see in her warnings the traditional complaints of the artist against the critic: the artist's denial of coherent or logical "patterns" in his work, the wariness of attempts at "placing" him (which inevitably look like pigeon-holing), and the fear that analysis will not often produce understanding and may destroy delight. While the critic admits, however, that he may be doing some injustice to the uniqueness of any single story in the process of showing the relationships among several, he recognizes that the relationships are unmistakably *there*, that one story does often illuminate another, that patterns emerge in the work of any good writer. The critic can also protest finally, and joyfully, that no amount of analysis can destroy the irreducible meaning and beauty of any real work of art, and (because of his faith that knowledge and understanding increase delight) that his analysis won't have "killed" the story for any reader.

Miss Welty, doubtless like any other artist, writes "in the ultimate hope of communication." This is the promise, the hope, the allurement. "Always in the back of our heads and in our hearts," she says in *Short Stories*, "are such hopes, and attendant fears that we may fail—we do everything out of the energy of some form of love or desire to please." But the peculiar, apparently perverse habit of the best artists, she says, is to be obstructionists, and in this they give the illusion of "hold[ing] back their own best interests." This is because "beauty is not a blatant or promiscuous or obvious quality—indeed at her finest she is somehow associated with obstruction—with reticence of a number of kinds."

Miss Welty *knows* she is mysterious and "obstructionist," but she is so because there is no other way for her to communicate what she must. She asks for a reader of "willing imagination" who will not insist on "a perfect Christmas tree of symmetry, branch, and ornament, with a star at the top for neatness," but will find "the branchings not what he's expecting, . . . not at all to the letter of the promise—rather to a degree (and to a degree of pleasure) mysterious." In explaining one of her own stories in "How I Write," she says, "Above all I had no wish to sound mystical, but I did expect to sound mysterious now and then, if I could: this was a circumstantial, realistic story in which the reality *was* mystery."

Miss Welty's stories are largely concerned with the mysteries of the inner life. She explains that to her the interior world is "endlessly new, mysterious, and alluring"; and "relationship *is* a pervading and changing mystery; it is not words that make it so in life, but words have to make it so in a story. Brutal or lovely, the mystery waits for people wherever they go, whatever extreme they run to." The term "mystery" has here to do with the enigma of man's being—his relation to the universe; what is secret, concealed, inviolable in any human being, resulting in distance or separation between human beings; the puzzles and difficulties we have about our own feelings, our meaning and our identity. Miss Welty's audacity is to probe these mysteries in the imaginative forms of her fiction. The critic's task is to try to follow her bold pursuit analytically and discursively, to state what the mysteries are, and to show how she tries to communicate them.

II

We begin with the story called "A Memory," which might be recognized as more or less autobiographical even if Katherine Anne Porter (in her sympathetic introduction to *A Curtain of Green*) had not suggested it first, because here in seminal form are some of the central mysteries which have occupied Eudora Welty as a mature writer. It is the *nature* of the child lying on the beach which suggests what is to come, her preoccupation and her discoveries. An incipient artist, the child has a passion for form, order, control, and a burning need to identify, categorize, and make judgments on whatever comes within her vision. She does this by making small frames with her fingers, which is her way of imposing or projecting order on a reality which she has already guessed but not admitted to be a terrifying chaos. She is convinced that reality is hidden and that to discover it requires perpetual vigilance, a patient and tireless scrutiny of the elusive gesture which will communicate a secret that may never be completely revealed.

Paralleled with this "intensity" is another equal intensity: that of her love for a small blond boy, a schoolmate about whom she knows nothing, to whom she has expressed nothing, but whom she holds fiercely within the protective focus of her love— a protection of him and of herself and her expectations which is enforced by the dreary regularity of school routine. But one day the boy suddenly has a nosebleed, a shock "unforeseen, but at the same time dreaded," and "recognized." It is the moment when she receives her first clear revelation of mortality, when she perceives the chaos that threatens all her carefully ordered universe, and the vulnerability of her loved one; she recognizes the sudden violence, the horror of reality, against which she is helpless. This event makes her even more fiercely anxious about the boy, for she "felt a mystery deeper than danger which hung about him."

This event is also a foreboding of the experience the girl has on the beach when a family-group of vulgar bathers comes crashing into the world of her dream. Here is wildness, chaos, abandonment of every description, a total loss of dignity, privateness, and identity. There is destruction of form in the way the bathers protrude from their costumes, in the "leglike confusion" of their sprawled postures, in their pudgy, flabby figures; there is terrifying violence in their abuse of each other, their pinches and kicks and "idiotic sounds," their hurdling leaps, the "thud and the fat impact of all their ugly bodies upon one another." There is a hint of a final threat to human existence itself when the man begins to pile sand on the woman's legs, which "lay prone one on the other like shadowed bulwarks, uneven and deserted," until there is a "teasing threat of oblivion." The girl finally feels "a peak of horror" when the woman turns out her bathing suit "so that the lumps of mashed and folded sand came emptying out . . . as though her breasts themselves had turned to sand, as though they were of no importance at all and she did not care." The girl has a premonition that without form—the kind she has been imposing on reality by her device of framing things like a picture—there is for human beings no dignity nor identity, that beyond the chaos of matter lies oblivion, total meaninglessness. This is the vision of reality which must be squared to the dream; and so the girl must now watch the boy, still vulnerable, "solitary and unprotected," with the hour on the beach accompanying her recovered dream and added to her love.

This is one of the sorrowful or "brutal" mysteries which Miss Welty presents in her stories. The "joyful" mystery is, of course, the careful, tender, ravishing love, the exquisite joy, and the dream. Chaotic reality does not displace the dream; though reality proves to be as terrifying as the child might have guessed, the dream cannot be totally destroyed.

The same mystery is explored in "A Curtain of Green," for the brooding, fearful, scarcely conscious anticipation of the girl in "A Memory" is the anguished knowledge of the bereaved young widow, Mrs. Larkin. In this story we have a similar careful, protective, absolute love, to which comes the violent affront of the most freakish and arbitrary kind of accident: a chinaberry tree simply falls on and kills Mrs. Larkin's husband. When she sees the accident, she assumes instinctively that the power of her love can save him: she orders softly, "You can't be hurt," as though, like God, she can bring order out of chaos. "She had waited there on the porch for a time afterward, not moving at all—in a sort of recollection—as if to reach under and bring out from obliteration her protective words and to try them once again . . . so as to change the whole happening. It was accident that was incredible, when her love for her husband was keeping him safe." Human love is finally powerless against chaos.

Now the young widow must penetrate deeply the meaning of this reality, which is simply to ask the question raised by any devastating accident: why did it happen? She plunges herself into the wild greenness out of which death fell: nature unpruned, uncultivated, formless in its fecundity. In the process of plunging, she hopes to discover the essential meaning of nature; the knowledge itself will give her a kind of power over it, even though paradoxically she must abandon herself to it, become a part of it, lose her identity in it, as she does with her hair streaming and tangled, her uncertain wanderings, her submersion in the "thick, irregular, sloping beds of plants." She must look to see what is concealed behind that curtain of green.

Into the focus of her attention comes Jamey, the Negro

gardener, and once again she tries to seize control of destiny and effect her will, to give some meaning to the confusion and disorder of reality. If her love cannot preserve life, at least her fury and vengeance can bring death. Jamey's mindless serenity, his elusive self-possession, his quiet, inaccessible apartness (which signifies his calm acceptance of life) goad her into wonder and fury. For a moment she experiences a terrible lust for destruction. "Such a head she could strike off, intentionally, so deeply did she know, from the effect of a man's danger and death, its cause in oblivion; and so helpless was she, too helpless to defy the working of accident, of life and death, of unaccountability. . . . Life and death, she thought, gripping the heavy hoe, life and death, which now meant nothing to her but which she was compelled continually to wield with both her hands, ceaselessly asking, Was it not possible to compensate? to punish? to protest?" Out of oblivion—without malice or motive —she can cause a death, as her husband's death has come, motiveless, out of oblivion; yet her destructive action would also be meaningless because it is *not* compensation for her husband's death: it is even too pointless to be a protest; what would the protest be against? Life and death are arbitrarily given and taken, pointlessly interchangeable—how then can her action, or any human action, have meaning? And yet, how can a human being *not* protest?

No rational answer comes to Mrs. Larkin. There is only release, touched off by the sudden fall of a retarded rain: thus it is a chance of nature which saves her from committing a meaningless murder, just as it is a chance of nature which kills her husband. The rain seems to bring out the quiet and lovely essences, the inner shapes of things in all the profusion of that green place, for "everything appeared to gleam unreflecting from within itself in its quiet arcade of identity." Mrs. Larkin feels the rush of love ("tenderness tore and spun through her sagging body"); she thinks senselessly, "it has come" (the rain and the release). She drops the hoe, and sinks down among the plants in a half-sleep, half-faint, which is resignation; a blissful surrender to the mystery of nature, to the inevitable, because "against that which is inexhaustible, there was no defense." But her sleep has the look of death: there is the suggestion that only by sinking herself into final oblivion will she ever be released from her burning compulsion to wrest meanings from nature, to impose order on chaos, to recover her loved one.

These dark mysteries are further explored in a story called "Flowers for Marjorie." The story takes place during the Depression, and Howard and Marjorie, a poor young Mississippi couple, have gone to New York City to find work. Marjorie is pregnant, and Howard has been engaged in a humiliating and fruitless search for a job. He has now reached a point of despair in which he imagines that nothing can ever happen to break the inevitability of the pattern of being without work, without food, without hope. In his view there is no slight possibility of change or chance, a stroke of good luck; time, like their cheap alarm clock, ticks on with a bland, maddening pointlessness, because for Howard time has stopped.

But Marjorie, a warm feminine girl with soft cut hair, quietly and literally embodies an assumption of the significance of time, change, and progression. She has the matter-of-fact, yet deeply mystical knowledge that her rounding body holds a new life. She looks forward to a birth, and to Howard she seems in a "world of sureness and fruitfulness and comfort, grown forever apart, safe and hopeful in pregnancy"—the one flagrant exception to the fixed pattern of hopeless and pointless repetition. As if to tease Howard with the knowledge of her enviable exemption from despair, she has by chance found a bright yellow pansy which she places in the buttonhole of her old sky-blue coat and looks at proudly—"as though she had displayed some power of the spirit." In her human hope and submission, her gentle and loving reproaches against Howard's anxiety, she seems to him almost "faithless and strange, allied to the other forces." He finally shouts at her, out of his deep love turned into terrible despair, "just because you can't go around forever with a baby inside your belly, and it will really happen that the baby is born—that doesn't mean everything else is going to happen and change! . . . You may not know it, but you're the only thing left in the world that hasn't stopped!"

Then in a moment of wild objection to the affront of time and change in her whole being, of her content, security, and easiness, he seizes a butcher knife and stabs her quickly and without violence—so quickly that the girl stays poised in a perfect balance in her seat at the window, one arm propped on the sill and hair blowing forward in the wind; the relative stillness and composure of her life now become the absolute, ironic stillness of death. Howard watches her lap like a bowl slowly filling with blood. Then he hears the clock ticking loudly, and throws it out the window. By his action he has taken a destructive hold of time and change, correcting the only apparent flaw in his desperate logic of futility.

The events which follow can only be described as monstrous. Howard, half-numb and hysterical, flings himself on the town, only to be confronted with a series of crazily ironic pieces of good luck. It is as though chance had seized him by the throat and said, "You suppose nothing can happen to change the pattern, and *you* try to seize control. Oh, the universe is full of surprises—only *see* what can happen!"—and then throttled him and taken a gleeful revenge by playing a series of ingenious tricks on him. What a surprise when the small bright world of the glass-ball paperweight is deluged in a fury of snow, and when a man unaccountably drops a dime in his hand! What a surprise when the slot machine at the bar responds to his last nickel by disgorging itself so profusely that one of the men says, "Fella, you ought not to let all hell loose that way" (for the crazy logic of hell *has* been let loose since Howard has committed the murder)! And what a finally horrifying surprise when he walks through a turnstile to an arcade and becomes "the ten millionth person to enter Radio City," covered with all of the honor and glory of arbitrarily conferred distinction and publicity ("What is your occupation?" "Are you married?"—as photo-lights flash) and given a huge key to the city and an armful of bright red roses!

He flees in terror back to the flat. There in the little fourth-story room, full of the deep waves of fragrance from the roses, he "knew for a fact that everything had stopped. It was just as he had feared, just as he had dreamed. He had had a dream to come true." Here he is with his gift of flowers for his lovely flower-loving wife (whose round and fruitful lap should be filled with roses instead of a pool of blood)—his good luck, his "break," his "dream come true." And here he is also with his nightmare come true. He now faces the impossibility of any personally significant kind of chance or change or hope, the absolute and unalterable fact of death.

If love and happiness seem to be permanently insured (as in Mrs. Larkin's case), chance may annihilate them at a stroke; if misery and destruction seem unalterable, so that from despair people act in accordance with what they suppose to be their tragic inevitability (as in Howard's case), chance may surprise them, belatedly and irrelevantly, with a shower of gifts. Human beings cannot predict, they cannot control, they cannot protest against, they cannot even begin to understand the inscrutable workings of the universe.

III

These are the darkest mysteries that Miss Welty ever explores, for in no other stories does she confront her characters with all the terrors of chance and oblivion. However inarticulate, plaintive, lonely, or frustrating she shows love becoming in the experience of a human being, she never again reveals it in its final and stark impotence against the implacable inhumanity of the universe. The stories tell us something about her philosophical vision, which might be identified (at the risk of giving her work the "tweak of fashion" she deplores) as pessimistic and existential.

Through the experience of her characters she seems to be saying that there is no final meaning to life beyond the human meanings; there is no divine "surround," no final shape to total reality, no love within or beyond the universe (for all its ravishing beauties), however much of it there may be burning in individual, isolated human hearts. Through an inevitable act of mind and heart (which is like a blessed reflex, because love comes willy-nilly, or a compulsion, because the mind must impose its order), the individual makes whatever meaning is to come out of chaotic reality, and this is the existential act. There are only fragments of shape and meaning, here, there, and everywhere: those created by all the world's lovers and artists (the terms often become interchangeable in her vocabulary). And in Miss Welty's catholic and charitable vision, the lovers and artists would probably include most people at least some of the time. Thus her deepest faith is couched securely in her deepest scepticism.

One other story in which she plunges into metaphysical questions is "A Still Moment." In this story three men try to wrest final meanings out of human life from three different points of view. Each of these men—Lorenzo Dow, the evangelist; Murrell, the outlaw; and Audubon, the naturalist—is consumed with a desire to know, or do, or communicate something of burning urgency; and each is essentially frustrated in his mission. Lorenzo, consumed by divine love, has the passion to save souls, but his efforts are mocked not only by lack of response —his inability to light up all the souls on earth—but by far more threatening internal struggles. These come from his awareness that nature mocks him in its simplicity, peace, and unconscious effectiveness; that he is more susceptible to nature than to divine beauty; and that in his frequent encounters with death he manages to survive less because of his sense of divine guidance and protection than because some strange savage strength and cunning overtake him in the moment of danger. He is saved by an instinct which he identifies as the word of the devil, not an angel, because "God would have protected him in His own way, less hurried, more divine." Because of his precarious and costly faith and the doubts and frustrations and waste places of his own heart, he flies across the wilderness floor from one camp meeting to the next, filled with the terrible urgency of his message: "Inhabitants of time! The wilderness is your souls on earth. . . . These wild places and these trails of awesome loneliness lie nowhere, nowhere but in your heart."

Murrell, the outlaw killer, who believes himself to be possessed of the devil, falls in beside Lorenzo and settles on him for his next victim. His method is strangely ceremonial, for he rides beside the victim telling long tales, in which a "silent man would have done a piece of evil . . . in a place of long ago, and it was all made for the revelation in the end that the silent man was Murrell himself, and the long story had happened yesterday, and the place *here*." Lorenzo's passion is to save the inhabitants of time before Eternity; Murrell's is to "Destroy the present! . . . the living moment and the man that lives in it must die before you can go on." In the moment of hideous confrontation with the victim just before the murder, Murrell tries to lay hold on the mystery of being. He murders for the same reason that Mrs. Larkin almost murders Jamey: "It was as if other men, all but himself, would lighten their hold on the secret, upon assault, and let it fly free at death. In his violence he was only treating of enigma." Approaching the point of climax which is to be the still moment, he and Lorenzo are like brothers seeking light; for Lorenzo's divine passion is darkened by his sense of the tempter within him, and Murrell is less guilty than his crimes would make him appear because he has no other motive for killing than pure quest for the elusive mystery of being. Evangelist and murderer, soul-saver and destroyer, seem to become as one.

Audubon's light step on the wilderness floor, his serene and loving gaze at the earth, and the birds and animals around him, suggest at first a sharp contrast with the desperate urgency of the two men. He is a man who seems in harmony with nature, "very sure and tender, as if the touch of all the earth rubbed upon him"; a man who needs no speech because it is useless in communicating with birds and animals. But Audubon is presently seen to have his own urgency. The sweet excess of love gives him a compulsive and insatiable need to remember, to record in his journal, and to convey all the varieties of nature about him. His vigilant probing of nature is a quest for origins and ends; he does not know whether the radiance he sees is only "closed into an interval between two darks," or whether it can illuminate the two darks which a human being cannot penetrate, and "discover at last, though it cannot be spoken, what was thought hidden and lost." His endless examination of the outside world may disclose to him the mystery of his own identity. "When a man at last brought himself to face some mirror surface he still saw the world looking back at him, and if he continued to look, to look closer and closer, what then? The gaze that looks outward must be trained without rest, to be indomitable."

Here gathered in the wilderness, then, are three fiery souls, each absolute in its consuming desire, for "what each of them had wanted was simply *all*. To save all souls, to destroy all men, to see and to record all life that filled this world—all, all. . . ."

Into the still moment comes the beautiful, slow, spiral flight of the snowy heron; with its unconscious freedom, it lays quiet over them, unburdens them, says to them, "Take my flight." To each comes a revelation, and these revelations are inevitably disparate and subjective. With swift joy Lorenzo sees the bird as a visible manifestation of God's love. Murrell has a sudden mounting desire for confession, and a response of pity; he wishes for a keen look from the bird which could fill and gratify his heart: as though the bird had some divine power, and its sign of recognition could accuse and forgive simultaneously. Audubon gazes at the bird intensely as if to memorize it; and then, because he knows he cannot paint accurately enough from memory, he raises his gun to shoot it. As he does so, he sees in Lorenzo's eyes horror so pure and final as to make him think he has never seen horror before.

Audubon shoots the bird and puts it in his bag. The three men disperse; and for each of them it is as though his destiny has been sealed, the basic issue of his life clarified. Murrell lies in wait for the next victim: "his faith was in innocence and his knowledge was of ruin; and had these things been shaken? Now, what could possibly be outside his grasp?" He is filled with his glorious satanic dreams of conquest and darkness.

Audubon knows that he will paint a likeness of the bird which will sometimes seem to him beautifully faithful to its original; but this knowledge comes with the tragic awareness that even though he alone as artist has really *seen* the bird, he cannot possess or even reproduce the vision because his painting will be a dead thing, "never the essence, only a sum of parts." The moment of beauty can never be communicated, "never be one with the beauty in any other man's head in the world. As he had seen the bird most purely at its moment of death, in some fatal way, in his care for looking outward, he saw his long labor most revealingly at the point where it met its limit." The final frustration of the artist is that he can never capture the final mystery of life, nor convey it to others; no matter how faithfully and sensitively reproduced, nature remains inviolable and unknown.

Riding slowly away, Lorenzo has a terrifying vision, for it suddenly seems to him that "God Himself, just now, thought of the Idea of Separateness." He sees no apparent order or scheme in the divine management of things, because God is outside Time, and He does not appear to know or care how much human beings who live inside Time need order and coherence which alone can bring the lover to a final union with the loved object. God created the yearnings, but He did not provide a way of meeting the need. He seems to Lorenzo finally indifferent:

> He could understand God's giving Separateness first and then giving Love to follow and heal in its wonder; but God had reversed this, and given Love first and then Separateness, as though it did not matter to Him which came first. Perhaps it was that God never counted the moments of Time; Lorenzo did that, among his tasks of love. Time did not occur to God. Therefore—did He even know of it? How to explain Time and

Separateness back to God, Who had never thought of them, Who could let the whole world come to grief in a scattering moment?

In terms of the incident Lorenzo is saying: "Why did you let me see the bird, which was inevitably to love it, and see in it your love become visible, and share that love with the other watchers, only to let it be suddenly and pointlessly destroyed, so that I am now separated both from the beloved object, and from all who saw it or who might have seen and loved it?" Which is like saying, "Why do you allow death to happen?"— the question which also tortures the young wife in "A Curtain of Green."

Yet the "beautiful little vision" of the feeding bird stays with Lorenzo, a beauty "greater than he could account for," which makes him shout "Tempter!" as he whirls forward with the sweat of rapture pouring down his face. This is because he has again felt in his heart how overwhelmingly sensitive he is to the beauty of nature, and also how pointless and baffling is any attempt to relate it to divine love or meaning or plan or purpose; how pointless, then, is his mission to save souls. But he rushes on through the gathering darkness to deliver his message on the text "in that day when all hearts shall be disclosed." His final desperate gesture of faith is that when Time is over, meanings will be revealed; then the breach between Love and Separateness, the source of human tragedy, will be eternally closed. It is a faith that Miss Welty herself nowhere affirms: she only shows us, in the richly varied characters and situations of her stories, the intensity of the Love, and the tragic fact of the Separateness in the only life we know, which is our present life in Time. Miss Welty is asking metaphysical questions, but she is attempting no answers. The only solution to a mystery is yet another mystery; cosmic reality is a nest of Chinese boxes.

IV

With a sensitivity as detached as it is tender, so that we may not even notice the sympathy because of the sure, cool objectivity of her art (like Audubon, she is a careful and relentless observer), Miss Welty brings to life a number of characters each engaged in the private quest for the identity of the self, and the self in relation to the other. She is concerned about what she calls "the mystery of relationship" in all stages of awareness. The questions asked are "Who am I and who are you?" These are related to the questions "How can I get my love out into the world, into reality"—that is, communicated and understood—and "How can I see and know what is going on in *your* heart," which is sometimes to say, "How can I see my love returned and shared?"

In "The Hitch-Hikers" and "Death of a Traveling Salesman," two salesmen have a flash of insight into their own identity, which is pathetically and paradoxically that they *have* no identity because they have no place and no focus of love to define them. Tom Harris, the thirty-year-old salesman of "The Hitch-Hikers," appears to have been born with a premonition of his coming isolation, for as a child he had often had the sense of "standing still, with nothing to touch him, feeling tall and having the world come all at once into its round shape underfoot and rush and turn through space and make his stand very precarious and lonely." He lives in a world of hitch-hikers, and the title suggests that Harris himself is one of the transients despite the relative economic security provided by his job.

Tom Harris is a wise, tolerant, generous sort; people naturally confide in him and women are attracted to him, but he will not be held back by anyone. He is beyond surprise or shock because of his wide experience. With a peculiarly detached kind of suspense he views the events surrounding a murder committed in his car by one of the hitch-hikers, and this is because any strong emotion or violence in his life has always been something encountered, personally removed. There had been "other fights, not quite so pointless, but fights in his car; fights, unheralded confessions, sudden love-making—none of any of this his, not his to keep, but belonging to the people of these towns as he passed through, coming out of their rooted pasts and their mock rambles, coming out of their time. He himself had no time. He was free; helpless." Without an ounce of exhilaration in the knowledge of his freedom, and embracing with apparent resignation his knowledge of helplessness, he is found in the last scene poised for yet another flight, a puzzling, touching American phenomenon, exceptional only in the degree of his self-awareness.

The salesman of "Death of a Traveling Salesman," R. J. Bowman, comes to this awareness belatedly, by perceiving with the acute eye of a stranger the essence of the simple, rooted life of the couple whose crude hospitality he briefly enjoys. The painful contrast with his own loveless, rootless ways kills him as much as does the protest of his troublesome heart. By the end of the story he is beautifully ready for love, but he cannot live to enjoy it. The best comment on the two salesman stories is Miss Welty's own in quite another context—her essay on the importance of place in fiction: "Being on the move is no substitute for feeling. Nothing is. And no love or insight can be at work in a shifting and never-defined position, where eye, mind, and heart have never willingly focused on a steadying point." Just *seeing* this truth is enough to kill a man, although his salvation may lie in having seen it.

The salesmen barely got started in their quest for love and identity; but Clytie, in the story by that name, though less self-aware, has made some small progress. She is ready to emerge, to reach out toward others: she is full of the wonder and mystery of humanity, and there is a kind of breathless, religious awe in the way she scans the faces of the townspeople, seeing the absolute and inscrutable uniqueness of each one. "The most profound, the most moving sight in the whole world must be a face. Was it possible to comprehend the eyes and the mouths of other people, which concealed she knew not what, and secretly asked for still another unknown thing? . . . It was purely for a resemblance to a vision that she examined the secret, mysterious, unrepeated faces she met in the street of Farr's Gin." To the people of Farr's Gin, Clytie is ready to give that most generous of all gifts—contemplation: the desire to know without using, the respect for "otherness," the awe of what is inviolable. But she is suffocated and nauseated, living in a house of disease and death with her vampire-like sister, her alcoholic brother, her apoplectic father, and the dead brother with a bullet hole in his head. These faces come pushing between her and the face she is looking for, which is a face that had long ago looked back at her once when she was young, in a sort of arbor: "hadn't she laughed, leaned forward . . . and that vision of a face—which was a little like all the other faces . . . and yet different . . . this face had been very close to hers, almost familiar, almost accessible."

After a horrible experience in which, with "breath-taking gentleness," she touches the face of a barber who comes to shave her father, only to find it hideously scratchy, with "dense, popping green eyes," she dashes out to the old rain barrel, which seems to her now like a friend, and full of a wonderful dark fragrance. As she looks in, she sees a face—the face she has been looking for—but horribly changed, ugly, contracted, full of the signs of waiting and suffering. There is a moment of sick recognition, "as though the poor, half-remembered vision had finally betrayed her." That knowledge compels her to do the only thing she can think of to do: she bends her head down over and into the barrel, under the water, "through its glittering surface into the kind, featureless depth, and held it there."

What does her action mean? First of all, that she sees the ghastly disparity between what she once was and ought to have been (the loving, laughing creature of her youth) and what she has become (ugly, warped, inverted). Also, perhaps, she realizes that the only love in that house, if not in that town, was the love *she* made: there was no one then to embrace, no nature to plunge into but her own, no love possible but narcissistic love, no reality but her own reality, no knowledge possible but the knowledge of death, which is the immersion into oblivion. It is another pointless joke in a pointless universe. The final image of her as fallen forward into the barrel, "with her poor ladylike black-stockinged legs up-ended and hung apart like a pair of tongs," is one of the most grim jokes Miss Welty has ever perpetrated: it is only our memory of the wild misfiring of Clytie's love which makes us hear the narrator say, "See her coldly as grotesque, but see her also tenderly as pathetic."

The situations in all these stories seem fundamentally tragic or pathetic. It is when the loving heart is awakened in finding an object that joy speaks out in the stories, almost inaudibly in "First Love," somewhat more clearly in "At the Landing," and loudly and triumphantly in "A Worn Path." Joel Mayes, the solitary little deaf-mute of "First Love," is dazzled into love by a single gesture of Aaron Burr's, a gesture which brings a revelation:

> One of the two men lifted his right arm—a tense, yet gentle and easy motion—and made the dark wet cloak fall back. To Joel it was like the first movement he had ever seen, as if the world had been up to that night inanimate. It was like a signal to open some heavy gate or paddock, and it did open to his complete astonishment upon a panorama in his own head,

about which he knew first of all that he would never be able
to speak—it was nothing but brightness. . . .

A single beautiful movement of human strength and careless
grace has crystallized a love which is fated to be as inarticulate
as it is sweetly wondering and intense. Quietly, night after
night, the little boy sits watching his beloved, adoring his nobility, his mystery, his urgency. The boy's presence is accepted
by the conspirators, but ignored. Joel has no way of expressing
his love, except by trotting like a little dog around his master,
sniffing out the dangers that lie in his path, for Joel constantly
senses the imminence of disaster, and the dread of coming
separation. "Why would the heart break so at absence? Joel
knew it was because nothing had been told." And yet even
if the moment of revelation *did* come, when love might speak
out, he knows there are no words for what it might say. Gazing deeply into the face of the sleeping Burr, he has a terrible
wish to speak out loud; "but he would have to find names for
the places of the heart and the times for its shadowy and tragic
events, and they seemed of great magnitude, heroic and terrible and splendid, like the legends of the mind. But for lack
of a way to tell how much was known, the boundaries would
lie between him and the others, all the others, until he died."
The most he can do for Burr is to quiet his nightfears by gently
taking his hand, stopping his nightmare ravings from the ears
of potential eavesdroppers. When Burr leaves town Joel feels
he will "never know now the true course, or the outcome of
any dream." His love never gets *in the world,* but it is less
pathetic than Clytie's because at least it has found an object,
it has flowered.

"In the world" is a key phrase in the story of Jenny Lockhart
called "At the Landing." It is the hearts of her family that are
locked: she is caught in the house of pride, tradition, "culture,"
and death, folded in the womb of that house by her grand-
father. Through the painful birth process of discovery and
experience she comes to the landing, the taking-off place, and
so out into the world. The world, the forces of life, are symbolized by the river and the flood, which inundate Jenny's
house and the graveyard where her relatives are buried. Billy
Floyd, a wild creature of mysterious origins who fishes on the
river, rides along on the flood and is master of it, is the one

who brings her into the world: not only by his sexual violation of her, but more quietly and surely through her adoring response to his wild beauty, through the revelations which come to her about herself and him, and about love, which are the chief concern of the story.

Jenny learns almost as much about love, about its mysteries and changes, and the mystery of human identity, as it is possible to learn. These revelations come to her by seeing, feeling, and guessing—by intuitive perception. For example, simply in watching Billy's innocence as he drinks deeply and then throws himself on the grass to sleep, she knows her innocence has left her: this is because a knowledge of innocence presupposes some knowledge of experience, of what might *not* be innocent, out of which contrast springs the recognition of innocence. Or she learns how love "would have a different story in the world if it could lose the moral knowledge of a mystery that is in the other heart": that is, if people who love were less aware of how both vulnerable and inviolable their lovers were, they could speak their minds more fully, ride over each other more freely with their aggressions, or attack each other more analytically; but they could not, of course, learn much more about each other, or achieve more satisfaction by doing so (even though, human nature being what it is, they inevitably *will* do so). Watching Billy ride the red horse becomes for her a kind of anticipation of the sexual act, through which she learns that "the vaunting [male] and prostration [female] of love told her nothing": that is, sexual experience in itself cannot disclose the mystery of human identity nor bring people together.

When she sees Billy Floyd in the village store, he seems changed: there is "something close, gathering-close, and used and worldly about him, . . . something handled, . . . strong as an odor, the odor of the old playing cards that the old men of The Landing shuffled every day over their table in the street." If she presses him now, corners him in that small place, she will discover his identity, and that will be something small, mean, and faintly dirty—for he is thought by the literal-minded to be "really the bastard of one of the old checker-players, that had been let grow up away in the woods till he got big enough to come back and make trouble." But he conquers her with his defiant look, and she wisely lets him escape, knowing that this is *not* his true and final definition: his origins are more wild and wonderful (is the Natchez Indian in his blood?—is he one of the people of the lost Atlantis?); his nature cannot be defined by the context of the village store and the odors of old playing cards.

She learns too the value of her love ("what my heart holds this minute is better than what you offer the least bit less"), and how enormously precious is her whole nature, which must be learned slowly, patiently, tenderly ("She looked outward with the sense of rightful space and time within her, which must be traversed before she could be known at all"). She knows also that "what she would reveal in the end was not herself, but the way of the traveler": that is, she has no final revelations to give to any lover; she is only herself, like every other human being, on a perplexing journey through life, engaged in the perpetual and difficult process of finding herself, her meaning, her destination. The most two people can do is to travel together for a while. Billy Floyd has his own search, and she has hers. These are only a few of the amazing discoveries Jenny makes in her birth process, the process of coming into the world; and each discovery is, of course, only the revelation of yet another human mystery. At the end of the story she is only starting her wait for Billy Floyd. She has "arrived," she has been born (and with what violence in that series of rapes at the hands of the river men); but she hasn't yet really begun the journey; she is "at the landing."

Jenny's love barely manages to get articulated; its actions in the world are fumbling and largely ineffectual; and at the end of the story she is left, like Joel, separated from her loved one. But the love of Old Phoenix in "A Worn Path" is most triumphantly realized "in the world." It has a clear object—her grandson; it is actualized, put out into reality, not only by her care of him, but in the periodic ceremonial act of her trip along the worn path into town to fetch the "soothing medicine." There are no significant barriers to the expressive love of old Phoenix, and this is reflected also in her sense of familiarity with nature—the ease with which she talks to the birds and animals—and in her ability to live as readily, interchangeably, and effectively in the realm of the fanciful and supernatural as she does in the realm of practicalities. She is, like Dilsey in *The Sound and the Fury,* a completely and beautifully harmonious person—something one does not often find in the fiction of either Miss Welty or Faulkner.

V

What happens when love finds fulfillment in the most natural and happy way possible, physically and emotionally, when it is both communicated and returned and is solidly "in the world" socially and legally through marriage? Is there then an end to the mysteries of the self and the other? In several of her stories Miss Welty shows there is not; she indicates, in fact, that the one thing any married person cannot do is to assume knowledge of the other, or try to force it in any way, or make a predictable pattern of a relationship, or block the independence, or impede the search of the other. A relationship of love can be kept joyful, active, free, only if each partner steps back now and then to see the other with a fresh sense of his inviolable otherness, his mystery, his absolutely sacred and always changing identity. Out of some deep need to establish the new perspective, to insist on freedom and apartness, one partner may simply run away from the other, withdraw, or go into temporary "retreat." This is a basic situation in "A Piece of News," "The Key," "The Wide Net," *The Robber Bridegroom, Delta Wedding,* "Music from Spain," "The Whole World Knows," and "The Bride of the Innisfallen." The quarrels and separations presented in these stories are not the ordinary distressing marital quarrels which spring from hate, aggression, and conventional domestic discord, for none of these lovers has ceased to love or want the other. Each of them is simply demanding in his own way: "See me *new.* Understand the changes in me, and see how I am apart from you, unknowable and not to be possessed: only when you see me new can you possess me fully again."

The theme is given a semi-comic treatment in "A Piece of News." Ruby Fischer, a primitive, isolated and apparently unfaithful young backwoods wife, chances on a newspaper story in which a girl with the same name is shot in the leg by her husband. Though Ruby knows such an action on her husband Clyde's part to be quite improbable—even though he knows of her infidelities—she is immediately struck with the imaginative possibilities of such a situation, and is marvelously impressed and flattered. Images of herself dying beautifully in a brand-new nightgown, with a remorseful Clyde hovering over her, play delightfully in her mind. The romantic view of herself extends to her whole body; and while preparing dinner after Clyde returns, she moves in a "mysteriously sweet . . . delicate and vulnerable manner, as though her breasts gave her pain." When she discloses to Clyde the secret of the newspaper story, there is a moment, before common sense triumphs, when the two of them face each other "as though with a double shame and a double pleasure." The deed *might* have been done: "Rare and wavering, some possibility stood timidly like a stranger between them and made them hang their heads." For an instant they have had a vision of each other in alien fantasy roles—an experience which is pleasing, exciting, and rather frightening.

The theme is again treated with tender humor in "The Key." Ellie and Albert Morgan are dramatically shut off from the outside world by being deaf-mutes. When the story opens, we find them sitting tautly in a railroad station, waiting for the departure of their train to Niagara Falls. Ellie, a large woman with a face "as pink and crowded as an old-fashioned rose," is by far the stronger of the two. Little Albert, "too shy for this world," seems to be Ellie's own "homemade" product, as though she had "self-consciously knitted or somehow contrived a husband when she sat alone at night." But he is neither defeated nor submissive: there is an occasional sly look in his eye which tells of a secret hope and anticipation, a waiting for some nameless surprise indefinitely withheld.

It comes at last in the form of a key accidentally dropped by a young man, a curious red-haired stranger who bears some kinship to Harris of "The Hitch-Hikers" and to George Fairchild of *Delta Wedding*. He is marvelously fiery, young and strong, compassionate, sensitive, with a lovingly humorous detachment. But the observer-narrator senses that he will "never express whatever might be the desire of his life . . . in making an intuitive present or sacrifice, or in any way of action at all —not because there was too much in the world demanding his strength, but because he was too deeply aware." His life is both full of giving and empty of permanent commitment; he has Harris' freely floating love and weariness.

The key, which drops apparently out of the sky at Albert's feet, immediately becomes the thing he has been waiting for, richly portentous—he sits there glowing with "almost incandescent delight." The young man senses this and doesn't reclaim the key; he stands apart watching the fingers go as Albert and Ellie talk in their own private language. What does it mean?

Maybe now they'll really fall in love at Niagara Falls; maybe they didn't have to marry just because they were afflicted and lonely; maybe they can love, be happy, like other people. They wait importantly and expectantly.

But they miss their train—they can't, of course, hear it coming and going so quickly. Shock! At once Ellie resumes her old mode of domination and organizes her "counter-plot" against the outside world, which is obviously hostile to their hopes and plans. But Albert refuses to be crushed now—he has the key; he is delightedly, securely inward. Ellie is baffled: she can't get through to him. Because the strange, funny, and pitiful little irony of their relationship is that Ellie "talks" too much. When they are on the farm together and she feels some unhappiness between them, she has to break off from her churning to assure Albert of her love and protection, "talking with the spotted sour milk dripping from her fingers." All her talk just makes the fluid, simple, natural farm life "turn sour." Security runs away in the face of Ellie's panic.

Ellie sits there, heavy with disappointment as she thinks about Niagara Falls, and her conviction that they would even *hear* it in their bodies through the vibrations. She is going to brood over the whole incident and the terrible disappointment, as she does over all their discussions, misunderstandings, agreements—"even about the secret and proper separation that lies between a man and a woman, the thing that makes them what they are in themselves, their secret life, their memory of the past, their childhood, their dreams. This to Ellie was unhappiness." She is afraid of Albert's private life, of all his secrets that cannot be hers. Loneliness and isolation compel her to claim *all*—to work herself into every corner of his pitifully limited experience. But Albert really isn't tamed despite his obedience—he stubbornly preserves his quiet, intensely personal identity, and he has the key to it in his pocket. Maybe the key wasn't, as he first thought, the symbol of a coming happiness through the Niagara Falls expedition; maybe it was "something which he could have alone, for only himself, in peace, something strange and unlooked for which would come to him." Poor Ellie.

But the red-haired stranger with his god-like compassion and omniscience (how much of all this does he guess?—the narrator seems to have infinite faith in his awareness), has a key for Ellie too. She is not to be left, literally or figuratively, out in the cold. The key he places in her hand bears the legend, "Star Hotel, Room 2." What could be neater or lovelier? The designated use to its owner of Albert's key is never disclosed. The imagination can soar on that one; it is appropriate as the symbol of Albert's secret hope, his own unique humanity, a thing shared with, endowed by the mysterious, god-like young man. Ellie's key to the young man's hotel room is appropriately practical—she is the one who "manages"; and yet it has its exciting edge. Why do honeymooners travel to Niagara Falls, after all, except to repair to hotel rooms? This room is in the *Star*, and that's what Ellie has been wishing on. Perhaps she will yet see her wish fulfilled for a "changing and mixing of their lives together."

But the story ends with the young man's faintly dismal, realistic vision, not of the possibilities, but of the probabilities. As he departs, lighting a cigarette, we can see his eyes by the light of the match, and in them, "all at once wild and searching, there was certainly, besides the simple compassion in his regard, a look both restless and weary, very much used to the comic. You could see that he despised and saw the uselessness of the thing he had done." He may have god-like prescience and compassion, but he hasn't the omnipotence—he can't *change* things.

Ellie and Albert are extraordinary, but their problem is not. People do not have to be deaf-mutes to be driven together by the felt hostility of the outside world, and the inevitable pattern then is one of a too insistent closeness. Ellie has to learn that Albert has a right to his secret—he'll keep that key in his pocket as long as he lives.

A version of this theme which bears some resemblance to the Cupid and Psyche myth appears in Miss Welty's romping fantasy, *The Robber Bridegroom*. Rosamond, the lovely heroine, has been kidnapped by a bold bandit of the forest; but she finds the arrangement much to her liking. The one prohibition —the forbidden fruit in her Eden—is any attempt to discover her bridegroom's identity, which is disguised by wild berry stain. Rosamond's idyllic state continues until the satanic stepmother tempts her to break the prohibition and provides her with a recipe for a brew to remove the berry stain. In the night when her bandit lover is sleeping, Rosamond wipes the stains off his face. He awakens, and she is distressed to find that he is only Jamie Lockhart, the well-scrubbed, dull, respectable young man who had come at the request of her father,

Clement, to search for and capture the robber bridegroom. Jamie, in turn, now recognizes Rosamond as "Clement Musgrove's silly daughter," and both of them are thoroughly disenchanted with each other. The truth, as old Clement has seen even with his upside-down version of his daughter's predicament, is that "all things are double, and this should keep us from taking liberties with the outside world, and acting too quickly to finish things off." Once human mystery and complexity are ignored or dissipated by a pressing for simple definitions, the residue is bound to be disappointing.

A "lovers' quarrel" is the cause of the falling out between William Wallace and his newly pregnant, young wife Hazel in "The Wide Net." Hazel is filled with her great experience of coming motherhood: she is elated, solemn, fearful, mysterious, "touchy." William Wallace hasn't taken sufficient account of this: in fact, to make matters worse, he has been out on a drinking spree with one of the boys. Hazel retaliates by writing a letter in which she threatens to drown herself. And so her husband must now go in quest of her, and find, swimming in the depths of the Pearl River, what is the "old trouble":

> So far down and all alone, had he found Hazel? Had he suspected down there, like some secret, the real, the true trouble that Hazel had fallen into, about which words in a letter could not speak . . . how (who knew?) she had been filled to the brim with that elation that they all remembered, like their own secret, the elation that comes of great hopes and changes, sometimes simply of the harvest time, that comes with a little course of its own like a tune to run in the head, and there was nothing she could do about it—they knew—and so it had turned into this? It could be nothing but the old trouble that William Wallace was finding out, reaching and turning in the gloom of such depths.

Though "The Bride of the Innisfallen" has been widely misunderstood, the real subject of that story is related to that of "The Wide Net." The point of view of most of "The Bride of the Innisfallen" is that of an observing narrator who obviously enjoys the human comedy in the train compartment full of richly varied "types" heading for Ireland, but it is a perspective subtly shared with that of one character singled out for special attention: a young American wife who is running away from her husband. Only at the end of the story does the narrator concentrate explicitly on the mind and experience of the young wife, but then we realize how what she has seen on the trip, and on her perambulations through glorious, fresh, wildly funny, dazzlingly lovely Cork (so it registers for her), *explain* both to us and to her what her "trouble" has been with her husband.

The "trouble" is her excess of hope, joy, and wonder at the mystery and glory of human life, all of which is symbolized to her in the lovely young bride who appears mysteriously on board the "Innisfallen" just as it prepares to land at Cork. This joy the American girl's husband apparently cannot see or share (as William Wallace cannot at first perceive Hazel's strange elation). "You hope for too much," her husband has said to her: that was "always her trouble." How can she preserve this quality which is so much and simply her definition that without it she loses her identity? The question answers itself, because joy and hope constantly bound up in her. "Love with the joy being drawn out of it like anything else that aches—that was loneliness; not this. *I* was nearly destroyed, she thought, and again was threatened with a light head, a rush of laughter. . . ." Her real problem is not how to preserve her joy, but how to communicate it to her husband, or to anybody:

> If she could never tell her husband her secret, perhaps she would never tell it at all. You must never betray pure joy—the kind you were born and began with—either by hiding it or by parading it in front of people's eyes; they didn't want to be shown it. And still you must tell it. Is there no way? she thought—for here I am, this far. I see Cork's streets take off from the waterside and rise lifting their houses and towers like note above note on a page of music, with arpeggios running over it of green and galleries and belvederes, and the bright sun raining at the top. Out of the joy I hide for fear it is promiscuous, I may walk forever at the fall of evening by the river, and find this river street by the red rock, this first, last house, that's perhaps a boarding house now, standing full-face to the tide, and look up to that window—that upper window, from which the mystery will never go. The curtains dyed so many times over are still pulled back and the window looks out open to the evening, the river, the hills, and the sea.

There is no "reconciliation scene" in this story as there is in "The Wide Net." The girl leaves the story wandering off happily into a bar. From it she hears a cry flung out "fresh

. . . like the signal for a song," and she walks into "the lovely room full of strangers"—people in whom she can delight without fear of exposure ("So strangeness gently steels us," Miss Welty has quoted a poem of Richard Wilbur). We do not know whether her husband will see her "new" when she returns to him, though we rather hope he may; for how can she possibly be resisted, this heavy-hearted little saint spinning so giddily toward heaven?

In a story called "Circe" (also from the volume titled *The Bride of the Innisfallen*), Miss Welty celebrates the human mystery by adopting the perspective of a superhuman being. The effort is a *tour de force*, because in her attempts to fathom the nature of Odysseus after she seduces him, Circe begins to look very much like one of Miss Welty's human lovers, more than one of whom gaze at the beloved when he is asleep, hoping at that unguarded moment to catch the elusive mystery of his identity. But as a sorceress and magician, though preserved from human frailty and tragedy, and all the uncertainties of time and circumstance (because she can predict the future), Circe envies the human condition. She first contrasts the way of her father with that of the earthly hero. Nature, here personified and deified, is seen to be enviably constant and serene, sure and effective, exempt from human pain, "suffering . . . no heroic fear of corruption through his constant shedding of light, needing no story, no retinue to vouch for where he has been." But in Circe's vision human beings have an equal, though different, glory. She thinks enviously,

I know they keep something from me, asleep and awake. There exists a mortal mystery, that, if I knew where it was, I could crush like an island grape. Only frailty, it seems, can divine it— and I was not endowed with that property. They live by frailty! By the moment! I tell myself that it is only a mystery, and mystery is only uncertainty. (There is no mystery in magic! Men are swine: let it be said, and no sooner said than done.) Yet mortals alone can divine where it lies in each other, can find it and prick it in all its peril, with an instrument made of air. I swear that only to possess that one, trifling secret, I would willingly turn myself into a harmless dove for the rest of eternity!

For what is the "instrument of air"—a metaphor? Possibly imagination, intuition, sensitivity, contemplation, wonder, love (whatever, one might guess, is the opposite of cold, rational, loveless, destructive analysis—the metaphor for which would be a blunt mechanical instrument). These delicate "instruments" are the means by which human beings can probe the human mystery, the means by which any lover may meet or be united with any object in the world.

VI

It is also with these "instruments of air" that Miss Welty approaches the persons and places and themes of her fiction; it is what makes for the distinctively lyrical quality of her style. "Relationship is a pervading and changing mystery," she says in "How I Write"; "it is not words that make it so in life, but words have to make it so in a story." Her problem as an artist has been to find the words to convey the mysteries, the elusive and subtle inner states of mind and feeling for which most people (and certainly the people of her fiction) have no words at all: she must be articulate about what cannot be articulated. She is out on a fringe, lonely place—as lonely as the wilderness in "A Still Moment"; there, like Lorenzo, Murrell, and Audubon, she must press for definitions: the meanings, the names of some of the most complex, elusive, and important of all human experiences. And it is inevitable that she should have her failures as well as her successes. Her language is not always adequate to the difficulty of what must be conveyed, which is perhaps the reason why she has often been accused of being coy, arch, perversely subtle, too nuanceful or precious.

The wonder is, after all, the large measure of her success. The reason for this we may trace as far back as to the habit of the child in "A Memory," the habit of close observation, of recording, identifying, "placing" things; or we may see it as recently expounded as in the small volume mentioned earlier, *Place in Fiction*. "Place in fiction," Miss Welty says, "is the named, identified, concrete, exact and exacting, and therefore credible, gathering-spot of all that has been felt, is about to be experienced, in the novel's progress." As she defines it, place is not only the region or setting of a story; it stands for everything in a story that fixes it to the known, recognizable, present, and "real" world of everyday human experience. It is like the solid flesh that both encloses (pins down) and discloses (reveals) the more elusive human thoughts and feelings. "In real life," she says, "we have to express the things plainest and closest to our minds by the clumsy word and the half-finished gesture. . . . It is our describable outside that defines us, willy-nilly, to others, that may save us, or destroy us, in the world; it may be our shield against chaos, our mask against exposure; but whatever it is, the move we make in the place we live has to signify our intent and feelings." In fiction this illusion of reality is created if the author has seen to "believability": "The world of experience must be at every step, through every moment, within reach as the world of appearance." The inner world and the outer surface of life must be interrelated and fused; the imaginative vision must glow through the carefully, objectively painted exterior world.

In her best stories Miss Welty has seen to "believability" by her use of the familiar local Mississippi settings; her close descriptions of the appearance, manner, gestures of her characters; her infallible ear for their speech rhythms and idioms; her use of plausible and logical plot structures; her concern with physical texture and psychological validity; her use of proper names which are always solidly realistic, local, devastatingly accurate, and at the same time, often richly allusive in their symbolism. The destination of the salesman in "Death of a Traveling Salesman," for example, is a town called Beulah. Surprisingly enough, there *is* such a place: population 342, Boliver County, N.W. Mississippi, according to the *Columbia Gazetteer;* but the higher validity of its use as a place name is that the salesman is on his way to the "Beulah Land" of the Southern Baptist gospel hymns.

Or her concern with "believability" may be shown again in the way "A Still Moment"—as formally patterned a story and as close to allegory as any she has written—is most solidly wedded to history in place and time. For the wilderness is not only the isolated, mythical desert setting appropriate to mystical revelations, but it is the old familiar Natchez Trace many years back in history; the characters are not simply abstract or apocryphal types of missionary prophet (the good man), criminal (the evil man), and naturalist (the artistic, detached, contemplative man), but they are three historical persons about whom Miss Welty has undoubtedly done her piece of "research."

Most of all, the style itself is the best illustration of her concern with "believability." The fusion of the elusive, insubstantial, mysterious, with what is solidly "real," can be seen in almost any passage selected at random from Miss Welty's fiction. The one chosen is a short and relatively simple description from "The Death of a Traveling Salesman." In this episode Sonny, the husband, has returned from a neighbor's with a burning stick in tongs; Bowman, the salesman, watches the wife lighting the fire and beginning preparations for supper:

> "We'll make a fire now," the woman said, taking the brand. When that was done she lit the lamp. It showed its dark and light. The whole room turned golden-yellow like some sort of flower, and the walls smelled of it and seemed to tremble with the quiet rush of the fire and the waving of the burning lamp-wick in its funnel of light.
>
> The woman moved among the iron pots. With the tongs she dropped hot coals on top of the iron lids. They made a set of soft vibrations, like the sound of a bell far away.
>
> She looked up and over at Bowman, but he could not answer. He was trembling. . . .

In this passage the simple actions, sights and sounds, are conveyed to us sharply and precisely and yet mysteriously and evocatively, through the mind of a man who experiences an unconscious heightening of awareness, a clarity of vision, because in these closing hours of his life he is approaching his moment of revelation. He is feeling more deeply than ever before, and hence everything he sees he also feels intensely. We know that throughout the story he is in a semi-delirious state, and thus in realistic terms, we are prepared for all the adumbrations and overtones, the exaggerations, blurs, and distortions of his perception. But strange and elusive meanings are coming to him through all he sees: each act and gesture becomes almost ceremonial; each sight and sound richly allusive, portentous, beautiful, and deeply disturbing. The lamplight registers to him as both dark and light, suggesting the states of dream and reality, his feeling of the warmth, welcome and shelter of this home and his fear of being left out, as well as the chills and fever of his illness. His sense impressions are blended as the golden light seems to him like a flower with an odor that pervades the walls; the trembling, rushing, and waving of the light are also extended to include the walls, suggesting the instability and delirium of his impressions. The woman does not simply "walk" or "step": she "moves among" the iron pots, like some priestess engaged in a mysterious ritual, moving among the sacred objects; the sound of the hot coals dropped on the iron lids is muted, softly vibrating; the comparison to the sound of a bell again suggests the ceremonial resonance these simple actions have for the salesman. It is no wonder that at the end of the passage we find him trembling and speechless. Through the evocation of the language we have felt into his complex emotional state of wonder, fear, longing, sickness, pain, love: we have seen it all through his eyes and experience. This is characteristically the way Miss Welty blends the inner world and outer surfaces of life—the way she sees to "believability."

In observing and recording the mysteries, Miss Welty creates a response of wonder, terror, pity, or delight. Her stories teach us nothing directly except, through *her* vision, how to observe, and wonder, and love, and see the mysteries; for brutal or lovely, they wait for us wherever we go.

CHAPTER 3

The Weather of the Mind

Down at the wharf, down out of the high heavens, [the gulls] stood solid as housewives, one large plump one to each little fishing boat, almost moral-looking, ready to pronounce judgment. It seemed sometimes that all sea gulls could not be the same, that they must be two varieties of birdkind, or the birds themselves must have two lives. Was it the sun or the fog, the time of day, that most often changed things, by changing their appearances? He supposed he had a horror of closed-in places and of being shut in, but in late afternoon he had seen Alcatraz light as a lady's hat afloat on the water, looking inviting, and he would almost wish to go to that island himself, and say to people, 'Convicts are Christ,' or the like.

— "Music from Spain"

I

ANYONE fortunate enough to have viewed a sizeable collection of Monet paintings, as was the privilege of those who visited the Monet exhibit at the Museum of Modern Art in the spring of 1960, will have been impressed by that painter's fascination with the effect of changing light, atmosphere, and season on a single motif.

Monet's custom was to set up many canvases before a favorite motif—haystacks, poplars, the Rouen cathedral, his famous water garden—and then paint it several times at different times of day and in varying seasons and kinds of weather, so that an object which on one canvas appears to the eye and imagination as dark and looming in grays, deep purples, and olives, may on a fourth or fifth canvas of the series appear gloriously transfigured in yellows, pinks, and pale blues. As one of his critics has summarized: "It is as if, within Monet's psyche, there were a scale analogous to that of the weather, grading from chromatic luminosity, vibrant with light and joy, through an infinite range of tinted and toned grays implying as many median emotional nuances, and finally down to blackness; nullity; immobility; non-being."[1]

If we were to abstract a set of "motifs" from Miss Welty's fiction, and think of them as the objects of her artistic vision, we could draw a useful analogy between the work of the two artists. In one kind of philosophical "weather" and according to one kind of light, the bright objects, the positive values, could be grouped to suggest order, form, control, rationality, discipline, knowledge, predictability: all these would provide the larger context favorable to meaning and purpose in life, to security and protection, to the flourishing of the prime value of love. Opposed to these values would be chance, confusion, disorder, chaos, catastrophe, oblivion: all these would make for exposure and vulnerability, they would be hostile to meaning and purpose in life, they would tend to discourage if not destroy love, and they would eventually be associated with death itself.

Human beings are immersed in this struggle, striving to make order out of chaos, but helpless in the face of the catastrophe which may spring out of nature; trying to live securely in love, but frustrated by the cosmic disorder of a time sequence which brings first the love and then the separateness, or the unpredictable and uncontrollable circumstance which brings separation. Furthermore, these opposing principles are not to be located merely in nature, cosmic reality, the outside world: the vulgar woman who rudely exposes her breasts in "A Memory" is an active though unconscious embodiment of the destructive principle of chaos, as the child is the embodiment of the principle of order. Mrs. Larkin in her submersion in the garden and wielding of the hoe and Howard in his murdering, become more self-conscious embodiments of the paradoxes, conducting their terrible and fatal experiments in meaning. The opposing principles form a continuum in man and the universe of which he is a part.

Now as if the light and weather had shifted over Miss Welty's shoulder, we find her engaged, in another set of stories, in painting similar motifs, but with a totally different "atmospheric" or value scheme. In these stories we find the bright tones of discipline, order, control, and rationality transmuted to the darker tones of repression, rigidity, or dullness; and the disordered, which in the process of metamorphosis goes through a stage of the ambiguously valued disorderly, at last pops up delightfully as the spontaneous, unconfined, wild, pagan, irreverent, irrepressible. By this changed light, chance and the unpredictable become surprise; abandon loses its former connotations of desolation and decay, and shines in the bright rays of carelessness and freedom; exposure and vulnerability dissolve with fear, and are displaced by challenge, mischievousness, and good-humored insolence. Glad welcome of the unknown supplants fear of the unknown; gloom is routed by joy; and all the tragic limitations of life and love, the conditions which threatened their destruction, have become opportunities favorable to their flourishing.

When one thinks of this second set of values in Miss Welty's stories, certain images come to mind. Perhaps one pictures Cash standing in Solomon's dignified front room, glorious and dazzling in his new Easter clothes, "all of him young" (the words sing to the delight in Livvie's heart), with a little guinea pig peeping out of his pocket. Or perhaps one pictures King Mac-Lain in irreverent attendance at the funeral of Miss Katie Rainey, cracking chicken bones with his teeth and putting out his bright pink tongue to cool from the hot coffee while the company sings "Nearer, My God, to Thee"; or maybe one sees little Jinny MacLain leaning curiously and boldly over the coffin with tiny green lizards hanging from her ears like earrings; or that funny, wicked old goat, "Papa" from "Going to Naples," who blasts every solemn, tender moment with a long "Tweet" from his weapon of impropriety—the raucous whistle. The mood, the atmosphere, is one of surging, irresistible, pagan joy—"the pure wish to live"—and it is an important atmosphere in Miss Welty's fiction.

II

The first clear statement of this view of the oppositions is to be found in "Asphodel" in *The Wide Net*. The story is a somewhat uneasy though fascinating blend of realism, mythology, allegory, and fantasy. Three old maids are on a picnic: they come in a buggy and sit on a hill at high noon in their fluffy, white dimity frocks; they have their baskets and spread cloth, and they eat their chicken, ham, cake, and fruit. Their setting is the golden ruin of the house "Asphodel"—six Doric columns with unbroken entablature on two—and they tell their story of Miss Sabina and Mr. Don McInnis, former owner of "Asphodel," in the manner of a Greek chorus: "their voices serene and alike," now one speaking, now another, and then all together.

The strong-willed, aristocratic Miss Sabina has been forced by her father to marry Mr. Don McInnis, "a great, profane man" with pointed yellow eyebrows, who is dangerous, uproarious, full of hope and laughter, and who stands "astride" everything at the wedding: the room, guests, flowers, tapers, even the bride and her father. He is "like a torch carried into a house." Miss Sabina, who represents the strictest order and control—the antithesis of everything wild, unruly, and sensual— tries to impose her will upon Mr. Don, but is necessarily defeated: he is not to be tamed and domesticated, and is flagrantly unfaithful. In a fury, Miss Sabina chases him, permanently unsubdued, out of "Asphodel," burns the place, and forbids further mention of his name or that of "Asphodel." She then concentrates on ruling the town, becoming, in fact, its presiding deity—its fate. She runs all its affairs, endows its monuments, names its children, predicts and prophesies each event, and holds everyone in awe of her power. When she passes by at the May Festival, the Maypoles become "hopelessly tangled, one by one"—showing that she has a way of spoiling anything pagan, such as an old fertility rite.

But the one place in town outside her domain is the post office, for there, say the old maids, "we might still be apart in a dream." The post office serves as a medium to the outside world, and the letters the old maids and townspeople clutch there are like "all far-away or ephemeral things," symbols of their "secret hope or joy and . . . despair too"—all that is privately sympathetic to the rebellious, pagan instincts Miss Sabina is trying to annihilate with her massive will. Hence her final assault is on the post office, "as if the place of the smallest and longest-permitted indulgence, the little common green, were to be invaded when the time came for the tyrant to die." In she goes, thrashing her lion-headed cane, crying "your lovers!" as she seizes the old maids' letters; she tears to bits with her bare hands every scrap of paper in sight, dancing and raging like one possessed, until she falls dead.

As if to show how ineffectual Miss Sabina's hold on the town has been, the old maids are already found on the day after her funeral picnicking at the forbidden spot, "laughing freely all at once," talking and dreaming in the bright sun when their tale is finished. Then suddenly an apparition appears in the form of a bearded man. "He stood motionless as one of the columns, his eyes bearing without a break upon the three women. He was as rude and golden as a lion. He did nothing, and he said nothing while the birds sang on. But he was naked."

The three old maids cry out and scatter off rather unconvincingly, looking back; Miss Cora identifies the apparition as Mr. Don McInnis, "buck-naked . . . as naked as an old goat." Then a number of goats come scampering through the columns of "Asphodel" and leap gaily over the fence toward the three old maids. The ladies scramble into their open buggy and appease the goats by throwing them a little baked hen to eat. As they ride home, Irene expresses satisfaction that Miss Sabina "did not live to see us then" and Cora observes decorously that Mr. Don "ought not to be left at liberty." But Phoebe, who has been all along the most susceptible of the three, laughs softly. She seems to be "still in a tender dream and an unconscious celebration—as though the picnic were not already set rudely in the past, but were the enduring and intoxicating present, . . . the golden day." The "golden age" of classical mythology has become Phoebe's golden day; Pan and his satyrs have been evoked in the appearance of Mr. Don and the chasing goats; order and control, the "civilized" virtues represented by the stiff-frocked, puritanical Miss Sabina, have been amusingly routed in that last but not so strong-hold of southern maidenhood.

In "Asphodel" the narrative method is rather puzzling, eclectic, and bizarre, but the theme of the story has a comic simplicity. Mr. Don McInnis, disorder, and the pagan values enjoy an unambiguous triumph: at least I should suspect that no reader would be tempted to much sympathy for Miss Sabina's cause. In the story "Livvie," however, we find the reverse: a narrative method disarmingly simple and clear, but a thematic structure far more complex and subtly adjusted to the ambiguities of actual human experience. The beautiful balance of the opposing values, their easy, natural embodiment in character and situation, the purity of the language, and the sympathy and detachment of the vision, give this story a deservedly high place among Miss Welty's works.

Livvie's return to life (the original title of the story was "Livvie is Back") through the death of her old husband, Solomon, and her surrender to Cash, the field hand who comes to claim her, is an obvious but not a complete and clear gain; for there is a corresponding loss and destruction of certain positive values.

As his name implies, Solomon stands for order, control, wisdom, security. His house is "nice"—neat and orderly. Patterns are delightfully worked out in groups of two's, three's, and four's. On each side of the porch, in perfect balance, is an easy chair with overhanging fern and a dishpan of seedlings growing at its foot; a plow-wheel hanging on one side of the door is balanced by a square mirror on the other side. In the house are three rooms; in the living room is a three-legged table with a pink marble top, and on it is a lamp with three gold feet; on the kitchen table are three objects: two jelly glasses holding spoons, knives and forks, with a cut-glass vinegar bottle between them; even the tiny blood-red roses which bloom on the bushes outside grow in three's on either side of the steps. And there are four baited mouse-traps in the kitchen, one in every corner. Each pictured detail of the house, inside and out, speaks of the balance and symmetry which characterize a dignified, well-disciplined, quiet and peaceful mode of existence.

Safety and security are suggested by the two safedoors which are always kept shut and by the bottled branches of the crape-myrtle trees, a precaution taken, as Livvie knows, to keep "evil spirits from coming into the house—by luring them inside the colored bottles, where they cannot get out again." Solomon's life is moral and pious—he seems to Livvie "such a strict man"; he has his Bible on the bedside table (and uses it); he keeps track of time like a clock, sleeping with his silver watch in his palm "and even holding it to his cheek like a child that loves a plaything."

As mistress of Solomon's golden palace, Livvie passes her days in serenity and comfort; in a sense she shares in Solomon's kingly opulence, though she serves her now ancient, fragile master by waiting on him in his illness. But since the "nice house" has also been her gilded cage for nine years, she is vaguely restless and discontent, unconsciously oppressed by the wintry atmosphere, by her barren and lonely existence. When she is busy at her churning, the sound seems to her sad, "like sobbing," and makes her homesick. Once she had ventured forth through the dead leaves in the deep Trace, and there, over a bank in a graveyard, she had had a vision both of her bondage and her possible release. She had seen "in the sun, trees shining like burning flames through the great caterpillar nets which enclosed them," even though "scarey thistles stood looking like the prophets in the Bible in Solomon's house." And she had thought, "Oh for a stirring of the leaves, and a breaking of the nets!"

Her release comes on the first day of spring, which brings a "little puffy wind," and on it the sounds of the distant shouts of men and girls plowing in the red fields and of the small piping cries of children playing. The harbinger of Livvie's release is Miss Baby-Marie, an amusingly vulgar, red-haired woman who travels around selling cosmetics to "white and colored" and is herself covered with "intense white and red" make-up. Livvie is tempted to apply some lipstick, and when she looks in the mirror, her face "dance[s] before her like a flame." The outside world has impinged on her secure, withdrawn world in a form crassly commercial, but its effect is romantically exciting. Pulsating with her new self-consciousness, Livvie is stirred to a further insight which she shares, unspoken, with Miss Baby-Marie as the two of them look at Solomon sleeping: he is about to die. Livvie rushes out for air.

Then Cash comes in his fine Easter clothes, and Livvie is purely dazzled. Cash is, as Robert Penn Warren has suggested, a black buck, a kind of field god;[2] but that identification overlooks the significance of his name, the fact that his gaudy clothes have been purchased with money stolen from Solomon, the fact that his luminous baby-pink shirt is the color of Miss Baby-Marie's lipstick. He is a commercially transformed field god, dressed in "the city way"; and if he destroys the nets which are binding Livvie, he is also destroying a certain decency and reserve, even a certain moral order. As she walks beside him, Livvie senses this threat in "the way he move[s] along kicking the flowers as if he could break through everything in the way and destroy anything in the world." Her eyes grow bright at that; she sees "hope in its insolence looking back"; but a little chill goes through her when he lifts his spread hand and laughingly brings it down, "as if Cash was bringing that strong hand down to beat a drum or to rain blows upon a man, such an abandon and menace were in his laugh." Soon afterwards when Cash sends a stone sailing through the bottle trees, the sounds of broken glass clatter "like cries of outrage"—the outrage perpetrated against Solomon's prevention and protection. Surely, by implication, a few more evil spirits have been released to wander freely and work their mischief in the world.

When Livvie rushes in to Solomon's bedside, she hears his watch ticking and sees him withdrawn in sleep, his old face looking "small, relentless, and devout, as if he were walking somewhere where she could imagine the snow falling." She feels the strength of his claims, his austerity, his pure dedication; and that is why the sight of Cash's bright, pitiless black face is "sweet" to her: she would have to be cruel to break with Solomon. Now as Solomon sleeps under the eyes of Cash and Livvie, his face tells them "like a mythical story that all his life he had built, little scrap by little scrap, respect." The images used to describe his purpose and method—that of an ant or beetle collecting, or an Egyptian builder-slave industriously working on the pyramid, so absorbed in his pursuit that he forgets the origins and meaning of his work—imply a curious blend of sympathy and criticism. Respectability, as Robert Penn Warren states, is "the dream, the idea, which has withered";[3] but nonetheless a simple wisdom and nobility characterize the process of this old man's life, the achievement of which is not entirely vitiated by the dubious value of its goal.

When Solomon wakes up, Cash raises his arm to strike; but the arm is fixed in mid-air as if held. A mysterious illumination flickers across Solomon's face: "It was that very mystery that Cash with his quick arm would have to strike, and that Livvie could not weep for." Though Cash is an impatiently pawing buck, he is momentarily stayed—if not by the sense of Solomon's mystery, at least because he feels "a pang of shame that the vigor of a man would come to such an end that he could not be struck without warning." Cash is sufficiently human to realize human vulnerability, if not dignity: he could not, without ceasing to be human, do violence to Solomon—push him over the trembling edge of life—in this moment of the old man's greatest strength and helplessness. Solomon must be permitted to surrender his ghost, and he does so with beautiful candor, grace, and dignity. Gently he reviews his own purpose for Livvie; without rebellion he faces the disagreeable fact of his failure (since there was "no prevention"), and the irony of its being Cash who has come to claim Livvie: "somebody I know all the time, and been knowing since he was born in a cotton patch, . . . Cash McCord, growed to size, growed up to come in my house in the end." With humility he confesses his fault:

"God forgive Solomon for carrying away too young girl for wife and keeping her away from . . . all the young people would clamor for her back." Finally he offers to Livvie his most valued possession, the symbol of his very life, his dignified, orderly existence; and the moment she receives the silver watch from his hand, Solomon dies.

The denouement is swift and joyful. Back in the front room, Cash seizes Livvie and drags her round him and out toward the door in a whirling embrace. As a final fleeting gesture of loyalty, Livvie keeps stiff and still the arm and hand holding Solomon's watch; then her fingers relax, the watch falls somewhere on the floor, all at once "the full song of a bird" is heard, and outside "the sun was in all the bottles on the prisoned trees, and the young peach was shining in the middle of them with the bursting light of spring."

The triumph of life, youth, passion would appear to be complete. But Miss Welty has shown us that just as Solomon's death is a necessary prelude to Livvie's new life with Cash, so all of Solomon's values and achievements must suffer a death. The new freedom and joy are not the uncomplicated pagan sort embodied in Don McInnis; they are, in part, a "cash" purchase, and their characteristic hue is a gaudy pink.

III

The juxtaposition and equal weighting of opposing sets of values which is found in "Livvie" is characteristic of Miss Welty's work as a whole. To return to the analogy from painting, a single canvas may contain dark, shaded areas and bright splashes of sunshine; it may contain more than a single kind of "weather." "At the Landing," for instance, shows the destructive violence which seems to be a necessary part of coming into life. As the flood ravages land and property, as the body is seized and raped, the human psyche, the mind and heart and soul, will be shaken to the very core of its being, undergo suffering and even death. But only as a result of this destruction can there be a birth of the knowledge and joy and fulfillment which comes from love, adult experience, and wisdom. In "The Winds," Josie recreates all the glorious diversions, rituals, superstitions, supreme ecstasies of childhood: all these must, in a sense, be destroyed if she is to become a "big girl" like that wistfully adored queen of her heart, Cornella of the golden hair. But

Josie is luckier than Cornella, who is lost in the equinoctial storm (the change from childhood to adulthood), because Cornella lacks the stability of home, the comforting presence of mother and father, through whose love and order and control Josie may be gently guided into the hazards of maturity.

What a variety of resonances even the word home has in Miss Welty's fiction: a womb, even a tomb, to Jenny; a stronghold of love and security to Josie; a gilded cage to Livvie; an enviable resting place to the traveling salesman; now a place to fight, to escape from, now a place to return to in *Delta Wedding;* now a narrow, stifling prison, now a focus of stability for the wanderers in *The Golden Apples*! As the lights and shadows play on that single concept, so variously embodied in Miss Welty's fiction, we see it as we have always experienced it: as a focal point of the most intense of human loves and hatreds.

To the two extremes of what has been called the philosophical atmosphere or weather of Miss Welty's fiction, the traditional literary terms of "tragic" and "comic" might well be applied. The weather of Miss Welty's comedy has its own peculiar fluctuations, ranging from humor and merriment to satire and irony. Some of the "seasons and moments" of this comedy are the next subject for our attention.

CHAPTER 4

Some Modes of Comedy

I

IN HIS INTRODUCTION to *A Subtreasury of American Humor*, E. B. White noted that "humor can be dissected, as a frog can, but the thing dies in the process and the innards are discouraging to any but the pure scientific mind. . . . [Humor] has a certain fragility, an evasiveness, which one had best respect. Essentially, it is a complete mystery."[1] Teachers in the classroom have repeatedly discovered what any good joke-teller knows by instinct: that if one has to explain what is funny, it ceases to *be* funny. The fact that the most useful comment a critic can make about Miss Welty's comedy is "read and enjoy," simply means that her comedy, like any good joke, is immediately and widely available; and the popularity of such stories as "Why I Live at the P. O." and *The Ponder Heart* demonstrates the point. The task left to the critic is that of distinguishing among the modes of comedy to be found in her work, of suggesting a few sources of her comic effects, and of describing methods and techniques of her comic writing.

In some of its manifestations, Miss Welty's comedy lightly evokes the mood and spirit of the most ancient rites of comedy: the Dionysiac feasts, the fertility rites of primitive cultures, the folk ceremonies which marked the changes in season or the celebration of birth and marriage. "The Wide Net" is an example of this kind of comedy. The clan's ritual of dragging the river takes place at the turn of a season, shortly before a birth, at a time of change in the life of the young hero who is about to become a father. The ritual is presided over by the leader of the clan (Old Doc), who lives on top of a hill and rules from his porch rocker, who rides the boat during the dragging, and makes philosophical comments on the change of season, the general proceedings, and the "problem" of the hero. For the hero, the ritual involves a testing of strength and fitness, an elemental struggle with potential alien forces or evil powers, and a discovery or revelation of the mysteries of life.

William Wallace's "testing" first comes through his repeated dives into the depths of the river, particularly one long dive into the "dark clear world of deepness" where he has a revelation as to the secret of Hazel's trouble. He finally emerges from this deep plunge "in an agony from submersion, . . . staring and glaring around in astonishment, as if a long time ha[s] gone by," and holding in his hand a small emblem of new life, a little green ribbon of plant, complete with its root. This episode is followed by a bacchanalian feast on the fish of the Pearl River, a brief sleep of satiety, and then the triumphal dance of the suddenly roused hero, who hooks a big catfish in his belt and leaps crazily about until everyone is laughing noisily.

Immediately after this incident the hero is put to his next test. A strange apparition rises out of the water in undulating loops. It is at once recognized by all as "The King of Snakes!" (the name is thrice intoned, mysteriously). First its old hoary head is seen, then hump after hump of the long black body appears briefly above the surface. It looks meaningfully at the hero, who stares back stoutly, then it disappears. The hero has faced up to the threatening evil powers in life, has stared down the King of Snakes, and this confrontation is part of his initiation to his new role as defender and protector of the family.

After the small company has endured a heavy thunder storm and witnessed the hazards of nature in the fiery fall of a great tree struck by lightning, it descends in triumphal procession to the town of Dover. Only two more "trials" remain for the hero. First, on the way home, he must prove to his officious friend, Virgil Thomas, that he, William Wallace, is the hero of the affair; beating Virgil in a fight, he makes his friend swear that it was *his* wife, *his* river-dragging, *his* net. Finally he must recapture his wife. This is easily accomplished by a scolding on either side and an affectionate paddling by William Wallace. When Hazel lies smiling in the crook of his arm, it is "the same as any other chase in the end."

Although the story moves along naturally and credibly within its own realistic terms of setting, event, and character (except for the King of the Snakes, whose literal proportions are somewhat mythical!), it contains many delicate allusions to archaic fertility ceremonies, with their celebration of the rebirth of the hero or king who survives his *agon* or conflict. Hence "The Wide Net" may be enjoyed as a modern recreation of comedy in its most ancient ritualistic forms.

In the appearance of the mask of Silenus—in any revival of the unruly, irrepressible Dionysian self in Miss Welty's fiction—we are again in touch with the ancient sources of comedy. In "Asphodel" we find him personified in the rude and golden Mr. Don McInnis, with his satyr's beard, whose career and appearances totally disrupt the Apollonian rule of Miss Sabina. In *The Golden Apples* the mask appears on the face of the merry and lascivious King MacLain, with his hard little horns butting against the walls of life. In this aspect of humanity the powerful life force is revealed; the resource and insolence of growing things; sexuality, fertility, birth and rebirth, pleasure, fulfillment; the triumph and progress of the race over the defeating forces of tragedy and death.

II

A second and more modern type of comedy which appears in Miss Welty's fiction concentrates upon eccentric characters who follow out their natures in humorous, repetitive action. Her best known story in this mode is "Why I Live at the P. O." The analytical terms of Henri Bergson, in his famous essay on "Laughter," are applicable to this story. According to Bergson, anything is laughable in a human being which suggests rigidity —the apparent mechanization of the human body or mind—so that his gestures, actions, ideas seem to become puppet-like, automatic and repetitive, rather than living, mobile, flexible.

The rigidity of the postmistress of China Grove takes the form of an *ideé fixe*. She follows up her single idea with relentless logic until it puts her in rebellious isolation from the world about her (the "world" being, in that small town, mostly her own family). Though acting and thinking with the insane logic of the paranoid, she is not felt to be so because of the marvelous energy, self-possession, and resourcefulness with which she carries out her revenge (so that our pity is not aroused), and because of the inescapable comedy in her situation, the members of her family and their behavior, and her mode of telling her story.

The motive of her particular obsession is as clear as it is unadmitted: vindictive jealousy of her sister. Stella-Rondo has repeatedly aggrieved and insulted her: by being a younger, favored sister; by stealing and running off with her boyfriend, Mr. Whitaker, the northern photographer; by reappearing not long afterwards with a two-year old "adopted" child; and finally, as she supposes, by setting the rest of the family against her, one by one. Her story is built on the logic of that steady progress of alienations: what Stella-Rondo did to bring them about, how she herself reacted to the mounting persecution—now with admirable forbearance, now with pacifying explanations, now with righteous indignation—and all the time with the assumed burden of running the family on that hot, hectic Fourth of July.

When the process of Stella-Rondo's evil machinations is complete and everyone is set against her, she saves her pride by moving out to the "P. O." Again she works with inexorable logic, disrupting the family as she systematically removes from the house everything that belongs to her: electric fan, needlepoint pillow, radio, sewing-machine motor, calendar, thermometer, canned goods, wall vases, and even a fern growing outside the house which she feels is rightfully hers because she watered it. Finally she is left alone at the "P. O.," secure in her knowledge of who in the town is for her and who against her; protesting loudly her independence and happiness, she works her revenge by shutting her family off from the outside world.

Her monologue is comic not only because of the apparent illogic of her logic, but because of her manner of speaking. One can see the fierce indignant gleam in her eye as the stream of natural southern idiom flows out of her; it is at once elliptical and baroque, full of irrelevancies, redolent of a way of life, a set of expressions, of prejudices, interests, problems, and human reactions which swiftly convey to the reader a comic and satiric portrait of this Mississippi family. The effect of "Why I Live at the P. O." depends not simply on the vividness of evoked scenes and sounds, but also on the implications of vulgarity which counter the comedy of the monologue in an ironic way. Marriage and family life are given their direction by the cheapest advertising, movies, and radio. Allusions to the "gorgeous Add-a-Pearl necklace," to the flesh-colored kimono "all cut on the bias" which was part of Stella-Rondo's trousseau, to the "Kress tweezers" she uses to pluck her eyebrows, and to Shirley-T., her tap-dancing, and her head-splitting rendition of "OE'm Pop-OE the Sailor-r-r-r Ma-a-an!" suggest some of the more macabre satiric effects of "Petrified Man."

In "Shower of Gold" (from *The Golden Apples*) and *The Ponder Heart*, Miss Welty again makes use of the comic monologue. In each case the narrator (Katie Rainey and Edna Earle) is a participant-observer, a garrulous woman with a position of some importance in the community. Each is alert to the most delicate social distinctions, a fountain of local expressions and opinions, stories, and legends; each is also a person of some tolerance and humanity, but possessing "a mind of her own." The auditor is someone who chances by, a stranger to the town who must be informed about persons and situations familiar to its inhabitants. Katie Rainey tells her story to a passerby while she does her churning; Edna Earle tells hers to the first guest who arrives at the Beulah Hotel after the trial and acquittal of her uncle.

The story each has to tell is that of a local "hero"; and in the telling each emerges as a comic type involved in a series of comic situations which develop from the collision of the ordinary world with his own particular, crazy "humour." King MacLain's "humour" is to take people (especially women) by surprise; willfully and outrageously he appears and disappears, according to his whim and appetite. He brings surprise gifts, he leaves behind surprising signs of his visits. On one of his surprise visits home, however, a comic reversal occurs. His own little boys, who do not recognize him, innocently pull a trick on him. They thoroughly confuse and frighten him with their Hallowe'en masks and pranks; King gets "up and out like the Devil was after him—or in him—finally." King resembles the practical-joker who eventually becomes victim of his own joke.

Uncle Daniel of *The Ponder Heart* has a Dickensian sort of eccentricity. His particular "humour" is his over-generosity: the compulsion to give away which springs from his enormous, "ponder"ous heart. But the incongruity of his nature is that this out-sized heart has no balancing counterpart of rational and moral intelligence. Lacking the wisdom of the serpent, Uncle Daniel is foolish as a dove; lacking a trace of "common sense," he borders on insanity. Out of the clash between the foolishness of Uncle Daniel's "wisdom" and the "foolishness" of the ordinary world of selfishness and calculation, zany relationships and muddles develop: the absurd marriage between Bonnie Dee Peacock and Uncle Daniel; the "murder" by tickling ("creep-mousie," Edna Earle calls it); the riotous disruption of a trial by the hero's explosive "give-away."

Again the comedy is inherent in the speaker's tone and manner of speech as much as in characters and situation, and again the comedy is mixed with irony. The "tragedy" develops because Bonnie Dee's heart isn't, either literally or symbolically, strong enough to match the strength of the Ponder Heart. "It may be," says Edna Earle, "anybody's heart would quail, trying to keep up with Uncle Daniel's." The townsfolk, in any event, are finally alienated from their most generous and entertaining citizen only because of their greed in keeping the money he gives away in the courtroom. But the story is not a parable; it is a light-hearted "murder mystery"—Miss Welty's single venture into that particular fictional mode.

Humorous characters in Miss Welty's stories—as is the case with most of their famous predecessors in Shakespeare, Fielding, Jane Austen, and Dickens—are "flat" in E. M. Forster's sense of the word: single-faceted, undeveloping. These characters are tagged by a particular set of actions or expressions, the recurrence of which we expect and meet with increasing delight. Among the passengers in "The Bride of the Innisfallen" and "Going to Naples" we find a rich array of these comic types: the man from Connemara who is always astonished, constantly exploding with "*Oh* my God!"; the fat, hovering little Mama Serto, enthusiastically sponsoring her daughter's romance on the boat going to Naples; and Gabriella herself, perpetually screaming in protest or mere delicious excitement.

III

Miss Welty often takes ritual action very seriously—especially the most simple and primitive rituals of the home, or the private rituals which come from a repeated performance of an action of love (Old Phoenix's trips down the worn path). But in the larger ceremonials which take place at community and family gatherings, she is likely to have an eye alert for the comic and satiric possibilities inherent in the manners and morals, social life and entertainment, of a highly organized and subtly stratified folk community. She perceives that whatever the purpose or occasion for bringing people together—a wedding (*Delta Wedding*), a funeral ("The Wanderers"), a courtroom trial (*The Ponder Heart*), a picture-taking ("Kin")— the product is pleasurable excitement for participants. For spectators, the occasion provides a rich and amusing display of the small actions, customs, modes of dress and speech, behavior and attitude, which go to make up the life of a southern town or family. With infectious zest and a genial humanity she crowds these group canvases like Brueghel paintings, exposing the small vanities, follies, blunders, incongruities of southern clans. Yet the most characteristic tone of this group comedy is tolerant, sympathetic, even affectionate: she enjoys the oddities and whimsicalities which become more obvious, because concerted, in these shared activities and rituals.

Each reader of her stories will have his own private collection of such comic pictures, which, although they may be ever so incidental to the essential meaning of a story, hang delightfully in odd corners of the mind. Among these may be the picture (from *Delta Wedding*) of an unbelievably enormous tubbed fern, fluttering and vibrating as though in a gale, and moving forward, apparently under its own power, through a dismayed group of Fairchilds (though it is actually borne on a broomstick by four small staggering Negro boys). The loan of this fern is a certain Miss Bonnie Hitchcock's idea of how to honor the Fairchilds on the occasion of Dabney's wedding: a double ineptitude and comic blunder, not only because of the unwieldy, virtually unplaceable size of the plant, but because of its having been sent only a few months earlier for the funeral of the bride's aunt. Or the following courtroom scene from *The Ponder Heart*, in which the intimate quizzing of Miss Teacake Magee, Uncle Daniel's first wife, is broken off by an immensely practical question:

"Why were you divorced, may I ask?" says old Gladney, cheerful-like.

"I just had to let him go," whispers Miss Teacake. That's just what she always says.

"Would you care to describe any features of your wedded life?" asks old Gladney, and squints like he's taking Miss Teacake's picture there with her mouth open.

"Just a minute," says the Judge. "Miss Edna Earle's girl is standing in the door to find out how many for dinner. I'll ask for a show of hands," and puts up his the first.

It was a table full, I can tell you. Everybody but the Peacocks, it appeared to me. I made a little sign to Ada's sister she'd better kill a few more hens.

From start to finish the trial is deliciously "hick," local and personal. The austerity and lofty justice of the law collapse utterly in the face of the intimacy and perversity of these southern small-town friends and neighbors.

IV

Tolerance and affection have been a constant element in much of Miss Welty's comedy: we find it in the first story of *A Curtain of Green*, "Lily Daw and the Three Ladies" (1937), as well as in "Going to Naples" (1954), the last story of *The Bride of the Innisfallen*. But a more caustic type of laughter can be found only in her first volume, and that chiefly in "Petrified Man" (1939), a story which has no close parallel among her other stories. Behind the "dramatic" narrative method of this story is a chilled, appalled recognition of abysmal vulgarity, and the scathing, annihilating laughter of satire.

The theme of "Petrified Man" is woman's inhumanity to man. As the title suggests, the men have been "petrified"—both terrorized and turned to stone (in effect, rendered impotent)—by the women. The scene of this satiric vision is a beauty parlor. Ironically it is in the ritual process of being feminized, made "beautiful," that they become physically horrible. For the women the beauty parlor is a "den of curling fluid and henna packs" in which they are "hidden" and "gratified."

But a peculiar sort of gratification it is. The apparatus, which suggests torture rather than indulgence, includes such things as wave pinchers, dryers, henna packs, cold wet towels, permanent machines, pungent fluids. The techniques are equally unpleasant, even brutal: strong red-nailed fingers press into a scalp; cold fluids trickle down the neck or into the eyes; a customer is "yanked up by the back locks and sat . . . up"; one complains, "You cooked me fourteen minutes"; another is complained about by an operator, "She always yelled bloody murder . . . when I give her a perm'nent." The place has not even the advantage of being clean. A little boy makes tents with aluminum wave pinchers on the floor; an operator flicks her cigarette ashes into a basket of dirty towels; an ashtray full of bobby pins spills on the messy floor. After as well as during the treatment, the women are made to look horribly ugly, big-headed, like a collection of Medusas—and the serpents' tongues are in their mouths. Their hair either stands out in a hideous electric frizz, or falls out, or both ("hennaed hair floated out of the lavender teeth like a small storm-cloud"). An operator gazes at herself in the mirror and observes, "I declare, I forgot my hair finally got combed and thought it was a stranger behind me"—indicating how far it stands out.

The three main characters in the story—a beauty operator, Leota; her customer, Mrs. Fletcher; and Leota's friend, Mrs. Pike (also a beautician before her marriage)—are the women whose petrifying domination of their respective husbands is exposed. Through a variety of physical, psychological, and cultural irregularities or perversities, the roles of male and female are ironically reversed. Leota is physically larger than her husband, Fred, and financially supports him. Mr. Pike, as well as Fred, is without work, and both men are loudly condemned by their wives for stupidity and indolence. Through a debasing intimacy and collusion with one another, and the divining powers of their fortune-teller "gods," these wives predict the future and manage the affairs of their husbands. They nag, accuse, thwart, force the men—who have reached the "bad age" of forty-two—into such male retreats as fishing trips. The favorite forms of entertainment of the women seem to be gossiping, reading romance and terror fiction, having beauty treatments, and viewing male freaks at traveling shows—pickled Siamese twins, forty-two-year-old pigmies, and a "petrified man" whose joints have been turning to stone since the age of nine.

Mrs. Fletcher, though belligerently asserting her own superiority to the other women in a hundred minutiae, is clearly another dominating female who prides herself upon her skillful management of her husband ("Mr. Fletcher can't do a thing with me"). She gets him to comply with her will by pretending to sick headaches, forcing him to do bending exercises to prevent him from becoming "petrified," and cleverly consulting his advice on "something important, like is it time for a permanent, not that I've told him about the baby" (she is pregnant).

The preoccupations of these women are all sexual and maternal, but in curiously perverted ways. Having destroyed the normal and natural in marital relations, their taste runs to the sensational and freakish. The petrified man is an object of pleasantly horrified speculation: "How'd you like to be married to a guy like that?" Pregnancy is shameful; to be accused of it is an insult; the condition is considered deplorable and concealed as long as possible; the husband is held vaguely culpable for this cruel assault on his wife's beauty. "Beauty," to these women, is more important than motherhood. Leota mentions the case of a certain Mrs. Montjoy who insisted, against the will of her helpless, frightened husband, on coming to the beauty parlor for her weekly shampoo and set on the way to the hospital after the onset of her labor pains. The children do not appear to be wanted or cared for: the one child we see in the story, Mrs. Pike's "Billy Boy," is rather nasty, prematurely "smart." Shunted around from hat shop to beauty parlor, he plays with such toys as wave pinchers and is made to feel disagreeably underfoot—as indeed he is.

It is, of course, the shrewd Mrs. Pike (as her name suggests, she is sharp-nosed and "cold as a fish")[2] who, from a picture in one of Leota's magazines, identifies the petrified man of the freak show as a former neighbor, a Mr. Petrie, wanted for a series of rapes ("four women in California all in the month of August"). The various reactions to this disclosure enforce the point of the story. Mrs. Pike is interested only in collecting her $500 reward, but Mr. Pike at first resists informing on a neighbor, remembering the kindness of the "ole bird" who was "real nice to 'em, lent 'em money or somethin'." Mr. Pike is simply told "to go to hell"; Mrs. Pike turns Mr. Petrie in and collects her reward. Leota is irrationally furious with Mrs. Pike for using her magazine to make the identification and for robbing her of the reward. Mrs. Fletcher, hearing about the dreadful Mr. Petrie, enjoys a pleasant revulsion and is somehow vindicated in her hatred of the woman who has divined the fact of her pregnancy.

The reader's reactions are more complicated. One is amused at the comically grotesque turn of events, and gratified that at least one man—Mr. Petrie—turned violently, if only briefly, against the collective monstrosity of female sexual action with a comparable male monstrosity of action. There is a certain depraved justice in his rebellious act of wild potency—the inhumanity of rape seems the only grotesquely appropriate answer to such feminine perversions. But then as one sees how this sole rebel, in becoming the petrified man of a freak show, settles literally and symbolically into the mode of impotence which characterizes his sex, one feels the pathetic defeat, the helplessness of the man, the horror of his victimized state. The man who becomes a freak is the symbol of a society in which relations between the sexes have become monstrous. This meaning is enforced by the title, which points a finger not at the particular person, but at the general appalling state of morals and manners—the traditional concern of satire. The brilliance of this story derives from the combination of its matter-of-fact, smile-producing fidelity to some of the most familiar types, attitudes, modes of behavior and speech of one level of modern American society, and its hallucinated, horror-producing vision of the modern Medusa turning to stone the man who gazes on her, the two of them frozen in the hideous postures of some piece of ancient grotesque statuary. We can say of this story what a critic has said of the comic spirit of Swift: it "frightens us out of laughter into dismay."[3]

The story ends with an intimation that the male has not been completely subjugated. Billy Boy, the only male present in this den of females, has the last word. Discovered in the mild disobedience of eating Leota's peanuts, he is caught and held on Mrs. Fletcher's lap while Leota paddles him with a brush. Women gather round from everywhere to witness the subduing of this small intruder from the enemy camp. With all the vigor of his three-year-old male defiance, Billy kicks Leota and Mrs. Fletcher; then he breaks away, stomps through the group of "wild-haired ladies," and flings back, "If you're so smart, why ain't you rich?" The remark is pure Pike; its cheap irony and cynical banality summon the voice and stance of his mother with her cleverly won $500; it hints that if there is to be a battle of the sexes, it will be fought at no high level, but with kicks and screams and remarks like these. The vulgar attitudes of his seniors have already infected this rebellious little male.

"A Visit of Charity" is also ironic and satiric, but its tone is less caustic than that of "Petrified Man." Marion, a fourteen-year-old campfire girl, is obliged to make a visit to an Old Ladies' Home in order to collect points. Her mood is anything but charitable: she approaches the undertaking with a legalistic sense of duty. Once inside, she is awed, frightened, disgusted. She is closeted in a dark, wet-smelling room with two rather terrifying old women. One reaches quickly with claw-like hands to snatch Marion's cap and the flowers from her hands; the other, lying in bed, bleats like a sheep and has its red eyes.

An initial comic contrast is made between the two women: the first is unconvincingly saccharine, flattering and ingratiating to the young visitor, calling the flowers "pretty—pretty"; the other, who is brutally frank, hostile to this and all other camp-fire girl visitors, announces sharply that the flowers are "stink-weeds." The comic and grotesque quickly shift to pathos, however, when we hear the reasons for the candid one's misan-thropy. Bleatingly she voices terrible accusations and desperate complaints against the violation of her privacy by the hated roommate and against the emptiness and indignity of their lives. "Your head is empty, your heart and hands and your old black purse are all empty. . . . And yet you talk, talk, talk, talk, talk all the time until I think I'm losing my mind. . . . Is it possible that they have actually done a thing like this to anyone—sent them in a stranger to talk, and rock, and tell away her whole long rigmarole?"

Then Marion suddenly looks at the bitter old woman intently, and for the first time she wonders deeply: it is apparently her first moment of genuine penetration of another. She breathes a soft inquiry—"How old are you?"—as she bends over the old woman, whose anger dissolves in the face of this unfamiliar attention and turns into a pathetic whimpering. Marion quickly flees from the room and escapes the final pleas of the first woman for a nickel or a penny "for a poor old woman that's not got anything of her own." It is about as large a dose of ugly reality as Marion can take. With the reflexive, cruel self-protection of youth against all the threats to its joy which human misery may present, she flies out to reclaim a hidden apple, boards a bus, and begins to eat.

The irony of the story—the discrepancy between the expected and the actual—is implied in the title. The Old Ladies' Home is supposed to be a charitable institution, but it is instead a final container and breeding-place of human misery, a hell for the living dead. The child's visit has none of the overtones of moral sweetness and light usually expected of visits of char-ity: the experience is one of terror, to be escaped, blotted out, as quickly as possible. It is as though the brutal fact of this place and its inmates, and the contrast between resilient youth and defeated old age, have been stumbled on and then recorded. No accusing finger is pointed, no one is particularly to blame. But in her biting into the apple there is a subtle hint that this little Eve has had her initiation to the knowledge of evil.

V

We have, in fact, left the realm of comedy altogether in those stories in which Miss Welty seems to be walking down a dark corridor opening doors on scenes and situations in which the characters are discovered in various painfully grotesque postures and actions induced by the brutal ironies of life. "The Whistle," "Clytie," and "Keela, the Outcast Indian Maiden" are examples of these stories and the last two doubtless contribute to the notion that Miss Welty is "preoccupied with the demented, the deformed, the queer, the highly spiced."[4] While it is true that Miss Welty often depicts the abnormal, especially in *A Curtain of Green*, it is scarcely with an eye to the sensational or melodramatic. The focus is never on the grotesque for its own sake, for the twinge of horror it evokes.

In "Keela, the Outcast Indian Maiden," however, we seem to be confronted with an external fact as grotesque and brutal as we could imagine. Significantly enough, it was not imagined at all; it was literally stumbled upon in the real world. Miss Welty has described the source of the story as follows: "One day I was on an assignment at a fair and talked to a man who was building a booth at the fair grounds. He told me the story I used in 'Keela, the Outcast Indian Maiden'—about a little Negro man in a carnival who was made to eat live chickens. That's the only actual story I've used. I guess if you read it you must have known that it was true and not made up—it was too horrible to make up."[5] The focus of the story is not, however, upon the central horrible fact but upon the reactions of the three principal characters both to the fact and to each other.

Steve, the young man who served as barker for Keela's "act" in the carnival, is driven around restlessly, cruelly burdened with a sense of guilt for a crime against humanity which he committed in relative innocence—relative because it had apparently never occurred to him that a savage "outcast Indian maiden" might also be an object for pity rather than commercial exploitation. But Steve had never viewed that frightening, alien creature as human, and moral enlightenment had come to him only when he had witnessed the effect of compassion working through the kindly stranger who identified Keela as a human being, familiar and near, a club-footed little Negro man sharing in the common human feelings. This is why Steve's imagination now broods compulsively on every detail which heightens the pathos of Keela's predicament, the outrage to humanity, the irony of his own guilty ignorance—the fact that the little deformed Negro was whipped up off a fence "like a cyclone happens," that "back in Miss'ippi it had it a little bitty pair of crutches an' could just go runnin' on 'em!," that "you could see where they'd whup it."

But no one can fathom the nature of Steve's anxiety: not the witness or "confessor," and still less the victim. The café proprietor, Max, is placid, even kindly; but his sensibility is closed to the deeper levels and nuances of human suffering, and he wants no trouble. Max sees his function simply as that of helping Steve find the man he wants, and he helps only because of his simple interpretation of Steve's anguished talk and behavior: to Max the man is "nuts." Steve needs a shared response of horror at his guilty action, a knowing, appalled sympathy, a moral judgment; but all he gets from Max is a bit of mild bafflement, bored patience and tolerance, tired little ironies, and irrelevant generosity. Because Steve isn't taken seriously, the fatal sense of responsibility settles on him more heavily than ever. He is even denied the satisfaction of making reparation, since he has no money to give Little Lee Roy.

But the final irony of Steve's moral predicament is that the victimized Negro himself has no comprehension of what his experience has meant. Steve quickly perceives this, and so scarcely addresses the little man, whose present attitude makes him irrelevant to Steve's whole problem. As Steve tells his story, Little Lee Roy sits quietly and happily, now and then emitting small murmurs and squeals of delighted recognition. He is flattered by the visit; pleased at the revival of this uniquely colorful episode in his life; tickled at the account of the debasing fraud, as though he had been party to some ingenious cleverness. The stranger who befriended him he has forgotten; Steve he "remembas" with obvious approval. Some anaesthesia seems to have numbed his memories of misery and an indignity which he may, in fact, never have felt. The smiling little man, his simplicity closely associated with that of the chickens who perch on either side of him on the stairs and the sparrow which alights on his "child's shoe," has no more than a child's moral intelligence, and even less than the child's capacity to remember pain. At supper that night he reports the day's interesting diversion to his children: "two white mens come heah to de house . . . . talks to me about de ole times when I use to be wid de circus—"; but the children, at least, understand, as is indicated by their cutting him off shortly with a "Hush up, Pappy."

Thus the reader's vision is shifted from the loud, shocking central fact of the story to a wondering contemplation of the strangely contrasting positions of the main characters in relation to it. As in "A Still Moment," the triangle of relationships is occasionally pointed up almost diagramatically when the narrator steps back to take a picture of the scene—for a fleeting moment freezes the relationships into a silently revealing shape. "The little man at the head of the steps where the chickens sat, one on each step, and the two men facing each other below made a pyramid." The dialogue is between the two men below; Lee Roy, with his chickens sitting like little mindless, instinctive vassals on either side of his perch, is "above" the other two, impervious; all three are, for different reasons, detached from each other, each occupying his own corner of the pyramid, not really communicating with the other two. It is another vision of "love and separateness": the love shown through Steve's pity and sense of responsibility, Max's imperturbable kindliness, and Little Lee Roy's childish delight in his visitors; the separateness, through their total failure to comprehend each other in and through the central fact of Lee Roy's terrible experience.

The grotesque and ironic are allied with pathos and tragedy rather than comedy in this story, as also in "Clytie," "Flowers for Marjorie," and "The Burning." These stories are included in a chapter about Miss Welty's comedy because much of her work seems to reveal the modern perspective on comedy, which is aware of its close relation to pathos and tragedy. In a discussion of "Our New Sense of the Comic" Wylie Sypher speaks of how "the direst calamities that befall man seem to prove that human life at its depths is inherently absurd. The comic and tragic views of life no longer exclude each other. . . . The comic and the tragic touch one another at the absolute point of infinity—at the extremes of human experience. . . . We have, in short, been forced to admit that the absurd is more than ever inherent in human existence: that is, the irrational, the inexplicable, the surprising, the nonsensical—in other words, the comic."[6] And is it not the absurd that confronts us through the experience of Howard ("Flowers for Marjorie"), who experiments "rationally" in an apparently irrational universe; or in the dilemma of Steve; or in the monstrosity of the women in "Petrified Man"; or in the alienation of the town of Clay from Uncle Daniel Ponder because of the affront of his generosity? In Miss Welty's fiction the absurd may evoke laughter or terror, pity or fear—more often in combination than singly. All of these feelings lie close together; all are part of the various and rapidly shifting "weather of the mind" which responds with clarity and immediacy to complex human experience.

That Miss Welty is not only intuitively but also consciously aware of the kinship between comedy and tragedy is apparent from her remarks in a review of one of Faulkner's novels: "Faulkner's veracity and accuracy about the world around keeps the comic thread from ever being lost or fouled, but that's a simple part of the matter. The complicated and intricate thing is that his stories aren't decked out in humor, but the humor is born in them, as much their blood and bones as the passion and poetry. Put one of his stories into a single factual statement and it's pure outrage—so would life be—too terrifying, too probable and too symbolic too, too funny to bear. There has to be the story, to bear it—wherein that statement, conjured up and implied and demonstrated, not said or the sky would fall on our heads, is yet the living source of his comedy—and a good part of that comedy's adjoining terror, of course."[7]

The terror adjoining the comedy—Miss Welty herself has shown us this, along with such disparate writers as Chekhov, Kafka, Faulkner, and Samuel Beckett. However, the fact that among her stories we may find such diverse manifestations of the spirit of comedy as those of ancient ritual and mythology, of the "humorous" character of nineteenth-century fiction, and of southern folk humor—as well as the satiric, ironic, and "absurd"—is evidence of the remarkable range and catholicity of Miss Welty's comic vision.

CHAPTER 5

The Season of Dreams

I

THERE IS in much of Miss Welty's fiction a special quality which cannot escape the notice of even the most cursory
reader. It is, in fact, the quality most immediately noted with
uneasy disfavor by many practical-minded American readers
upon what may be their single encounter with a Welty story
in a textbook anthology. The uneasiness may register for them
as a dim sense of not knowing exactly where they are in relation to the "hard facts" of the story; they may feel that the
secure centers of gravity have shifted on them almost imper-
ceptibly, as if they had taken a drink too many, or during the
course of a smooth plane ride had suddenly hit an air pocket,
or as if, now and again, they were being mysteriously plunged
underwater and treated to a faintly distorted and wavering
view of things.

The trustworthiness of sight, the confidence that a person
knows when he is asleep and dreaming and when he is awake,
the distinct difference and comforting gap between dream and
reality, irrational and rational, illusion or fantasy and fact, are
continually being threatened by Miss Welty's fiction. With a
story like "Death of a Traveling Salesman," the feeling may
remain subliminal and register only in the vague complaint that
there is "something queer" about the whole narrative; the uneasiness may dissolve when it is pointed out that the salesman's
perceptions are influenced by his sick, semi-delirious state,
only to reassert itself even more strongly when a disturbing
suggestion of Mark Schorer is introduced: that all the events
of the story may be hallucinatory, taking place in Bowman's
mind as he lies on his hospital bed.[1] With "A Worn Path" the
reaction may begin with irritation, but quickly turn into tolerant amusement at a shrewd old woman's occasional fantasies;
with "Powerhouse" it may break into heated argument and

dogged insistence that Powerhouse's wife Gypsy positively *is* or positively *is not* dead; with "Old Mr. Marblehall" it may result in sheer frustrated puzzlement.

In Miss Welty's exploration of the inner life, hard and fast lines are not always drawn between the world of fact and fantasy; there are half-states, mixtures of dream and reality, or rapid shifts between the two worlds. The facts may lie around somewhere to be pieced together by the diligent, but they may not be insisted on or even particularly interesting or relevant to the meaning of the story. The reader who recognizes this blurring of the lines as *in itself* a demonstrable and intensely personal fact of human experience, who accepts this tendency in human beings because of the release and enrichment fantasy brings into a reality which may be drab or cruel, and who perceives its power to crystallize an insight or convey a truth not available to the literal mind in the rational world, approves of this special form of "realism" and of the special techniques which project it. On the other hand, the reader who is disinclined to mix the two worlds, or to perceive how others mix them, often rejects fiction which presents the state of uncertainties; he is also perhaps unsettled at discovering to what extent the two worlds interpenetrate.

Robert Penn Warren (who, it goes without saying, does not fall into the latter category) has perceived a basic difference between the stories in *A Curtain of Green* and *The Wide Net*. He suggests that from the first sentence of the second volume —("Whatever happened, it happened in extraordinary times, in a season of dreams. . . .")—we have entered a "special world," in which the author purports not to be completely sure of what happens, in which "the logic of things . . . is not quite the logic by which we live, or think we live, in our ordinary daylight lives."[2] While it is true, as Mr. Warren observes, that *A Curtain of Green* displays greater variety in subject matter and mood than does *A Wide Net*, the tendency to fantasy and the depiction of dream life in Miss Welty's fiction is apparent from the outset. In the earlier stories, however, fantasy is most likely to be presented as a habit of mind of one of the characters; it tends to be a subjective phenomenon which does not distort for the reader the external reality presented. Thus in "A Memory" the child lives in a dream world which is coexistent with the real world, as does the heroine of "Clytie"; the former is made to square the two worlds to her moral and emotional growth; the latter, to her complete destruction. Again in "A Worn Path" Old Phoenix is seen to have her little dreams and abstractions, to slip over into the fantasy world and exist there briefly in a mode as simple and natural as in the real world: she reaches out her hand for a slice of marble-cake offered by a little boy who disappears as suddenly as he appears; she takes the scarecrow for a ghost and so addresses him; she seems to herself to be walking in the sleep of the strings of silver trees and cabins boarded shut, "all like old women under a spell sitting there."

But already in "Powerhouse" and "Old Mr. Marblehall," both from *A Curtain of Green,* the two worlds of dream and actuality are becoming less clearly distinguishable. Powerhouse not only has his fantasy life, but wields it masterfully; he prods and shapes it and then makes music out of it. He has his own brilliant completeness, which in itself is fantastic, and he has a resounding effectiveness "in the world." Through a remarkable and devastating series of descriptive images, Miss Welty manages to convey what he is: a person who has, all intuitively, encompassed an unbelievably wide range of knowledge and experience—much of it savage, terrorizing, much of it tender, most of it closed to white people, except insofar as he conveys it through his music.

With enormous delight and prodigality the narrator presses for definitions of the nature of Powerhouse, who himself perpetrates a mystery on the crowd, out of which he makes a musical conversation with his quartet. The piece is "Pagan Love Song," the theme is "My wife is dead," and elaborate · variations are played upon it as he debates with Little Brother, Valentine, and Scoot, who respond with appropriate horror, sympathy, scepticism (appropriate, that is, to both their temperaments and their instruments). In the Negro-town café to which the band repairs for refreshment during the intermission, the theme is again taken up, and more variations—this time spoken—are played upon it. Powerhouse luridly describes how his wife Gypsy, in a fit of loneliness, jumps from a window in her nightgown, "bust her brain all over the world," and is found by Uranus Knockwood, "that no-good pussyfooted crooning creeper, that creeper that follow around after me, coming up like weeds behind me, following around after me everything I do and messing around on the trail I leave."

The waitress, gloriously impressed, breathes, "It must be the real truth." Powerhouse puts his hand to his pocket teasingly, as though to pull out the fatal telegram; but he never produces it. "No, babe, it ain't the truth," he says. "Truth is something worse, I ain't said what, yet. It's something hasn't come to me, but I ain't saying it won't. And when it does, then want me to tell you?" Then he turns up his eyes, smiles dreamily, and the waitress screams in terror and delight.

In this story the line between fact and fantasy has begun to blur. We may reach the safe conclusion that the conventional "gory details" and all the hocus-pocus about the jinxing Uranus (originally a star—Titan of the sky) Knockwood (knock-on-wood) indicate that Powerhouse has only made fantasy of his general and specific fears in order to relieve himself and to entertain his audience; but no provision is made for an unequivocal assertion that Gypsy either has or has not on account of loneliness been unfaithful to Powerhouse or killed herself. For "fact" we should trust Powerhouse's mysterious denials no more than his mysterious assertions, but the point is that we aren't expected to be interested in trusting either literally. We are only meant to perceive and enjoy Powerhouse as everything that his name implies: a tremendous human dynamo that is capable of taking in any raw fact of nature— even sudden death by violence—and with the energy he generates in the "Powerhouse" of his blood and his imagination, of pouring out the wild order of his music. Fantasy is his product, an important mode of his being, the necessary ingredient of what he is; "the facts of the case" have simply ceased to be relevant. The narrator of the story, assuming the implicitly collective point of view of "civilized" but fascinated white people toward the Negro jazz musician, abandons herself to the fantasy observed and created, and we are swept along in that abandonment, as we would have been swept into the jazz itself had we actually heard it. Thus both the mode of narration and the subject of the narrative participate in, or project, the fantasy.

"Old Mr. Marblehall," which exhibits an even more marked ambiguity in the relation of fact to fantasy, is the story of an old man's battle against public unconcern and the private sense of boredom and insignificance. Through delicate and complex maneuvers in point of view, the narrator shows us both the public attitude of Natchez, the "little party-giving town" he lives in, and Mr. Marblehall's rebellious reaction to this attitude. To the town Mr. Marblehall is nothing ("Nobody gives a hoot about any old Mr. Marblehall")—he is just a little old man from an ancestral house who goes out walking or is driven in his carriage, who is supposed to travel for his health, and who remains insultingly alive and well preserved year after year when he might as well be dead. Mr. Marblehall is determined, however, to be noticed; so he takes a wife and produces a son in his old age, and then looks about furtively for reactions. But nobody gets excited, nobody pays any attention, and nobody is likely to discover that Mr. Marblehall is really leading a double life.

For down in the poorer section of town, Mr. Marblehall has another house, another wife, another son: an identical arrangement, but with curious contrasts. The second wife, short and solid and "combustible," is always complaining; the first, tall and disquieted, hovers nervously. The second little boy has the shrewd monkey look, the tantrum-throwing obstinacy of the first son, but he is even more cunning than the first. Mr. Marblehall's name here is Mr. Bird, and his wife tells the neighbors about the horrible and fantastic tales Mr. Bird reads in bed late at night under a naked light bulb—*Terror Tales* and *Astonishing Stories*.

One day, Mr. Marblehall imagines, his secret will be discovered. One of the shrewd little boys will trail him across town, or perhaps Mr. Marblehall himself will make a public confession—then what astonishment there will be! He consoles himself by thinking how electrified his two wives and sons will be, "to say nothing of most men over sixty-six." He has "caught on, he thinks, to what people are supposed to do. This is it: they endure something inwardly—for a time secretly; they establish a past, a memory; thus they store up life." Having done this, he now waits for "some glorious finish, a great explosion of revelations . . . the future."

But people may never find out, the climax may never come, and nobody cares anyway about being deceived by old Mr. Marblehall. "He may have years ahead yet in which to wake up bolt upright in the bed under the naked bulb, his heart thumping, his old eyes watering and wild, imagining that if people knew about his double life, they'd die."

We may question whether Mr. Marblehall is leading his double life in fact or only in fantasy. But whatever conclusion may be reached, the double life is the important fact of Mr. Marblehall's existence. His rebellion and his pathetic, comic, and yet residually courageous attempt to give his life glamor and significance and the irony of the futility of his effort in the face of public indifference, are the kernel of the story.

II

If Miss Welty's predilection for fantasy was already suggested in *A Curtain of Green* (1941), this interest became loud and clear in her second volume, *The Robber Bridegroom* (1942). The short novel is a riotous blending of European fairy tales and folklore with the tall tales and legends of the Mississippi River country of pioneer days. It reveals the child's unabashed delight in the world of fantasy and legendary history; but in its hints of satire, the way in which human foolishness, envy, greed, and destructiveness are explored, we see the adult's critical intelligence.

From Grimm's *Fairy Tales* (such stories as "The Robber Bridegroom," "The Little Goose Girl," "Rumpelstiltskin," and "Snow White and the Seven Dwarfs"), Miss Welty drew several familiar character types, themes, and situations: the beautiful golden-haired heroine, the wicked ugly stepmother, the bandit bridegroom, the forest hideout, the warning raven, the locket talisman, the talking head in a trunk, the counting out of gold in the robber's lair. From Mississippi history and legend are drawn such folk heroes and types as Mike Fink, champion keelboatman; the Harpe brothers, bandits noted for their barbarous cruelty ("Harpe's Head" being to this day the name of a place where the decapitated head of one of these bandits was placed as a warning to other outlaws); Clement Musgrove, the innocent and successful planter; and Indians, outlaw bands, mail riders, and rich New Orleans merchants.

The links with actuality in this fantasy are, in fact, provided largely by its setting in the historic past. Bandits of all sorts did roam the forest in those days; berryjuice disguises were used; and bragging contests, Indian dances, and massacres actually took place. The atmosphere, the types of events and characters we meet in the story are real, therefore, to that time and place, just as the descriptions of nature are still faithful to the setting. An amusing witness to the "historicity" of this wild little fantasy of Miss Welty's is the fact that it is listed, along with a few soberly historical works, in the bibliography which concludes an *Encyclopedia Americana* article about the state of Mississippi.

"Whatever happened, it happened in extraordinary times, in a season of dreams"—the opening lines of Miss Welty's third volume to which Robert Penn Warren referred—imply a variety of contexts and methods in and through which illusion, fantasy, and the dream world are presented in that collection of stories. "Whatever happened" suggests that actual events may not always be unambiguous, as is the case in "Powerhouse" and "Old Mr. Marblehall," and also, as we shall presently see, in "Asphodel" and "The Purple Hat."

"It happened in extraordinary times" introduces another reason for and variety of the break with strict realism in two of the stories: the events of "First Love" and "A Still Moment," like those of *The Robber Bridegroom,* take place in the legendary past, which for the Natchez Trace and River Country of frontier days (the early 1800's) was indeed extraordinary. Even the historian cannot be sure exactly what happened at the time of the famous Burr conspiracy, nor what motivated the designs of that fabulous rebel; he cannot know with certainty what wild schemes drove the lawless Murrell to his quest for a kingdom of outlaws, or Lorenzo Dow to his for a kingdom of souls. "The times"—that specific period in American history—were favorable to dreams of ambition and conquest, to mad, glorious, heroic and demonic schemes. And in projecting these legendary dreams, Miss Welty is assuming fiction's right to guess, to deal with the elusive mysteries of motivation, while admitting fiction's helplessness or even its unwillingness to define with factual exactitude.

In its literal sense, "the season of dreams" suggests, further, that the particular weather or atmosphere that a season brings is conducive to all sorts of dream states. In "First Love" the season is winter, a deadly cold and bitter one: the screaming north wind is followed by a preternatural calm in which there is "a strange drugged fall of snow"; the Mississippi "shudder[s] and lift[s] from its bed, reaching like a somnambulist driven to go in new places," and in the "fastness" of Natchez it seems that "the whole world, like itself, must be in a transfiguration." This trance-like atmosphere is appropriate to the story of the deaf-mute whose early journeys to the frontier had affected him as "a kind of childhood wandering in oblivion," and whose "first love" will be breathless, lonely, unspoken, existing only in the dream-country of his heart.

In "Livvie" and "At the Landing" springtime becomes the

"season of dreams": the stir of spring excites Livvie, and is "as present in the house as a young man would be"; Jenny's violent initiation to sexual experience takes place when spring floods are ravaging the land, and her sweet, wistful dreams of Billy Floyd are spun out in a sunny springtime pasture. The sleepy noon of a golden day in hot summer is the season for the sensuous, timidly erotic dreams of the three old maids of "Asphodel." In "The Wide Net" Hazel's dreams and hopes of coming motherhood—producing the secret elation "that comes of great hopes and changes, sometimes simply of the harvest time"—and William Wallace's quest for her in the Pearl River, take place when the fully ripened summer edges on autumn. And in "The Winds" little Josie's dreams of childhood and futurity, her instinctive groping on the restless brink of adolescence, are part of the violent equinoctial storm which seizes and shakes her home and shatters the sky with "strangely flowing lightning."

These examples show that every season can be "a season of dreams" in *The Wide Net*, that Miss Welty's characters often tend to be dreamers, that their dreams are beautifully adjusted to their times and seasons, and that the clear focus of her verbal lens upon these worlds of the dreamers (first observed, or conjured up, by means of her own artistic vision) often produces a ravishing effect available to those readers of "willing imagination" whom she covets. For within these dim and lovely flowering places of the human mind, the mysteries may be seen walking about freely.

III

A focus on the dream-world, both waking and sleeping, does not imply a break with actuality, though it necessarily implies a shift in emphasis from the "daylight" world of ordinary, rationally perceived events and actions to the inner world of hopes, fears, desires. In addition to this general shift to the inner world of dreams, we find in *The Wide Net* a few tentative, a few more bold and explicit excursions into the kind of fantasy which involves a break with actuality. The title story, for instance, contains a brief, slightly fantastic episode in the appearance of the King of the Snakes. The allusions of "Asphodel" are frankly mythological, the mode hints of allegory (the pagan forces are arrayed against the "civilized" forces); but the story contains enough of what Henry James would call "solidity of specification" to evoke a clear image of the small southern town dominated by, but eventually defeating the strong-willed aristocrat. (As a type, Miss Sabina bears a family resemblance to Faulkner's Miss Emily.)

"The Purple Hat" comes closest to pure Gothic supernaturalism; but it also contains a solid admixture of realism in the setting of the New Orleans bar which frames the story, and in the descriptive details used to convey the nature of the storyteller and his two listeners. These two listeners are a passively curious bartender and an intensely involved young alcoholic who is obviously an active participant in the fantastic events and their import.

The fat storyteller is an armed guard who circles the little catwalk beneath the dome of a large New Orleans casino, the "Palace of Pleasure." From his uniquely exalted vantage point, he has seen a rather old, shabby woman with a strange purple hat who has been coming to the casino for years and has been luring a series of young men with the intrigues of her fabulous crown—an "ancient, battered, outrageous hat" decorated with "awful plush flowers" and "a little glass vial with a plunger." The catwalker is convinced that the woman is a ghost, because he has seen her twice murdered by one of her young men—once shot point-blank; the second time stabbed by the long flashing jeweled hatpin which she wears to balance the weight of the attractive little plunger. But each time after an absence of a week or two, she reappears, and the whole process is repeated. As the story is told, the young man drinks feverishly and listens intently: it is apparent that he has already been victimized and already ruined by the fascinations of the purple hat, that he is to be the next murderer that very night, and that he and the fat man know it.

The story is obscure, but it invites a loosely allegorical interpretation. The "Palace of Pleasure" is the fantasy world to which old women flee to escape boredom and to which young men who are born victims (New Orleans is "the birthplace of ready-made victims") are drawn in pursuit of what is exotic and sinfully pleasurable. There they fall in love, not with the concrete woman herself (though she is a "lover," a *femme fatale* who knows all the tricks of seduction) but with the tawdry image of beauty, the hat she wears on her head. That crown attracts them because of the dangerous, ineluctable mystery of the little vial which might contain who knows what magic love potion or poison—some secret path to pleasure—some absolute, dangerous, forbidden knowledge or sensation which is perpetually luring and is yet perpetually denied them. But after they have fallen, and "love has blossomed," and the hat is "thrilling to the touch"—after they have become thoroughly victimized by the pursuit of pleasure—they reach a point of frustration. They can "no longer be sure about the little vial" because in privacy they may find it empty. "It is her coquettishness, you see. She leads you on. . . ." The dream, the feverish hope, may turn out to be without content, as empty as the vial. Then the young men seek revenge by trying to destroy the agent of temptation and promise, but their attempt is necessarily futile, because she is as deathless as is man's pursuit of pleasure.

The catwalker is the fascinated but detached spectator who now and then has a strange illusion of power—"the feeling . . . that you could put out your finger and make a change in the universe." He is not sympathetic as is another such god-like spectator of the human comedy, the young man in "The Key." The catwalker is symbolically as well as literally fat: he fattens on his curiosity, his superior knowledge, his powers of prediction, and he contemplates the symbol of his power, the large red ruby on a fat finger of his puffy, powerless little hand (the stone being a miniature of the red-carpeted criss-crossing aisles of the gem-like Palace). He seems almost to enjoy the idea that the old woman's blood has soaked into the red carpet unnoticed and that all crimes pass without concern because "nobody cares"; he teases the next victim, the alcoholic youth, into a shattering awareness of his plight and the fact of his detection. The sense of terror in the story is produced not only by the use of supernatural events, but even more by the uncanny sense of this distant watcher of the glamorous, luring, fatal "Palace of Pleasure," who would not lift a little fat finger to help, whose curiosity is passionless and unsympathetic, and whose knowledge is therefore horribly exposing, indecent, abysmal.

After *The Wide Net* one does not again find in Miss Welty's work such clear excursions into fantasy as those of *The Robber Bridegroom* or "The Purple Hat." "Circe" might be counted as a single exception, but in this story the myth is assumed from the outset and the viewpoint of the sorceress is adopted chiefly as a way to investigate what it means to be a human being. This deliberate inversion in perspective is designed to create amazement and wonder, not at the mystery of what is supernatural or superhuman, but at the mystery of what is wholly natural, human, actual.

IV

A significant tendency, a distinct power of the human mind, is the ability to create dreams and fantasies, and with this tendency Miss Welty has always been in sympathy. How she has gone out to meet it, lovingly spied, reported on it, and shared in it may be seen not only throughout her fiction but in two non-fiction sketches written about some representatives of that great southern race of fantasy-builders, the Negroes. One sketch, "Pageant of Birds" (*New Republic,* October, 1943), is an account of how the members of a Negro congregation, with no other materials than some bright tissue paper and their own lively imaginations, create a colorful and fascinating pageant of birds, themselves *become* birds, and so "bedazzle" both themselves and their spectators.

The other sketch, "Ida M'Toy" (*Accent,* Summer, 1942), is a characterization of a fabulous old Negress of Jackson who was for thirty-five years a midwife and practical nurse and then for the next twenty-five years was a dealer in second-hand clothes. The woman emerges as a kind of prophetess or sibyl who is full of the joy and wonder of life, proud of having for so many years assisted in the mysteries and rites of human birth: her "most constant gestures today still involve a dramatic out-thrust of the right hand, and let any prominent name be mentioned . . . and she will fling out her palm and cry into the conversation, 'Born in this hand!' "

Although the second or commercial phase of her career might appear to vitiate the first half, since the old woman makes a 25 per cent profit on everything she sells and frequently bewitches her customers into buying gaudily ornamented and practically useless garments, her life forms a beautifully organic whole. What could be a "grubby enough little business" is not so, Miss Welty says, because Ida's handling of it "has become an affair of imagination, . . . an expression of a whole attitude of life as integrated as an art or a philosophy." Ida has a way of making her customers feel like queens: very beautiful and noble, very important. She sends them out "wrapped . . . in some glowing raiment of illusion. . . . With some little flash of scarf, some extra glitter of trimming for which they have paid dearly, dressed like some visions in Ida's speculations on the world, . . . all rampant and somehow fulfilled by this last touch of costume as though they have been tapped by a spirit when Ida's thimble rapped them, they float dizzily down the steps and through the flowers out the gate; and you could not help thinking of the phrase 'going out into the world' as if Ida had birthed them anew."

What human joy, what renewal of spirit grows out of the fantasy life Ida has touched off in those magic moments spent in her conjurer's shop! Miss Welty's sketch of Ida M'Toy speaks of the value, even the dignity, of such dreamers and fantasy-makers.

Even in her portrayal of dream-life, Miss Welty again exhibits the shaping influence of place. Something about the South encourages dreaming—less its history and legends, possibly, than the heat and fragrance of its long summers. "Southern summer is nostalgic," she once wrote, "because even when it happens it's dream-like. Find the shade of the biggest tree; in it your hammock is dreaming already, like a boat on the stream."[3] In "No Place for You, My Love," an Eastern business-man contrasts the open, naïve face of a Midwestern young woman—a face which says "show me," and "now-watch-out-everybody"—with the faces of the other women sitting in that New Orleans restaurant—faces wearing "the Southern look—Southern mask—of life-is-a-dream irony, which could turn to pure challenge at the drop of a hat. . . ." The generalization is tempting to pursue, faintly damning, faintly praising in both directions. Perhaps in the perception we may again discern the northern and southern blend in Miss Welty's perspective: its end product, earnestness and candor, as well as sophistication and irony, are visible too on the face of her fiction.

In all the manifestations, forms, and degrees of dream and fantasy life which Miss Welty projects in her stories, there is, however, one constant element: a firm rooting in reality. The observer in her always coexists with the sympathetic dreamer. In *Place in Fiction* Miss Welty remarks: "Fantasy itself must touch ground with at least one toe, and ghost stories must have one foot, so to speak, in the grave." It is probably because she has always somewhere "touched ground" that Miss Welty has been successful in fantasy as well as in that other means to human refreshment and insight, the mode of comedy.

CHAPTER 6

Delta Wedding: "A Comedy of Love"

I

THE BRIDE of *Delta Wedding*, Dabney Fairchild, receives from her two maiden aunts the wedding gift of a tiny porcelain lamp with a delicately painted cylinder chimney on top of which rests a perfect small teapot. On this cylinder is a picture of a little town with trees, towers, people, windowed houses, a bridge, and a sky full of clouds, sun, stars, and moon. But when the candle inside the cylinder is lit, there appears a glowing redness from within and the little town amazingly takes fire, since the heat of the candle produces the illusion of the motion of flames. This beautiful little lamp resembles a kind of china night-light familiar in her childhood to Miss Welty, which she describes in her essay on *Place in Fiction*, and then uses as a metaphor of what happens in fiction. "The lamp alight is the combination of internal and external, glowing at the imagination as one; and so is the good novel." In real life these inner and outer surfaces lie close together, are "implicit in each other"; and to render that reality, the novel must be "steadily alight, revealing."

The metaphor is applicable to much of Miss Welty's own work, and especially to *Delta Wedding*. In this novel the surface shapes, the pictures, the external life presented are so extraordinarily plentiful, however, that our attention may be devoured by this inexhaustible richness. To begin with, we have the Fairchild clan—Battle and Ellen Fairchild and their eight children (the second of whom is to be married to the plantation overseer Troy), and a dozen or more of aunts, uncles, and cousins, all of whom live in nearby family homes or have collected for the wedding; in addition, there is an array of Negro servants attached to the family. "Shellmound" is a burgeoning home, as thoroughly lived in as any house in fiction

or out, with its large collection of high, shabby old rooms,
floral rugs and matting, rocking chairs, and "little knickknacks
and playthings and treasures all shaken up in them together"
as the family steadily swells in size: a house "where, in some
room at least, the human voice was never still." There is also
the ceaseless variety of chatter and activity which works up
to a pitch unusual even for "Shellmound" as the wedding day
approaches and trains are met, relatives visit back and forth,
embrace and kiss, dances are attended, cakes baked, children's
games played, and enormous meals consumed. (A typical Fairchild menu consists of "chicken and ham and dressing and gravy,
and good, black snap beans, greens, butter beans, okra, corn
on the cob, all kinds of relish, and watermelon-rind preserves,
and that good bread," and, since the family is having "just a
pieced dessert, without George to fix something special for—
some of Primrose's put-up peaches and the crumbs of the coco-
nut cake.") A bright rainbow of color is provided by clothing
and flowers; and the fecundity of earth, the soft ripeness of
plantation cotton, the profuse natural growth in the warmth
of the Delta September season, enforce the pervasive sense of
plenitude. But all this busyness is still only surface, the external painting on the cylinder chimney; inside the flame is glowing, with all the beauty, excitement, and danger that fire con-
notes: and that fire—the inner life of the central characters—
is the essential life of the novel, lighting up the rich surface
texture.

The focus is generally on the nature of the Fairchild family:
on what distinguishes the men from the women, the insiders
from the outsiders (that is, those who have "married in"), the
perplexities of their relationship to each other, and the solitary,
unique, joyous or painful growth of each private sensibility,
both as it reflects the others and as it begins to discover itself.
Despite all their family warmth and shared activity, the Fairchilds are intensely private identities. Their significant thoughts
and feelings seldom break into words, their perceptions are
intuitive, their "analysis" is internal. Sitting around together in
the "closest intimacy," they yet bask in the "greatest anonymity";
at times they seem "more different and farther apart than the
stars"; and even the bride and her mother have "gone into shells
of mutual contemplation—like two shy young girls meeting in
a country of a strange language." When the music of Mary
Lamar Mackey's nocturne comes from another room, the house

becomes "like a nameless forest, wherein many little lives live privately each to its lyric pursuit and its shy protection." Though the baffling, frustrating, lonely side of "separateness" is shown in the novel, its attractive rather than its tragic aspect is stressed. "Separateness" protects the vulnerable and provides a shell against exposure, so that within each shell the tender life may silently evolve with trembling or joy, enduring its burdens of pleasure or of pain.

The specific event that points up several problems of identity and relationship in the novel takes place two weeks before the opening events. Most of the family have been picnicking, and on the way home, tired and singing, they walk on the railroad track. One of the cousins, a simple-minded child named Maureen ("funny in her head"), catches her foot in the trestle; and as Uncle George kneels down to try to release the foot, a local train, the "Yellow Dog," comes bearing down. The others jump, but George does not: he wrestles with the caught foot while Maureen senselessly spreads her arms out across the path of the engine. The train comes to a stop; there is a "tumbling denouement"; and then Robbie Reid, George's young wife, who has been viewing the impending tragedy with terror, cries out in violent protest, "George Fairchild, you didn't do this for *me!*"

The complex implications of this incident reverberate through the story, for right after it Troy and Dabney go up the railroad track and get engaged; Robbie bursts into open rebellion; Shelley shames herself by revealing a symptomatic cowardice. Thinking of it later, Ellen feels that "perhaps that near-calamity on the trestle was nearer than she had realized to the heart of much that had happened in her family lately—as the sheet lightning of summer plays in the whole heaven but presently you observe that each time it concentrates in one place, throbbing like a nerve in the sky."

The "hero" of both the trestle incident and the novel is George Fairchild. His action defines his nature, which is scrutinized and contemplated endlessly, patiently and impatiently, with awe and vexation, with detachment and devouring. He is seen always from the outside, and it is exactly because of the thoroughness with which he is seen through the minds and hearts of his wife, sisters, and nieces that we realize the depth and breadth both of love's knowledge by intuitive penetration, and its helpless ignorance. Miss Welty has walked her readers round George several times over—the relative length of the novel form gives her an opportunity for leisure, amplitude, and variety of circumspection—so that we seem to know everything about him. But in the end she is, by implication, throwing up her hands and saying, "See how much *can't* be known—who and what *is* he, or anybody?"

George is the family idol and the inheritor and living exponent of the legend about Denis (brilliant, free, intense, squandering of his love), the brother who had been killed in World War I: the two of them had been "born sweet." Dabney perceives that Uncle George, "the very heart of the family," is different from the rest of them; and once, thinking about him, she recalls a couple of incidents which seem to clarify his rare and precious nature:

> She saw Uncle George lying on his arm on a picnic, smiling to hear what someone was telling, with a butterfly going across his gaze, a way to make her imagine all at once that in that moment he erected an entire, complicated house for the butterfly inside his sleepy body. It was very strange, but she had felt it. She had then known something he knew all along, it seemed then—that when you felt, touched, heard, looked at things in the world, and found their fragrances, they themselves made a sort of house within you, which filled with life to hold them, filled with knowledge all by itself, and all else, the other ways to know, seemed calculation and tyranny.

She remembers too an incident from childhood in which she had unexpectedly come upon George in the woods, naked, fresh out of the bayou, catching a knife flung by one of two little Negroes, stopping their violent and dangerous wrestling, and then "disgracefully" taking them both against his side. Dabney had protested against that—"all the Fairchild in her had screamed at his interfering—at his taking part—*caring* about anything in the world but them." She is awed at the kind of sweetness which could be "the visible surface of profound depths—the surface of all the darkness that might frighten her. . . . George loved the *world*, something told her suddenly. Not them! Not them in particular." Her fear springs from her awareness that deep, universal love can never be made to focus singly, simply, protectingly, on any one family or person: the Fairchilds can never possess him, he can and will not exist solely for them. It springs too from her unfaced sense that this kind of love is an end product of an active, courageous participation in all human life, of suffering sustained, of terrors met and subdued. George the beloved, the peacemaker, is apart from the family which mothers him indulgently and yet relies upon him as its conscience and protector.

There are others in the family who perceive this special quality in George. Shelley records in her diary: "I think Uncle George takes us one by one. That is love, I think." Laura, the little motherless cousin who comes to "Shellmound" for the wedding, thinks how "it was right for him to stand apart" because his kindness, unlike that of the other Fairchilds, was "more than an acting in kindness, it was a waiting, a withholding, as if he could see a fire or light, when he saw a human being—regardless of who it was, kin or not, . . . and had never done the first thing in his life to dim it." She wants to protect him from the crowding in of the Fairchilds. If "Shellmound" would only burn down, she wildly dreams, she could rescue him and then "give him room"—let him be "mean and horrible— horrible to the horrible world." Laura too is experiencing the desire individually to protect and be protected by this strangely detached, universal love.

George has, of course, already broken loose from the family bonds (if they ever held him) in taking as his wife little Robbie Reid, a local store clerk. The marriage is considered shockingly "beneath" a Fairchild, and Dabney too is breaking the social code by marrying Troy, an overseer. Robbie loves George deeply and knows his "real and forgetful and exacting body," "the heat of his heavy arm, the drag of his night beard over her"; she responds to his pure, helpless need of her. But she is greatly troubled by the continual and insistent demands of the Fairchild women, who seem to ask "small sacrifice by small sacrifice, the little pieces of the whole body!" It seems to Robbie that in his action on the trestle, George is making an instinctive if not a conscious choice between the Fairchilds and herself; it is as if all the Fairchilds, and George himself, assumed that the final sacrifice of love and loyalty had to be made unhesitatingly to the idiot child of the legendary Denis rather than to his own wife.

To Robbie her husband's rescue of Maureen seems related to all the intangible, aristocratic loyalties which she cannot feel or understand and which she therefore deeply resents. George "evidently felt," she thinks, "that old stories, family stories,

Mississippi stories, were the same as very holy or very passionate. . . . He looked out at the world, at her, sometimes, with the essence of the remote, proud, over-innocent Fairchild look that she suspected, as if an old story had taken hold of him—entered his flesh. And she did not know the story." Ever since her marriage Robbie has felt terribly "out of it," and now her resentment springs into open rebellion when it seems that the Fairchilds may demand even the life of her beloved, which would, in fact, be her own life, since she loves him enough to want to "turn into him."

After the trestle incident, she runs away from George in a fury, leaving him in solitary, noncommittal hurt and puzzlement on the eve of Dabney's wedding. During the process of her long spiritual journey back to him, the agony of which is symbolized by her long walk on the killingly hot, dusty road from the store to "Shellmound," she tortures into fully recognized existence the reasons for her fear and hatred. The Fairchilds' family love of George is too fiercely possessive and binding; it is threatening, unworthy of him. George needs a love of "pure gold, a love that could be simply beside him—her love. Only she could hold him against that grasp, that separating thrust of Fairchild love that would go on and on persuading him, comparing him, begging him, crowing over him, slighting him, proving to him, sparing him, comforting him, deceiving him, confessing and yielding to him, tormenting him, . . . those smiling and not really mysterious ways of the Fairchilds."

But if she supposes she must save him from the Fairchilds, from dedicating his life to the family myth, she knows, to her humiliation and pain, that it cannot be by more of her own pleading and demanding. With shame she recalls her own weakness, when she had, by her look of terror, called out to George "to come back from his danger as a favor to her," and had seen him thrust away "the *working* of the Fairchild mask," which was the mask of pleading for more and more of his giving. "Unless," she thinks, "pleading must go on forever in life, and was no mask, but real, for longer than other things, for longer than winning and having."

Robbie has seen the family demands on George's potential sacrifice and indulgence, and she has observed as well his rejection of whatever is selfish in those demands. She even has the wisdom of recognizing herself, briefly, as neither better nor worse than the other Fairchilds in her pleading for and to George. She must resign herself to the fact of the inexhaustible human need for love and to the final elusiveness of the beloved in the face of love that is greedy or pleading. George may appear to be granting special favors to this one and that, but he is not—even to his most passionately loving wife. There is both dramatic and moral propriety in Robbie's having to come back to *him;* for if a heroic action ever appears wrong, it is wrong only to the person whose identity has been so completely emptied into that of the hero that the two lives seem risked instead of one. The awe-filling poise, the seemingly inhuman detachment of a universal love, is a source of frustration or even of terror to any human being who loves in the "normal"— that is, the personal, "attached"—way. Dabney and Laura touch this mystery only lightly because of their relational distance from George; Robbie, as his wife, is plunged into it fully.

And yet Robbie knows that the very quality which makes George's love independent will also make him take nothing for granted in their relationship. He will woo her all over again when she comes back to him, "as if she were shy"; he will need to come back to her "as a little spring where he had somehow cherished only the hope for the refreshment that all the time flowed boundlessly enough." The traveler, the proud, independent adventurer, the detached lover, is the supplicant too. She knows that he needs her, wants her, loves her in a simple lover's way—she has that to fling at the Fairchilds and to protect her pride.

As a favored center of consciousness in the novel, Ellen is the most balanced of the major characters, the most mature and objectively "reliable." She stands in the midst of the family as mother, wife, sister; but she is not a Fairchild, not by nature a plantation mistress; she is only, "in her original heart, . . . a town-loving, book-loving young lady of Mitchem Corners" (Virginia). Out of her frantically busy life, she watches with tender concern the growth of her children and all the developing relationships around her; and she sees everything: Dabney's wild hope and expectation of life; Laura's pathetically eager desire to be drawn into the family and stay on at "Shellmound"; Shelley's emotional tightness, her inward fear and outrage at her younger sister's marriage; Battle's and his sisters' disapproval of Dabney's marriage to an overseer; Robbie's grievances against the Fairchild's; George's apartness ("she felt that he was, in reality, not intimate with this household at all"). Through love's observation she knows everybody from the inside, hopes for everybody, and with exquisitely gentle tact and grace, works for harmony in patient ways which are rather like those of Mrs. Ramsey in *To The Lighthouse.*

The climax of the novel occurs in the scene following Robbie's return to "Shellmound." As luck would have it, George is out visiting the two maiden aunts, and the rest of the Fairchilds are finishing dinner. Half sick, dirty and tired, Robbie must suffer the humiliation of joining them at the table and hearing one of George's older sisters, Tempe, voice the family accusation: "*Why* have you treated George Fairchild the way you have? . . . Except for Denis Fairchild, the sweetest man ever born in the Delta?" Robbie's immediate response is a stout inward rebellion against what she considers their insufferable vanity, their inability to feel deeply, their injustice in demanding from her a penitent attitude, and their intolerance and refusal to love outside the family.

Just then a little crisis occurs. One of the Negro servants rushes in crying, "Miss Rob' come in lettin' bird in de house!"; another cries, "Bird in de house mean death!" The family jump up from their chairs, and a chase ensues during which are heard cries of excitement, distress, challenge—"Get it out! Get it out!" Ellen is left to confront Robbie alone in a meeting supremely taxing to Ellen's honesty, tact, courage, and love. For a potentially destructive force has indeed come with Robbie's entrance into the family and the outcome of her relationship with George is somehow both harbinger and omen of the coming relationship of Dabney with Troy. To the sound of beating wings, and with a muffled sense of excitement and danger, Ellen "has it out" with Robbie, hears the reason for all her hurt and protest, and admits: "There is a fight and it's come between us, Robbie." But she insists that the fight is not over George, who would be hurt and shamed to know of the quarrel and who should not be "pulled to pieces, and over something he . . . very honorably did." The real fight, she says, is "*in* us, already, . . . *in* people on this earth, not between us, and there is a fight in Georgie too. It's part of being alive. . . . The fight in you's over things, not over people. . . . Things like the truth, and what you owe people." Ellen sees that the internal fight is a condition of life itself, and so necessarily George struggles as he tries to live honorably and independently as well as lovingly, as he tries to reconcile his various loyalties and to resist what is merely possessive in the Fairchilds or his wife.

As she speaks, Ellen has subconsciously blended the throbbing, beating sound of the bird wings with a memory of the sound of fire bells ringing; the cries of pursuit and the general sense of danger and climax with another time of panic when the gin had caught fire several years back and she had fainted and miscarried a child. Now George suddenly appears at the door, shirt torn back, shoulders bare, "looking joyous." Ellen cries "Is it out? Is the fire out?"; then to George, "Don't let them forgive you, for anything, good or bad. Georgie, you've made this child suffer." Finally relief sweeps over Ellen; she has said what needed saying, a series of catastrophes has been miraculously avoided. "The Yellow Dog had not run down George and Maureen; Robbie had not stayed away too long; Battle had not driven Troy out of the Delta; no one realized Aunt Shannon was out of her mind; even Laura had not cried yet for her mother. For a little while it was a charmed life. . . ." Ellen faints, but is revived after a half hour; the bird is caught; and it turns out, appropriately, to be a brown female thrush.

Ellen's further reflections on the meaning of what has transpired form a major part of the concluding sections of the novel. In odd moments she thinks about George's "resembled indifference"—his apparent lack of intense concern over such major events as Dabney's marriage or Robbie's anguish; "but little Ranny, a flower, a horse running, a color, a terrible story listened to in the store in Fairchilds, or a common song, and yes, shock, physical danger, as Robbie had discovered, roused something in him that was immense contemplation, motionless pity, indifference." There is a "wild detachment" in him which she finds akin to her own feeling—"perhaps she had fainted in the way he was driven to detachment."

Ellen's sense of kinship with George has been deepened by their shared experience of separate encounters with a mysterious, incredibly beautiful girl found roaming in the woods. The very fact of his also meeting her by chance had amazed Ellen because "it was a thing she had never learned in her life, to expect that what has come to you, come in dignity to yourself in loneliness, will yet be shared, the secret never intact." Even more amazing is George's direct statement that he had taken

the girl "over to the old Argyle gin and slept with her." Ellen
is rocked at this (as is the reader), but she quickly recovers,
knowing George to be incapable of any degrading action;
despite his "fierce energies" and "heresies," he leaves the world
"as pure . . . as he [finds] it; still real, still bad, still fleeting
and mysterious and hopelessly alluring to her." Later their
secret is darkly extended when they learn that the girl in her
wanderings has been accidently killed on the railroad track,
as if to prove that George's challenge of death was no harmless joke, because a train on a track could indeed kill.

Watching George at the dance after the wedding it seems to
Ellen as though "any act on his part might be startling, isolated
in its very subtlety from the action of all those around him,
springing from long, dark, previous abstract thought and direct
apprehension, instead of explainable, Fairchild impulse." Given
this complexity of mind, it is inevitable that George should
act in such careless defiance. "He was capable—taking no more
prerogative than a kind of grace, no more than an ordinary
responsibility—of meeting a fate whose dealing out to him he
would not contest; even when to people he loved his act was
'conceited,' if not absurd, if not just a little story in the family."
And so, too, George was "capable of the same kind of love.
Indeed, there danced Robbie, the proof of this. To all their
eyes shallow, unworthy, she was his love; it was her ordinary
face that was looking at him through the lovely and magic veil,
little Robbie Reid's from the store."

What George is and what he does seem to constitute an
important answer to the problems raised in some of Miss Welty's
earlier stories: problems about how to exist in the face of
potential accident or catastrophe, vulnerable to the whims of
fate; how to act freely and without fear; how to live through
and out of love. Again it is the existential act which makes life
significant, beautiful, even heroic. Deeply felt through Ellen's
perspective is an admiration of this divinely careless attitude;
this joyous or courageous embracing of experience; this throwing of the self in the way of every kind of potential danger,
"ready for anything all the time," "magnificently disrespectful";
this unflinching confrontation of death in all its myriad forms,
physical or emotional: a state which looks simple and spontaneous, but is in fact supremely sophisticated, fully aware,
lying beyond infinite complexities of thought and experience.
Seeing George's glorious independence, Ellen knows how use-

less is even her own form of solicitude for him, her tolerance
and compassion:

> He appeared, as he made his way alone now and smiling through
> the dancing couples, infinitely simple and infinitely complex,
> stretching the opposite ways the self stretches; . . . but at the
> same time he appeared very finite in that he was wholly sin-
> gular and dear, and not promisingly married, tired of being a
> lawyer, a smiling, intoxicated, tender, weather-worn, late-tired,
> beard-showing being.

Miss Welty's vision of both the enormous possibilities and
limitations of love, the theme of "love and separateness," have
also been fully explored in this novel, and under optimum conditions: namely, where the characters are fully aware adults;
where there is a great deal of love and the possibility of communication to begin with, because of the existence of social and
personal contexts and relationships favorable to its flowering;
because the novel form provides space for more extensive analysis of the complex thoughts and feelings involved than would
a short story. It is, on the whole, not a tragic vision of love's
possibilities; the novel, as John Crowe Ransom has named it,
is a "comedy of love."

II

The question remains how all this "inner glow" of the novel
is seen through, or fused with, the profuse "outer surface."
Since the "plot" is largely a matter of the internal development
of the characters, some readers have found the novel episodic,
crowded with minor events, lacking in structural coherence, and
anticlimactic in the way its central external event—the wedding
itself—is reduced to the plainest sentence: "Mr. Rondo married
Dabney and Troy." The structural coherence of the novel is
found, however, in the internal developments already described:
in them we find the basic situations, complications, tension,
crisis and resolution that we look for in well-constructed fiction.

But it must be admitted that the fusion of the outer and inner
life in the novel is not always complete. There is a good deal of
skipping back and forth, which at its worst produces this kind
of writing:

> As Ellen put in the nutmeg and the grated lemon rind she
> diligently assumed George's happiness, seeing it in the Fairchild
> aspects of exuberance and satiety; if it was unabashed, it was

the best part true. But—adding the milk, the egg whites, the flour, carefully and alternately as Mashula's recipe said—she could be diligent and still not wholly sure—never wholly. She loved George too dearly herself to seek her knowledge of him through the family attitude, keen and subtle as that was. . . .

That intelligent and sensitive housewives engage in such analysis of their loved ones while baking cakes is undeniable, but the realism of the narrative method in this instance remains fundamentally awkward. The noble function, the glory of language in literature—as we have heard from Coleridge, T. S. Eliot, and others—is to reconcile opposites, to make a unity of things disparate in real life; and there is nothing in the language of this passage to weld the two different sets of experience. The fusion, where and when it occurs, comes through the creation of atmosphere, and the free use of metaphor and symbol. Miss Welty informs and infuses her descriptions of the physical world—woods, river and field, time and texture of day or night, house interiors, even external events—with the emotions of her characters. The language which projects the inner world is sympathetic to the language which conveys the outside world. Two examples of this correlation have already been suggested: an atmosphere of cruel and killing midday heat on a dusty road is related to Robbie's sense of terrible exposure, hurt, ordeal, as she takes the long hot walk in the boiling sun; and the atmosphere of panic and excitement caused by the bird chase provides a counterpart to Ellen's sense of crisis in confronting Robbie on her return.

But the technique may be seen functioning already, and more delicately, in the opening pages of the novel. Laura is riding the train into the Delta country, which is closely and beautifully painted; but the description is charged throughout with the intense, compressed anticipation and excitement of the little traveler—who feels terribly grown up (all of nine years old), yet is a bit frightened and young, as she reviews each delight of landscape: the tones and colors of field and sky which open themselves upon her eye, memory, and imagination. With an almost dizzying joy and solemnity she re-enters the land of enchantment, so that the train seems to be racing with the yellow butterflies outside the window; the slightest, gayest note of panic is sounded when a white foxy farm dog runs beside the train barking sharply; the large clouds seem "larger than horses or houses, larger than boats or churches or gins, larger than anything except the fields the Fairchilds planted"; the land lies flat and level, but it shimmers "like the wing of a lighted dragonfly"; it seems "strummed, as though it were an instrument and something had touched it." In order both to endure and increase the pleasure, Laura sinks her teeth delightedly into a banana; then later she watches the sky color change till "all that had been bright or dark was now one color," a glowing "like a hearth in firelight." At the conclusion of the opening passage we find the explicit statement: "Laura . . . felt what an arriver in a land feels—that slow hard pounding in the breast." But we have felt the little heart beating excitedly all through the description.

The scene of Dabney's early morning ride out to view "Marmion" is another illustration of the creation of picture and atmosphere as a correlative to inner experience. Dabney is as young, fresh, and lovely as the fully described morning. She is much in love with Troy, but more with "sweet life" itself. With the same free, bounding spirit she exhibits in riding her red filly across the plantation, she throws off the burden of the family honor in her thoughts (as she will presently in her action by marrying Troy); for she hates whatever kills or limits life and is determined "to give up nothing" to prove her happiness. But the whirlpool in the Yazoo River, into which she later gazes broodingly for a few moments, remembering stories about its many victims and watching the alien life of twisted cypress roots and water snakes turning and moving there, represents her fears about the dark and threatening aspects of her uncertain future as mistress of "Marmion." In this manner Miss Welty fuses inner and outer event, external atmosphere and internal feeling in the novel.

Atmosphere becomes symbol in many of these instances, and so it is with the patterns of light and dark in the novel. Isolated lights surrounded by darkness suggest human isolation or mystery; light from within, shining out from or illuminating a surface, may suggest insight or communication. Out in the night after the wedding Ellen sees the whirling dancers "burning as sparks of fire to her now, more different and apart than stars"; but a moment later she sees George's mind "as if it too were inversely lighted up by the failing paper lanterns—lucid and tortuous." In the closing scene of the novel, after their supper picnic, the family are lying on the grassy blanket beside the

Yazoo River, singing "softly, wanderingly, each his way," looking at the stars falling. The insects all over the Delta are noisy,
and "a kind of audible twinkling, like a lowly starlight, per-
vade[s] the night with a gregarious radiance." So the family is
"gregarious"; the desultory chatter, teasing, and relaxed specu-
lating about the future provide the "audible twinkling"; but each
person is essentially drawn up into quiet reflection and soli-
tude; each is a bright star, a beautiful, separate, mysterious
identity in the wide dark sky.

According to another pattern, light may suggest what is familiar and comforting, the security of childhood and innocence,
over against which darkness suggests what is terrifying or potentially destructive in life—passion, experience, change, the unknown future. The night-light is used according to this symbolic
pattern. As a little family treasure, a delight to children, a gift
of the two maiden aunts, who call it "a friendly little thing," it is
something cherished by the innocent, a stay against darkness and
fear, a thing enjoyed within the light and warmth of the family
circle. Riding back beside her sister, India makes a circle with
her fingers, imagining she holds the lamp carefully; it seems
to her "filled with the mysterious and flowing air of night."
When Dabney accidentally drops it while running forward to
meet Troy (who appears to India as "a black wedge in the
lighted window"), she is symbolically shattering not only her
innocence and childhood within the family, but a part of the
family unity itself, its "coziness," one of its legends in a concrete object—all that the two aunts would like to preserve intact,
along with their own and their nieces' virginity. "It's all right,"
Dabney says "cooly enough" after the accident (though she
weeps later as if feeling it "part of her being married that this
cherished little bit of other people's lives should be shattered
now"). But it isn't all right to India, who flings herself sobbing
against George's knees and has to be consoled and teased about
"an old piece of glass that Dabney would never miss." George
protects and comforts the women of his family, but he cannot
and will not preserve them from the "facts of life"—from experience or the wrong-headed fear of it.

The trestle incident, which undergoes continual metamorphosis from fact to legend and back again to fact, also has symbolic
functions related to the theme of innocence and experience.
The train is on a track coming from the outside world; George
has gone to this outside world; he now comes back as a visitor

into the enclosed, protected, self-sufficient world of the Fairchilds—"Shellmound," a mound of shells, an isolated group of essentially private, inwardly sensitive people, who are living more or less on top of each other in a large, white, overcrowded house. The train which comes from the outside is only the familiar "Yellow Dog," but it is a train that *can*, and later *does*, kill. George's act of heroic abandonment on the track is both a protective action and an invitation to experience, or a similar abandonment, to all his young viewers (significantly the adults are not along). He is showing them all clearly that danger *is* involved in living a free, courageous life, but that is the kind of life he himself embodies, and unconsciously challenges them to share.

Troy and Dabney respond by immediately taking their own pledge for a leap into experience—they decide to marry. Shelley responds with an initial terrorized retreat from experience, sexual involvement, mature relationships, and accident and death. For a while she closes even more tightly into her own "shelley" self and into her family shell, "communicating" only with her diary, setting her will against her sister's plunge into experience. She is greatly troubled, feeling that "alarm and protest should be the nature of the body," that life is "too easy" and can change too quickly, that it is never "inviolate." But during the course of the novel she begins to mature, becomes reconciled to the closing of her girlhood relationship to her sister, and is earnestly trying to conquer her various fears. In the end as she is driving the car along the trestle, she is struck all at once with the idea that it would be "so fine to drive without pondering a moment into disaster's edge"—so up and over the trestle she goes before the "Yellow Dog." Mr. Doolittle patiently stops a second time, and Shelley is thoroughly humiliated. The minute she gets over the trestle, she despises her action, "as if she had caught herself contriving." She is learning that genuine fearlessness does not need to make its own occasions for abandonment, or play a game of Russian roulette; life provides such occasions without willful invitation. She should meet experience courageously, not force it.

Hence, to those who witness, react to, ponder the trestle incident, there follows a new view of reality and experience: a clear image of the way to face their threats fearlessly in the life and action of the beloved uncle, husband, brother; a refined potential for significant communication and meaningful relationships; a clearing of the air of illusion, but a deepening of the awareness of mystery.

III

Because the focus of *Delta Wedding* was taken by some readers to be the way of life of the traditional South (or at least what southern plantation society had become by 1923), it was attacked by such northern liberal critics as Isaac Rosenfeld (in the *New Republic*, April 29, 1946) and Diana Trilling (*Nation*, May 11, 1946). They complained that the novel failed to show the relationship between the world of the Fairchilds and southern society as a whole, and that the attitude taken toward the Fairchild mode of life was neither critical nor morally discriminating. Even John Crowe Ransom (*Sewanee Review*, Summer, 1946), though generally admiring of the sensibility and "high art" of living achieved by the Fairchilds as the end-product of their socially and economically structured society, wondered whether they were not being "heedless of the moral and material shortcomings of their establishment." Miss Welty's readers, he said, would surmise that she had witnessed such a society in her youth and had identified herself with the child Laura (as being roughly Laura's age in 1923); he wondered whether the reader might not even conclude that "there was no strategic conception behind this novel other than that Miss Welty was nostalgic for a kind of life that already had passed beyond recognition"—a time before either the introduction of mechanical cotton-pickers and cultivators or the rise of racial tension.

These critics were complaining about the apparent lack of social criticism in the novel, but none of them, I think, had seen clearly that "the South" as such was no part of its concern. Nor was the "southern problem" assumed *not* to exist by reason of exclusion, since no attempt was made to present the Fairchilds as socially or economically typical of any large or significant sector of southern society.[1] "Shellmound" is a separate place, "inside"; "the world" (always, to be sure, the southern world) is "outside": it is Memphis, the city where George has his lawyer's practice and lives with Robbie Reid in a "nice two-story flat," the city to which the beautiful lost girl is headed; it is Ellen's original home in Mitchem Corners, Virginia; Troy's hill country; Jackson, the home of Laura and her father, where the air is different from "Shellmound's" air of "pleasure and excitement." The author's perspective, in actual life as well as functionally in the novel, is that of an "outsider." Miss Welty never lived in the Delta country, and she visited it only once (the town of Greenville, overnight), while she was writing *Delta Wedding*. Her story was partly based on stories and legends of the Delta country told by the old people in her community, and it was probably as much a product of creative and imaginative guess-work and "research" as "A Still Moment" or "First Love."

Miss Welty has made the life at "Shellmound" convincing, but she has not presented it with a total lack of moral discrimination. An implied affection for the Fairchild way of life is balanced by an implied criticism of its tendency to self-protective isolation, its snobbery, the piety surrounding its legends. This criticism is embodied in the stance of George and in the thoughts and actions of the "outsiders" in the family—particularly Ellen and Robbie, and to a lesser extent, Troy. Even Dabney comes to the perspective of an "outsider"; for, reflecting on a chapter in the family history which involved a duel over land, she thinks, "Honor, honor, honor, the aunts drummed it into their ears. . . . To give up your life because you thought that much of your *cotton*—where was the love, even, in that? *Other* people's cotton! Fine glory! Dabney would not have done it." The question perpetually raised in the novel is "where is the love?" in any action or attitude. The central heroic action of George on the trestle is suspect until "the love in it" is disclosed; family loyalty, the basis of family cohesion, is everywhere suspect. The vision which produces the society also provides its testing ground.

Miss Welty's account of why she set her story in 1923 is instructive.[2] She used that date, after some preliminary research, as the only year in which there had not been, either in the world at large or that region in particular, some external catastrophe such as a war, a depression, or a flood. The novel was published in 1946: it was then presumably written during the last stages of World War II. In apparent defiance of the immediate facts of time and history (such a monstrous fact, for instance, as that of the dropping of atomic bombs), Miss Welty lifted a particular place and time out of history in order to learn what might be continuing and permanent in human relations.

We might think of the characters in "Shellmound" as forming a kind of "control group" in an experiment designed to isolate and discover what the possibilities of human love are under the best possible circumstances. In this small, closely knit society there are no outside causes for grief or pain: no war or natural catastrophe, no extremes of poverty or wealth, no sense of rootlessness or insecurity which are by-products of competitive urban society, no serious racial or social disharmony. Furthermore, there is no marked tendency to moral ugliness in any character: we find rather less than the usual human selfishness, rather more than the usual affection and tenderness. In short, the "givens" of the novel are wholly congenial to the flourishing of every sort of love—romantic, conjugal, domestic, filial. (This is in contrast to such stories as "Clytie," "A Curtain of Green," and "Flowers for Marjorie," in which an impossible home situation, sudden death by accident, and a major economic depression—all external causes—ruin the possibilities for human happiness.)

But even in the secure world of "Shellmound" catastrophe threatens, and in every heart are the potentials of fear, distrust, selfishness, introversion—all of which produce the "separateness." "The fight is *in* us, *in* people on this earth," says Ellen, telling us, in effect, where the battles are fought in this novel: telling us to look not simply at the pretty paintings on the china lamp, but through the surface to the dangerous and beautiful flame within, "steadily alight, revealing." *Delta Wedding* is a gentle inquiry into the workings of human love, reaching conclusions that are credible and balanced as well as joyful. As such it may be rediscovered by readers who have dismissed the novel as a social document.

CHAPTER 7

The Search for the Golden Apples

I

THE MOST COMPLEX and encompassing of Miss Welty's works is *The Golden Apples,* a book which can be read not merely as a collection of short stories but as a novel which gathers up several of the motifs of her earlier fiction. The unity of the book derives not only from its focus on the characters who within a forty-year span live and die in one small Mississippi town, Morgana, but from its richly thematic, symbolic, mythical patterns of organization. The best approach to that unity is through the Yeats poem from which Miss Welty draws her title:

THE SONG OF THE WANDERING AENGUS

I went out to the hazel wood
Because a fire was in my head,
And cut and peeled a hazel wand,
And hooked a berry to a thread;
And when white moths were on the wing,
And moth-like stars were flickering out,
I dropped the berry in a stream
And caught a little silver trout.

When I had laid it on the floor
I went to blow the fire aflame,
But something rustled on the floor,
And some one called me by my name:
It had become a glimmering girl
With apple blossoms in her hair
Who called me by my name and ran
And faded through the brightening air.

Though I am old with wandering
Through hollow lands and hilly lands,
I will find out where she has gone,

And kiss her lips and take her hands;
And walk among long dappled grass,
And pluck till time and times are done
The silver apples of the moon,
The golden apples of the sun.

The poem concerns the quest of one of Yeats's favorite Celtic hero-gods, Aengus, who is associated with youth, beauty, and poetry, and who becomes, in the present poem, an alter-ego of the poet. The speaker is "possessed," passionate and restless, and he goes out in the starlit night on a ritual fishing expedition. He catches a silver trout, which changes into a "glimmering girl," a beautiful visionary invitation and lure, who calls out his name, then disappears. Now he is forever in quest to find and possess her, to enjoy eternal happiness, to pluck the apples of which the blossoms in her hair gave promise—the apples which are silver by moonlight, golden by sunlight.

Snatches of this poem appear in the story called "June Recital," welling up in the thoughts of Cassie Morrison when memories of the past, set off by the *"Für Elise"* theme, break over her. She knows that both Miss Eckhart and Virgie Rainey are "human beings terribly at large, roaming on the face of the earth," and she knows that there are others like them, "human beings, roaming, like lost beasts." In the middle of her sleep that night she sits up, says a snatch of the poem (*"Because a fire was in my head"*), then falls back to sleep. The chapter concludes: "She did not see except in dreams that a face looked in; that it was the grave, unappeased, and radiant face, once more and always, the face that was in the poem." The face that looks in on Cassie looks out at us in many guises on every page of the book, for the search of the passionate, tireless, wandering Aengus is the search of all the wanderers in *The Golden Apples:* a search for the glimmering vision which is love, adventure, art, through the achievement of which the golden apples may be plucked, or individual fulfillment realized. And yet, to any Morgana son or daughter, a dream of fulfillment may be only a Fata Morgana—a bewitcher like Morgan the Fay—a mirage, an illusion.

We might think, from the title and content of the opening story, that this fulfillment had already come in the "Shower of Gold" which pours from King MacLain; and we would not be entirely wrong. In this book, as in life, the golden apples are everywhere plucked, and everywhere eternally withheld and pursued: this is the paradox of the glory and comedy of man's achievement and joy, and the tragedy of his frustration and failure.

King MacLain is the first of the wanderers to whom we are introduced, comically, through the monologue of the wise and garrulous Katie Rainey, busy at her churning. Her gossipy idiom plunges us at once into the middle of the life and ethos of this small southern town, and it conveys exactly the mixed admiration and sense of outrage felt by Morgana folk as they contemplate King's amorous career. King stands boldly opposed to what is moral and orderly in their society, mocking both wives and husbands in their respectively submissive roles, tempting and triumphantly seducing the wives, flouting and cuckolding the husbands, appearing and disappearing freely and mysteriously at whim. In his pagan abandon and sensuality, his open defiance of sobriety and decorum, he is allied with such characters as Don McInnis of "Asphodel" and Cash McCord of "Livvie" (curiously, all three surnames are Irish or Scottish Gaelic). Though outrageous like Don McInnis and still another "outrage," Uncle Daniel of *The Ponder Heart* (to whom he is related in warmth, generosity, and an apparent lack of rational and moral intelligence), like both of these men he is courteous and courtly in manner, and like them he also appears in a dazzling and impeccably crisp white suit.

King's mythical counterpart is the Zeus of the roving eye, who involved himself in a series of *amours* with mortal women. His wife, Snowdie Hudson, is obviously related to Danäe, who, according to the Greek myth, was confined by her father in a subterranean chamber or brazen tower and was visited and impregnated by Zeus in a "shower of gold," a glorious stream of sunlight. Snowdie has been established in a house built especially for her by her father. She is an albino, with eyes susceptible to light; a sweet, gentle girl who appears "whiter than your dreams" in her wedding dress. And when, shortly after one of King's visits, she comes to inform Mrs. Rainey that she is expecting a child, Mrs. Rainey says, "It was like a shower of something had struck her, like she'd been caught out in something bright. . . . There with her eyes all crinkled up with always fighting the light, yet she was looking out bold as a lion that day under her brim, and gazing into my bucket and into my stall like a visiting somebody."

King is widely adored for his mystery, his legend, his exoticism (like some ancient merchant he travels, selling tea and spices), his coming by surprise ("Fate Rainey," Mrs. Rainey complains of her husband, "ain't got a surprise in him, and proud of it"), his bringing of gifts, his sexual prowess; and above all, perhaps, for his ability to make of every woman a goddess, a queen, a legend to herself. It is this achievement that King boasts of at the end of the novel when he is old and appears at the funeral of Mrs. Rainey: he tells how he had once given her a swivel chair to use at her selling post on the roadside. "Oh, then, she could see where Fate Rainey had fallen down, and a lovely man too; never got her the thing she wanted. I set her on a throne!" But he is also considered both a show-off and a scoundrel not only for deserting his faithful and courageous wife but also for irresponsibly populating the countryside: "children of his growing up in the County Orphan's, so say several, and children known and unknown, scattered-like." The clearly "known" children are Snowdie's twins, Randall and Eugene; the identity of some of the "unknown" children will be a matter for further speculation.

On the whole, Miss Welty treats the career of King MacLain in a comic manner, with little attempt at complexity of characterization. King is more absurdly human than supernaturally heroic. On one of his surprise visits home he arrives on Hallowe'en, and is himself surprised by the twins, who are frighteningly masked for the nonce and chase round him on their roller skates like little possessed demons, scaring him off in a panic. On another visit, described in the story titled "Sir Rabbit," he cleverly outwits the stupid husband of his willing and gleeful victim, Mattie Will Sojourner (Mattie "will," and she *will* wander) in a hunting encounter in some woods near Morgana. The scene of King's assault of Mattie Will evokes the experience of Leda in Yeats's famous "Leda and the Swan" sonnet. Miss Welty seems to be working simultaneously with what is common and uncommon in the action—the quality that makes it at once actual and mythic. The use of Mattie Will's consciousness makes possible both wonder ("when she laid eyes on Mr. MacLain close, she staggered, he had such grandeur") and a reduction to the commonplace ("she was caught by the hair and brought down as suddenly to earth as if whacked by an unseen shillelagh"). When she has "put on her, with the affront of his body, the affront of his sense too," and finds "no pleasure in that," it is possible that she feels King's need and compulsion as painful to him: there is something of the victim as well as the conqueror in King, with "his whole blithe, smiling, superior, frantic existence." When he has finished with her, she feels she has become "Mr. MacLain's Doom, or Mr. MacLain's Weakness, like the rest, and neither Mrs. Junior Holifield nor Mattie Will Sojourner"; she is part of the legend, "something she had always heard of."

But the tone of the story is largely comic; the prepotent male can't be allowed to be Olympian, except for a moment or two to the dazzled girl. Later, after Mattie Will has come upon him snoring against a tree, his once fiery limbs looking to her "no more driven than any man's, now," she thinks of a depreciatingly funny little rhyme:

> In the night time
> At the right time
> So I've understood,
> 'Tis the habit of Sir Rabbit
> To dance in the wood—

In the last story we find, to our surprise, that King has returned home from his wandering voluntarily and permanently at the age of "sixty-odd." Snowdie, having spent all her parents' money unsuccessfully tracing him through the Jupiter Detective Agency of Jackson, is curiously discontent—ashamed of herself for having tried to find him, confessing in private to Virgie Rainey, "I don't know what to do with him." But despite the visible signs of old age and senility in King (a coffee cup trembles in his hand, his mind is a wandering storehouse of anecdotes from the past), he is permanently defiant; his stiffly starched white suit looks "fierce—the lapels alert as ears," recalling the impudent rabbit in this old gentleman. He retains the irresponsibility of amorality; he can never be coerced or wheedled. And when at Mrs. Rainey's funeral he makes a hideous face at her daughter Virgie Rainey, it is to her like "a silent yell at everything"—propriety and decorum, law and order, human misery, the implications of time's passing, fate, tragedy—a yell at death itself, "not leaving it out." It is a simple joyous assertion by an old man with an untamed spirit of "the pure wish to live."

Among the wanderers, King seems to have plucked more than his share of the golden apples; but then he is a "flat" character, undeveloping, mythical, existing outside the complex moral world which we and the other main characters in the book know to be real and pressing; nor is he offered seriously as a type of the ideally fulfilled man.

II

In the second story, "June Recital," we are introduced to several other Morgana wanderers, chief among whom are the piano teacher, Miss Eckhart; Virgie Rainey, in her rebellious sixteenth year; and Loch Morrison. The point of view in this section is divided between that of Loch Morrison and his sister Cassie. Loch is a restless youngster supposedly confined to his bed with malaria, but through a telescope and later from the branches of the tree into which he scrambles from his window, he curiously views the events which transpire in the large abandoned MacLain house next door. Cassie, who in her own room is busy dyeing a colorful scarf in preparation for a hayride, has a more limited view of the activities in the MacLain house from her window, but through her consciousness and memory we learn the implications of the mysterious goings-on next door. Throughout, the reader enjoys a richly multiple, almost cinematic perspective, from which he sees both the Morrison and MacLain homes; the variety of persons, rooms, and activities in and around both; and the comings and goings on the street. Loch's eyes and boy's imagination record, sometimes inaccurately; Cassie remembers and ponders; the reader is left with the delightful task of sorting, constructing, relating the parts, interpreting.

From his window and tree posts Loch observes with proprietary interest what at first appear to be two unrelated little dramas taking place on two levels of the MacLain house (a possible third is sheer comic by-play: Old Man Holifield, a night-watchman from the gin mill, sleeps through everything). In one of the bedrooms upstairs Virgie Rainey is gaily romping with a young sailor—making love on a bare mattress, eating pickles from a bag, chasing and being chased. Downstairs an old woman, whom Loch mistakenly takes to be the mother of the sailor, comes in; with quantities of shredded paper, she elaborately and ritualistically "decorates" the room in preparation for burning. On the piano she places a large magnolia and later a ticking metronome. Before lighting the fire she plays, three times over, the opening bars of a piece called "*Für Elise.*" Cassie hears the theme, and from a kind of conditioned response she murmurs, "Virgie Rainey, *danke schoen.*" Then, through Cassie's thoughts, we learn how the two little dramas are related: the old lady is really Miss Eckhart; the mysterious and grotesque ceremonial below is her desperate, vindictive act of thwarted love, hope, ambition, which is directed against the breezy, abandoned young lady upstairs.

Miss Eckhart has traveled the farthest of all the wanderers, and she has achieved the least obvious fulfillment in her lifetime. "Home" to her must once have been Germany, and how the large, dark-haired, iron-willed and passionate woman with her alien tongue happened to come with her old mother to this small southern town, no one ever learns. But she takes a room with Snowdie MacLain and sets up a "studio" in which she gives piano lessons, the annual climax of which is the gala "June Recital." Miss Eckhart's life, one gathers, is largely boring and frustrating since her pupils are without talent, and she has no other interest or occupation save the care of her old mother. She is a stern and exacting teacher: one after another, each little girl sits quivering under her bosom "like a traveler under a cliff," waiting for the sharp smack of the fly swatter on the back of her hand (Miss Eckhart hates flies), yielding to the discipline of the metronome. But Virgie Rainey is in every way exceptional. Unlike the others, she is musically gifted and sensitive, obviously Miss Eckhart's one bright hope among her pupils (hence her refrain after Virgie finishes playing, "Virgie Rainey, *danke schoen*"). Unlike the others, Virgie is also spirited, independent, and fearless; she rejects the use of the obnoxious metronome, displays temper and "bad manners" at her lessons, asserts her will about the playing of certain pieces. She reveals that "Miss Eckhart, for all her being so strict and inexorable, in spite of her walk, with no give whatsoever, had a timid spot in her soul. There was a weak place in her, vulnerable, and Virgie Rainey found it and showed it to people."

The "vulnerable" place had also become apparent in Miss Eckhart's passion for Mr. Hal Sissum, a shoe department clerk who played the cello each evening in the Bijou (the local movie house). Mr. Sissum had discovered Miss Eckhart's surprisingly pretty ankles, and when he had played one sweet soft summer evening at a "speaking-night," plucking the strings above her while Virgie had ceremonially looped her with a clover chain, Miss Eckhart had sat "perfectly still and submissive." But Mr. Sissum had drowned in the Big Black River, and at his grave during the funeral Miss Eckhart had expressed her grief by a strange, hysterical rocking back and forth—as though she had become a living metronome. Once only, during a thunder storm, had Cassie and Virgie witnessed and heard the release of that passionate nature in Miss Eckhart's playing of a Beethoven sonata, a self-exposure which was alarming because "something had burst out, unwanted, exciting, from the wrong person's life. This was some brilliant thing too splendid for Miss Eckhart. . . ."

Virgie becomes Miss Eckhart's last hope for vicarious fulfillment—the child must go out into the world, Miss Eckhart repeats over and over; she has "a gift." "In the world, she must study and practice music for the rest of her life. In repeating all of this, Miss Eckhart suffered." Because she knows the independent nature she is dealing with, she senses, even before it happens, that Virgie will flout her and determine her own way. From studying serious music, Virgie goes straight to playing the piano at the Bijou, and her hand immediately "loses its touch." She matures overnight: "with her customary swiftness and lightness she had managed to skip an interval, some world-in-between where Cassie and Missie and Parnell were, all dyeing scarves. Virgie had gone direct into the world of power and emotion. . . ." No awkward, tentative adolescence for Virgie: she plunges herself directly into an affair with a sailor. Poor Miss Eckhart, her ideals, her discipline, her music, are abandoned.

In being so confounded in her career as in love, Miss Eckhart is proving herself once more a natural-born victim, plaything of a hostile fate. This tendency to disaster had revealed itself early in her Morgana career when she had been attacked and beaten one night by a Negro. After she recovered, people had expected and hoped she would move out: "perhaps more than anything it was the nigger in the hedge, the terrible fate that came on her, that people could not forgive Miss Eckhart." But she stayed on, "as though she considered one thing not so much more terrifying than another"—being beaten or murdered physically was no worse than being emotionally tortured. Not only fate but the town itself seems opposed to her fulfillment, just as the townspeople are indifferent to Virgie's flowering as a pianist; they are hostile, as small towns always are, to artistic impulse, idiosyncracy and "foreignness," ambition, restlessness—to hunger for the golden apples. "Perhaps nobody wanted Virgie Rainey to be anything in Morgana any more than they had wanted Miss Eckhart to be, and they were the two of them still linked together by people's saying that. How much might depend on people's being linked together?" Fate clips wings, sometimes through disaster, but more often slowly and subtly through provincial blindness and narrowness.

When Snowdie sells her home and returns to MacLain, Miss Eckhart is put out of the house. She has no more pupils; and after her mother dies, she is a pathetically lonely creature, eventually winding up a charity case on the County Farm. Somehow, we gather, she has learned that Virgie is using the abandoned MacLain house for her rendezvous with the sailor, and Miss Eckhart's intent now in her attempt to burn the studio, the old piano, the metronome, the magnolia blossom (Virgie had often come to lessons bearing one of these exotic blossoms) is suicidal as well as murderous; she is destroying all that was once precious to herself but is now meaningless and lost because of Virgie's infidelity. She is lighting, in effect, her own funeral pyre.

To complete the pattern of the ineffectuality of her life, her attempt at a glorious, retributive finish is thwarted by fate and the town in the form of a timely (or untimely) appearance of King MacLain and a pair of town comics, Old Man Moody, the marshal, and Mr. Fatty Bowles. They put out the fire, and Miss Eckhart, having suffered the indignity of having her hair burned off in a second desperate attempt to revive the fire, is taken away in full view of the town, her head wrapped in "some nameless kitchen rag," her gray housedress "prophetic of an institution." Virgie and the sailor run out of the house; the sailor, still only half dressed, darts toward the river. Virgie clips up the street in a defiantly bright apricot, voile dress, swinging a mesh bag on a chain, clicking her heels "as if nothing had happened in the past or behind her, as if she were free, whatever else she might be."

The ladies coming from their "Rook" party look on unsurprised: "people saw things like this as they saw Mr. MacLain come and go. They only hoped to place them, in their hour or their street or the name of their mother's people"—that is, to make something known and fixed out of this event, a story or a legend; to take the sting, the surprise, the comedy or tragedy, out of the glorious, pathetic, baffling humanity around them. "Then Morgana could hold them, and at least they were this and they were that. And when ruin was predicted all along . . . even if they mightn't have missed it if it hadn't appeared, still they were never surprised when it came." The town is giving "the treatment" to Virgie and Miss Eckhart: the treatment of "placing" that is tantamount to indifference, dismissal, or "not caring." It is the fate, in an earlier story, of old Mr. Marblehall.

Only Cassie and Loch, who have excitedly run out in front in petticoat and nightie, are surprised and shocked, which is the same, in this context, as "caring." When Cassie sees Virgie clicking along toward Old Man Moody's party, she knows there will be a confrontation of the two principals of the drama:

> "She'll stop for Miss Eckhart," breathed Cassie.
> Virgie went by. There was a meeting of glances between the teacher and her old pupil that Cassie knew. She could not be sure that Miss Eckhart's eyes closed once in recall—they had looked so wide-open at everything alike. The meeting amounted only to Virgie Rainey's passing by, in plain fact. She clicked by Miss Eckhart and she clicked straight through the middle of the Rook party, without a word or the pause of a moment.

The reader recoils at what seems a heart-shattering snub to the lonely, brave, ruined woman who had counted on and hoped so much for the girl. But later in her moonlit bed Cassie, who thinks about the strange meeting, realizes that it is much too late for any sign or communication between the two. They are too far apart: neither can, any more, blame, or thank, or help the other:

> What she was certain of was the distance those two had gone, as if all along they had been making a trip (which the sailor was only starting). It had changed them. They were deliberately terrible. They looked at each other and neither wished to speak. They did not even horrify each other. No one could touch them now, either.
> *Danke schoen.* . . . That much was out in the open. Gratitude—like rescue—was simply no more. It was not only past; it was outworn and cast away. Both Miss Eckhart and Virgie Rainey were human beings terribly at large, roaming on the face of the earth.

Virgie's roaming has only begun, but Miss Eckhart's is nearly over. Two more journeys for her: one to a mental hospital in Jackson, and then her last, through the kindness of Miss Snowdie, to her long rest in the MacLain graveyard. It is a painful career to contemplate.

III

In contrast is the career of the third wanderer to whom we are introduced in "June Recital," Loch Morrison. His adventurous and rebellious spirit does not show itself in explicitly sexual activity, as does King MacLain's, but he is a boy-wonder with a heroic name, a youthful Perseus. He may be a son of King, though the evidence for this possibility—tenuous and inconclusive—depends largely upon our interpretation of the character of his mother. A dainty, light-hearted, faintly lawless creature, she makes a favorite of her son, calls him "*my* child," and often stops in at dusk to speak to him in a softly abstracted way. Perhaps dissatisfied with her efficient and preoccupied editor husband, she ends her life by suicide.

Loch is staunchly independent and scornful of girls, of the "civilities," of danger; lonely and apart in his activities and imagination, "all eyes like Argus, on guard everywhere," he is restlessly waiting for the glorious, heroic opportunity. His possessive love of the abandoned MacLain house springs from its appealing, romantic wildness and its invitation to adventure. Opportunity blossoms excitingly with Miss Eckhart's attempt at arson, and provides Loch with his first occasion for a heroic rescue mission: he dives head first out of the tree branches to capture the "time-bomb" metronome.

This action is a comic foreshadowing of the serious and effectual rescue which he carries out in "Moon Lake" when he dives into the murky lake bottom to bring back the half-dead orphan, Easter, and resuscitates her through the drawn-out ordeal of artificial respiration. The adults who witness this process—the indignant Miss Lizzie Stark who shouts, "What's he *doing* to her? Stop that," and Ran MacLain, who sets the "seasoned gaze" of the twenty-three-year-old on Loch's rhythmical movements over Easter on the table—note the oddness of the act. The incident is a superb example of Miss Welty's mastery of delicately ambiguous tone and of gently intimated symbolism, since the reader is both amused at the varied human responses to sexual suggestion, and yet moved and sobered by the deeper implications of this strange physical correspondence. The stakes are really life and death, and the young boy-scout is as fully and passionately, even though as mindlessly and mechanically, engaged in giving life as he would be if involved in the act of love.

Like the Perseus of the picture hanging in Miss Eckhart's studio, Loch must be allowed his pride and his vaunting. This vaunting is partly witnessed, partly imagined, by two of the young camp girls, Nina and Jinny Love, when they wander toward the boy scout's tent on the evening after all the excitement, and see him in silhouette, undressing by candlelight. After he examines his case of sunburn in the Kress mirror, he comes naked to the tent opening where he stands leaning on one raised arm, his weight on one foot, looking out quietly into the night:

> Hadn't he, surely, just before they caught him, been pounding his chest with his fists? Bragging on himself? It seemed to them they could still hear in the beating air of night the wild tattoo of pride he must have struck off. His silly, brief, overriding little show they could well imagine there in his tent of separation in the middle of the woods, in the night. Minnowy thing that matched his candle flame, naked as he was with that, he thought he shone forth too. Didn't he?

He is as plausibly human as his possible sire, and a youth of undoubtedly heroic parts; but he is beyond no one's gentle laughter, and looks, in the end, self-consciously gawky, "rather at loose ends." Yet his restless heart drives him away from restricting Morgana to New York City, where, as his sister Cassie notes wistfully, he has "a life of his own."

IV

Throughout *The Golden Apples* we find juxtaposed two sets of characters. There are the wanderers who are expressive in action, wild, rebellious, free, over-flowing, self-determining; but they are driven by fierce hungers and yearnings. The characters who serve as their foils appear to be re-actors more than actors. They tend to be passive, helpless, outreaching; their characteristic activity is quietly unobtrusive and inward, for they observe and learn, feel and wonder. But they have their own kind of power since they achieve insight about life, about themselves and others, through their exercise of the moral imagination and through the patient work of their soft, giving hearts. They admire the strong characters; they both sigh for and are frightened by freedom and by the large, bold gestures of their independent loved ones who come and go at will or impulse—the gods among them with their noble, godlike gestures. These characters exist to know and adore; they are the "still points" in humanity, resting places, stable and secure, for all their inward growing and sympathetic roving after the wanderers. Their instincts are cautious and protective: they want to ward off the disaster which inevitably threatens the freely experimental life. By definition they are almost necessarily feminine, or very young. Examples of the type are Jennie Lockhart of "At the Landing," Joel Mayes of "First Love," and Laura and Ellen of *Delta Wedding*. In *The Golden Apples* we find Snowdie MacLain, Cassie Morrison, and Nina Carmichael, though some of the softness and sensitivity of the type may also be seen in Eugene MacLain.

In her relation to Miss Eckhart, Virgie, and her brother Loch, Cassie—admiring, timorous, sensitive, virginal—is the reflecting "still point." Even as a child Cassie finds in Virgie "her secret love, as well as her secret hate"—she envies the glorious freedom and the careless assurance of Virgie's musical talent. Out of this love springs her power of perception. She knows, for instance, what Miss Eckhart is feeling. "She found it so easy— ever since Virgie showed her—to feel terror and pain in an outsider; in someone you did not know at all well, pain made you wonderfully sorry." At one point she even wonders whether this secret knowledge might not have provided her with an opportunity to help the woman. "Somewhere, even up to the last, there could have been for Miss Eckhart a little opening wedge—a crack in the door. . . . But if I had been the one to see it open, she thought slowly, I might have slammed it tight for ever. I might." She is wise enough to perceive that knowledge of another's heart may be a formidable weapon and that no outward or inward law determines that it shall necessarily be used kindly rather than ruthlessly.

In her relationship with her brother Loch, Cassie is the adoring, passive spectator. The time when he was a child and she had wanted "to shield his innocence" is past, even though she bursts into tears because of worry about his malaria when she sees him out in front in his nightie with a row of big pepper-

and-salt colored mosquitoes perched all along his forehead. But Loch is already out on a limb figuratively as well as literally when she watches him cavorting in the tree overhanging the MacLain house. Unlike her brother, she is not a wanderer: "She could never go for herself, never creep out on the shimmering bridge of the tree, or reach the dark magnet there that drew you inside, kept drawing you in. She could not see herself do an unknown thing. She was not Loch, she was not Virgie Rainey; she was not her mother. She was Cassie in her room, seeing the knowledge and torment beyond her reach, standing at her window singing. . . ." As we might expect, she remains unmarried and at home in Morgana; she cares for her psychotic father, tenderly regards the careers of the wanderers from a distance, and patiently constructs memorials for the dead. She is one of those characters who, like Snowdie MacLain, might make the word "home" connote security and love, rather than stifling confinement, to any wanderer.

In "Moon Lake" we are introduced to another wanderer, Easter. She is dominant among the orphans and "advanced" for her age both physically ("she had started her breasts") and experientially; she is a wild tomboy who plays mumblety-peg and runs around with an enviable ring of "pure dirt" on her neck. Easter is quite possibly another offspring of King MacLain; but the evidence in her case is somewhat more conclusive than in Loch's case. First of all, there is Katie Rainey's remark that several of King's children are growing up in the County Orphan's. Then there is the "withstanding gold" of Easter's hair, which forms a crest on top of her head and seems to "fly up at the temples, being cropped and wiry" (the golden crest may be associated with King's golden panama hat, and the pompadour cap so fiercely loved by Loch Morrison). Finally, there are Easter's own remarks about her parentage: "I haven't got no father. I never had, he ran away. I've got a mother. When I could walk, then my mother took me by the hand and turned me in, and I remember it."

Like a true daughter of King, Easter is independent and adventurous, wandering away from camp into the woods, smoking a piece of cross-vine, seeking out new forms of excitement with Jinny Love and Nina, running about with her dress stained green behind, dreamily floating out on the lake in an abandoned boat. Her eyes, which are "neither brown nor green nor cat," have "something of metal, flat ancient metal" in them,

so that their color could have been found "somewhere . . .
away, under lost leaves—strange as the painted color of the
ants. Instead of round black holes in the center of her eyes,
there might have been women's heads, ancient." This strange,
half-mythical child with her ancient eyes also has her secret
ambition: she is going to be a singer.

Nina Carmichael stands in relation to Easter as Cassie does
to Virgie in "June Recital." Nina is tremendously impressed,
admiring, envious of Easter's "beatific state" of being "not
answerable to a soul on earth"; yet she is protective and pity-
ing—or rather wanting to pity—for she is waiting for her heart
to be twisted by the knowledge that her delightful new companion is an orphan. Easter serves for Nina as Virgie does for
Cassie in being a means to growing moral insight by way of
imaginative projection. Lying on her cot in the tent at night,
Nina thinks and dreams of the exciting possibilities of "slipping
into" the experience of persons quite different from herself; she
wants "to try for the fiercest secrets. To slip into them all—
to change. . . . To *have been* an orphan."

Nina then has a sense of the night personified and of holding
a special relation to Easter. The passage which follows is significant both as a foreshadowing of coming events and as a
symbolic account of the nature and destiny of the two types
of characters juxtaposed in the novel: the wanderers, and their
static, reflective counterparts:

Nina sat up on the cot and stared passionately before her at
the night—the pale dark roaring night with its secret step,
the Indian night. She felt the forehead, the beaded stars, look
in thoughtfully at her.

The pondering night stood rude at the tent door, the opening fold would let it stoop in—it, him—he had risen up inside.
Long-armed, or long-winged, he stood in the center where the
pole went up. Nina lay back, drawn quietly from him. But the
night knew about Easter. All about her. Geneva had pushed
her to the edge of the cot. Easter's hand hung down, opened
outward. Come here, night, Easter might say, tender to a giant,
to such a dark thing. And the night, obedient and graceful,
would kneel to her. Easter's callused hand hung open there
to the night that had got wholly into the tent.

Nina let her own arm stretch forward opposite Easter's.
Her hand too opened, of itself. She lay there a long time motionless, under the night's gaze, its black cheek, looking immov-
ably at her hand, the only part of her now which was not

asleep. Its gesture was like Easter's, but Easter's hand slept and her own hand knew—shrank and knew, yet offered still.

"Instead . . . me instead. . . ."

In the cup of her hand, in her filling skin, in the fingers' weight and stillness, Nina felt it: compassion and a kind of competing that were all one, a single ecstasy, a single longing. For the night was not impartial. No, the night loved some more than others, served some more than others. Nina's hand lay open there for a long time, as if its fingers would be its eyes. Then it too slept. She dreamed her hand was helpless to the tearing teeth of wild beasts. At reveille she woke up lying on it. She could not move it. She hit it and bit it until like a cluster of bees it stung back and came to life.

The night in this passage may be related to the "dark magnet that kept drawing you in" which Cassie sees as her brother's lure, but not her own. It is the dark or unknown side of life, attractive and beautiful, yet dangerous, leading to possible death, either death of the heart or a literal death: the fate which threatens persons who live with the hand and the heart thrown carelessly open, freely, experimentally, courageously. The fact that the night "loves" and "serves" these persons indicates their paradoxical relation to experience and fate: they are partly victimized by it, partly inviting, even controlling and subduing it. The figure of night as a giant Indian, summoned by Easter and kneeling at her side, indicates that susceptibility to both love and death is a significant element in the fearless nature. The night comes as a great wild lover to woo the maiden, but he is also reminiscent of *"Der Tod"* in Schubert's famous song, who sings to the maiden, *"Gib deine Hand."* The child is clearly marked either for some special tragedy or some special escape and fulfillment—perhaps for both.

Nina's hand imitates the careless gesture, but it is distinguished from the orphan's hand in being aware, in "knowing," yet "offering still." Nina is filled with "a single ecstasy and longing"; she wants herself to be open to love and experience, to accept the fate of the wanderer. Out of "compassion" she yearns to suffer tragedy with and for the other; out of a desire to live fully and freely she "competes" with the other. "Instead . . ." she prays to the dark unknown presence; "me instead. . . ."

When Nina finally goes to sleep, the hand also "sleeps."

During the night the open hand lives its entire life symbolically, independent of the girl, yet attached to her, making her suffer sympathetically the pain and terror of experience. When she awakens in the morning, the hand is dead; the life in it seems over. But she brings it back to life by the ruthless action of hitting and biting it. Thus its brief night's history has anticipated Easter's coming ordeal of death and resurrection (by a similarly cruel method); and in addition, it has shown forth the entire life process of such wanderers as Virgie Rainey and Ran and Eugene MacLain, who will experience their own deaths by despair and rebirths by a resurgence of joy and hope.

The nature of Easter's near-tragedy again shows the large part played by chance or accident in Miss Welty's vision of the universe. The orphan is standing high up on the diving board, watching the swimming lesson, when Exum, a little Negro boy bent on nothing but sheer mischievous fun, gives Easter's heel "the tenderest, obscurest little brush" with a green willow switch. She drops as though hit in the head by a stone, and apparently the heavy fall of her body causes it to be imbedded deep in the muddy lake bottom. Only after Loch has made several attempts to find her and has come up with "long ribbons of green and terrible stuff, shapeless black matter" in his hands is he finally successful. When Easter is brought up she is not only more dead than alive, but hideously disfigured —tongue rolled backwards, teeth smeared with mud, wet hair lying over her face in "long fern shapes," a dark stream of water rolling from her mouth down her cheek. All the little girls have a long solemn look at the "berated" and "betrayed" figure, "the mask formed and set on the face, one hand displayed, one jealously clawed under the waist"—they have seen, most of them for the first time, the ugliness of death. When Easter is finally revived after hours of work, Nina thinks: "At least what had happened to Easter was out in the world, like the table itself. There it remained—mystery, if only for being hard and cruel and, by something Nina felt inside her body, murderous." Catastrophe has been seen and faced as a *fact*. The change is not in the horror or mystery itself, but in the girl's attitude toward it. Catastrophe or death which is actually visible or recognized is less terrifying than catastrophe which is imagined: the threatening, the "unknown" has been objectified, fully met "in the world"; it can be survived both by victims and spectators.

V

The careers of Randall and Eugene MacLain, the twin sons of King and Snowdie, are presented in "The Whole World Knows" and "Music from Spain." In the earlier sections of *The Golden Apples* the twins are almost indistinguishable: they are seen from a distance as rather mischievous, feebly disciplined little monkeys who always leave their doors "wide open to the universe" when they go out to play, and let in the flies so annoying to Miss Eckhart. They are next seen in "Sir Rabbit" as a pair of fair-banged fifteen-year-olds who come trotting up like a pair of matched circus ponies to engage Mattie Will Sojourner in a spring-inspired sexual romp—an incident which serves as a prelude to Mattie's greater adventure with King, and shows the twins, in actions as well as appearance, to be "the very spit of their father." But in the stories devoted to each, the two brothers are clearly differentiated; they are alike only in a common woe: marital discord, failure in love.

"The Whole World Knows" is an almost unrelieved lamentation, a singularly distressing account of a sordid scandal into which Randall is unwillingly swept. It takes the form of a soliloquy which is half confession, half supplication, as though spoken to a priest or even to God. To his wandering, unhearing father, King, Ran pours out the tale of his estrangement from his wife and his tragic affair with Maideen Sumrell. His words are drenched with confusion, grief, loneliness, a sense of guilt, a desire for self-justification, a need for the paternal understanding and guidance which we know will never be forthcoming.

Before all the trouble begins, Ran has apparently been on his way to becoming an established citizen of Morgana. He has married young Jinny Love Stark (some ten years his junior) and is working as a teller in the Morgana bank. Then one summer Ran leaves his wife and returns to a hot, dismal room in his old home, the MacLain house, now run for boarders by a Miss Francine Murphy. Why has he left Jinny? The "up-and-down of it, . . . the brunt of it," according to Miss Perdita Mayo—one of the town's leading old maids, gossips, and general opinion-makers and takers—is that "Jinny was unfaithful to Ran" with young Woodrow Spights, who works beside Ran in the Morgana bank. But Miss Perdita, for all her common sense and humanity ("I'm a women that's been clear around the world in my rocking chair") cannot see what lies behind the fact of Jinny's infidelity, nor, apparently, can anybody. Jinny's mother, who has had her own trouble with an alcoholic husband, provides a clue when she says to Randall, "You men. You got us beat in the end. . . . We'd know you through and through except we never know what ails you. . . . Of course I see what Jinny's doing, the fool, but you ailed first. You just got her answer to it, Ran." To this Ran responds in bafflement, "And what ails me I don't know, Father, unless maybe you know."

The reader is able to divine what is ailing Ran only by watching his reactions to Jinny's character. Jinny is one of Miss Welty's favorite types—what I should like to call a "joy-girl." Another example of such a type, rendered more somber by circumstance, is Marjorie of "Flowers for Marjorie"; a thoughtful, sensitive variation is Dabney of *Delta Wedding;* a pure example of the type is seen in the American wife of "The Bride of the Innisfallen." These girls have somehow been born, and remain, content, if not effervescently happy. Free spirits who cannot be touched by misery, frustration, tragedy, they won't—they can't—take life really seriously; their hearts are constant springs of joy and pleasure. They radiate delight into the hearts of their lovers, but at the same time they baffle and enrage, simply because they are so completely untouchable, unmalleable, closed to all those terrible dark worlds of deep inward suffering. Their gayety and carelessness are a stinging, unconscious reproach and mockery. Living with such a person, we conclude from Ran's experience, must involve equal parts of irritation and delight: it must have been when the irritation became too annoyingly evident that Jinny retaliated by having an affair with Woody Spights.

The element of joy in Jinny's nature was already established in "Moon Lake." In contrast to the sober, reflective temperament of Nina Carmichael, Jinny's temperament was carefree and resilient; she was a child who skipped gaily because even the swamp sounds came to her as "a song of hilarity." It is not surprising to come upon her next, some ten years later—a young woman who ought to be somewhere in a corner weeping because her husband has left her—standing in front of a mirror, smiling frivolously, and carelessly hacking off chunks of her pretty brown hair as she says lightly, "Obey that

impulse——." Ran's reaction to her on this first visit back to the
Stark house after the separation is inevitable: "That lightness
came right back. Just to step on the matting, that billows a
little anyway, and with Jinny's hair scattered like feathers on
it, I could have floated, risen and floated."

The rage which counterpoints Ran's delight is seen most
clearly in an incident which takes place on another of his
visits. A button is missing from his sleeve, and he asks Jinny
to sew it on for him. While she performs this intimate domestic task, the girl is agonizingly close to him; yet she is so exas-
peratingly untroubled that his thoughts become murderous.
With inward violence he imaginatively shoots her full of bullet
holes:

> I fired pointblank at Jinny—more than once. . . . But Jinny
> didn't feel it. She made her little face of success. Her thread
> always went straight to the eye. . . . She far from acknowl-
> edged pain—anything but sorrow and pain. When I couldn't
> give her something she wanted she would hum a little tune.
> In our room, her voice would go low and soft to complete dis-
> paragement. Then I loved her a lot. The little cheat. I waited
> on, while she darted the needle and pulled at my sleeve, the
> sleeve to my helpless hand. It was like counting my breaths.
> I let out my fury and breathed the pure disappointment in:
> that she was not dead on earth. She bit the thread—magnifi-
> cently. When she took her mouth away I nearly fell. The cheat.

To Ran, Jinny is a cheat because she refuses to be affected or
frustrated; she refuses to feel deeply or to suffer with or for
him or anyone else—least of all herself; and that is, perhaps,
"cheating" on an important area of human experience.

Ran takes up with an eighteen-year-old country girl named
Maideen Sumrall, partly for the sake of company, but mostly
because Maideen looks like a fresh and "uncontaminated"
version of Jinny herself: Jinny without the mockery in her face
and with lovely brown hair shoulder-length rather than butch-
ered by scissors and "ruined." Maideen is simple and good-
natured, but Ran makes a literally fatal mistake in supposing
that "there was nothing but time between them." Not only does
Maideen turn out to be malleable to his will but far worse,
she reveals herself to be as disastrously vulnerable as Jinny is
invulnerable. After the Vicksburg adventure which the two
have shared, they collapse in a roadside cabin, where Ran's
suffering reaches its climax. During the night he attempts suicide

unsuccessfully with an old pistol of his father and then takes Maideen in a quick, loveless conjunction. Later he awakens to hear her weeping beside him, "the kind of soft, patient, meditative sobs a child will venture long after punishment." Now in soliloquy to his missing father he wails, "How was I to know she would go and hurt herself? She cheated, she cheated too."

Maideen has "cheated" in taking her experience altogether too seriously, too tragically, in ironic opposition to Jinny's kind of cheating. It is Maideen's breast, rather than Jinny's, which ends filled with "the bright holes where Ran's bullets had gone through." Only in the last chapter do we learn how irrevocably the girl has "hurt herself": soon afterwards she dies by suicide, found on the floor of the place where she works by Old Man Moody. But the fact of her suicide gives point to Ran's desperately futile plea, "Father! Dear God, wipe it clean. Wipe it clean, wipe it out. Don't let it be."

The final cry of Randall's soliloquy—"And where's Jinny?"—is apparently answered, for the two are seen back together a decade later at Mrs. Rainey's funeral. At one point during the afternoon Virgie is subjected to Jinny's insistence that she marry—everybody ought to marry, Jinny seems to feel, because "only then could she resume as Jinny Love Stark, her true self," careless and independent, not bound by marriage. Virgie smiles faintly as she suddenly senses, "without warning, that two passionate people stood in this roomful, with their indifferent backs to each other." The union at this stage almost resembles that between Robbie and George Fairchild in *Delta Wedding;* and as if to prove that at least an armed truce has been achieved, we find at the funeral their curious and delightful children.

Randall's "wanderings" have been largely confined to Morgana—he knows he belongs there, even though his mother has called him to come back under her roof in the town of MacLain, and even though he sets off restlessly for Vicksburg because he has "looked at Morgana too long." Morgana has been the scene of his triumphs as well as his scandals, defeats, and disasters. The son of King has become reigning prince (mayor) of Morgana, a man whose career, like that of his father, is a legend to the community:

Didn't it show on Ran, that once he had taken advantage of a country girl who had died a suicide? It showed at election time as it showed now, and he won the election for mayor over Mr. Carmichael, for all was remembered in his middle-age when he stood on the platform. . . . They had voted for him for that—for his glamour and his story, for being a MacLain and the bad twin, for marrying a Stark and then for ruining a girl and the thing she did. . . . They voted for the revelation; it had made their hearts faint, and they would assert it again. Ran knew that every minute, there in the door he stood it.

"The whole world knows" (because Morgana is the whole world to Morgana) about Randall MacLain.

"Father, Eugene! What you went and found, was it better than this?" asks Randall in his soliloquy. If his brother, the twin who grew up gentle like his mother, could have heard that question, he would have had to shake his head and answer sadly, "No, no better." The reasons for his answer are provided in "Music from Spain," the one story of *The Golden Apples* which is not set in Morgana. This story is told in the third person, mostly from Eugene's point of view. It has a natural simplicity and economy of structure, since Eugene's odyssey takes place on a single day in San Francisco, and the carefully related internal and external events lead with a gradual and controlled crescendo to the climax and resolution. The central action is initiated by a sudden, instinctive move on the part of Eugene, which expresses and unleashes in him a long accumulated sense of protest and rebellion. One morning at breakfast when Eugene is opening his paper and his wife makes some "innocent" remark to him—"Crumb on your chin" or the like— he leans across the table and, with no idea of why he does it, slaps her face. Then without giving her either the paper or the usual goodbye kiss, he leaves the apartment and steps out on the street to walk and reflect about the meaning of his strange, aggressive action.

Eugene has traveled so far from Morgana only to find himself more effectively trapped in a marriage gone bad than he might ever have been at home. His wife Emma is in every way a curious contrast to Randall's wife Jinny. Older and heavier than Eugene, she is a plump, fussily feminine, busy-tongued, self-indulgent little woman whose traits are in contrast to Jinny's youth, slim boyishness, and mocking abandon. Furthermore, Emma has the disease of oversensitivity and self-crucifixion, which naturally means that she crucifies everyone around her. In sharp contrast to Jinny, she is an indefatigable, noxious, almost professional sufferer. (Proverbs 15:15 types the two exactly: "All the days of the afflicted are evil: but he that is of a merry heart hath a continual feast.")

Not that Emma hasn't some reason for suffering: a year earlier, little Nan, their sunny, lovable child, had died. But that loss has been Eugene's as well as Emma's, and there has been no relief from her prolonged, narcissistically bloated grief. Because Emma is so "touchy," Eugene cannot attack her response to the loss: "A quarrel couldn't even grow between him and Emma. And she would be unfair, beg the question, if a quarrel did spring up; she would cry. That was a thing a stranger might feel on being introduced to Emma, even though Emma never proved it to anybody: she had a waterfall of tears back there." As a result, there is no more love between them. Out of his layman's reading of his unconscious, Eugene produces the awareness of his frustration. "*He struck her because he wanted another love. The forties. Psychology.*" His life, his need and his ability to love and to enjoy are not over and done with, though his wife is acting as if hers died with the child. The slap he feels has been "like kissing the cheek of the dead. . . . How cold to the living hour grief could make you."

The initial gesture of protest made, Eugene follows with another and decides not to work at Bertsingers' Jewelers that day. Beginning his wanderings, he passes through Market Street and notes with disgust and shame the tawdry, pathetic appeals of this Vanity Fair, for "Market had with the years become a street of trusses, pads, braces, false bosoms, false teeth, and glass eyes. And of course jewelry stores." Just beyond Bertsingers' the doorway of a market is crowded with flowers. Eugene wishes he could have worked there—cracked crabs with a mallet or grown flowers instead of bending all day like a little drudge over "meticulous watches." Watching the "daily revelation" of the fog lifting from the city, he is filled with a fresh longing, such as he had felt years ago in Mississippi, to wander and see distant places, or once again to return to "that careless, patched land of Mississippi winter, trees in their rusty wrappers, slow-grown trees taking their time, the lost shambles of old cane, the winter swamp where his twin brother, he supposed, still hunted." His eyes are freshly opened to every detail of the glorious natural and human variety about him as he walks the streets, and he experiences a strange sympathy with the lawless, chaotic life of the big city: "he would know anything that happened, anything that threatened the moral way, or transformed it, even, in the city of San Francisco that day: as if he and the city were watching each other—without accustomed faith. But with interest . . . boldness . . . recklessness, almost."

Just then Eugene spies walking ahead of him in traffic the Spanish guitarist he and Emma had heard in solo recital the previous evening at Aeolian Hall. Suddenly the Spaniard is almost hit by an automobile: Eugene springs forward, seizes the man's coat, and saves him from a possibly fatal accident. The two men shake hands in relief and delight, but Eugene suffers a shock of disappointment when he sees that the Spaniard cannot speak English. Since no words of thanks or deprecation can be spoken, the two stroll on together. Eugene notes that the big fellow has remained imperturbable, and he reflects that the Spaniard "had walked out in front of the automobile almost tempting it to try and get him, with all the aplomb of—certainly a bull fighter." Thus the Spaniard is immediately established as one of life's fearless ones; like that other fabulous musician, Powerhouse, this man is self-possessed, bold, generous of spirit. And again, as with Powerhouse, Miss Welty joyously turns the lavish power of her descriptive gift on this admirable, inscrutable creature of paradoxes: wild and primitive with his thick black hair, crude table manners, and fierce bull-like nostrils, but dignified and tender with his music, large and noble in his gestures and bearing.

Although Eugene doesn't know it, the Spaniard is a perfect companion for him on this day of pilgrimage to freedom and rebirth. Articulate, the old fellow would probably have been of little use to Eugene: it is difficult to conceive of his having any sort of vocabulary and experience to deal with the nuances of Eugene's complex marital problem. Rendered mute by the language barrier, Eugene is eventually pressed to a more basic and primal form of communication, an almost physical blood-knowledge, the special mysterious mode of knowledge that we usually associate with the vision of D. H. Lawrence.

With Eugene serving as host, the two advance from the streets to a restaurant for lunch, where Eugene's mind grows fantastical thinking up possible clues to the stranger's secret life, the exotic, perhaps sinful and dangerous acts perpetrated, "and always the one, dark face, though momently fire from his nostrils brimmed over, with that veritable *waste* of life!" Out of these aroused thoughts spring images from his own past—a favorite piece of music played when he was Miss Eckhart's student; an engraving of "the kneeling Man in the Wilderness . . . in his father's remnant geography book, who hacked once at the Traveler's Tree, opened his mouth, and the water came pouring in"—the Traveler he had once believed to represent his unknown father, and with whom he now identifies himself.

When the two return to the street they witness an accident. A dumpy little woman trips on high heels in the street, sinks "in an outrageous-looking pink color" in the streetcar's path, is pitched and thrown ahead on the track, and is instantly killed. People close round in morbid curiosity: "they were going to have been there." The Spaniard shakes his head, but there is no sign that he has made a connection between his own near-accident and this one. Miss Welty has only shown, as in *Delta Wedding* when George is saved and the young girl killed, that real accidents occur as well as near-accidents; she has shown again how little security there is for the individual in a universe which seems largely governed by chance.

Eugene takes his guest on a streetcar out toward the edge of the city, and the two walk up and down hill after hill in a steady progress toward the sea. Once they come to a high point where the Spaniard suddenly swings around to survey the world behind them through which they have just come. "He tenderly swept an arm. The whole arena was alight with a fairness and blueness at this hour of afternoon; all the gray was blue and the white was blue—the laid-out city looked soft, brushed over with some sky-feather. Then he dropped his hand, as though the city might retire; and lifted it again, as though to bring it back for a second time. He was really wonderful, with his arm raised." The gesture is heroic, suggesting divine powers of creation and benediction, as if the Spaniard were bringing the city into its beautiful being. The raised arm is related to Perseus' vaunting in Miss Eckhart's picture and to that youthful heroic reflection in Loch; in *The Golden Apples* it is the symbolic gesture of men who have gloriously achieved and conquered.

The two men advance until they come to the beach and cliffs of "Land's End" and begin scrambling over brown rocks with the sea exploding wildly beneath and a strong wind blowing against them, turning back the gulls in their flight. While the sun slowly sets, the Spaniard leads a tortuous progress through rough paths and caves. Eugene has begun throwing out remarks like "You assaulted your wife" from the safe position of not being understood, thus objectifying and trying to work out his dilemma. At last they arrive at a perilous point on the edge of a cliff, where a touch from Eugene could topple the Spaniard over the edge. Then in some strange ecstasy Eugene seizes and clings to him, "almost as if he had waited for him a long time with longing, almost as if he loved him, and had found a lasting refuge." The Spaniard lets out a "bullish roar," followed by a "terrible recital" of incomprehensible words which strike Eugene as fearless and shameless. Eugene nearly falls and has to pull himself back by seizing the big man. He then runs to chase the Spaniard's big black hat (caught in the wind), puts it on his own head, runs back to the Spaniard, and this time is himself held with "hard, callused fingers like prongs." He has an odd sensation of being disembodied, weightless; he feels himself lifted up in the strong arms of the Spaniard and swung around "pillowed in great strength." The whirling and exciting dizziness affect his body like the coming of passion, and he thinks of Emma turning around and advancing to meet him on the stairs, her arms lifted in the "wide, aroused sleeves," closing around him, "returning him awesome favors in full vigor, with not the ghost of the salt of tears." If only he could explain to Emma—this is the way it should be:

> If he could have spoken! It was out of this relentlessness, not out of the gush of tears, that there would be a child again. Could it be possible that everything now could wait? If he could have stopped everything, until that pulse, far back, far inside, far within now, could shake like the little hard red fist of the first spring leaf!
>
> He was brought over and held by the knees in the posture of a bird, his body almost upright and his forearms gently spread. In his nostrils and relaxing eyes and around his naked head he could feel the reach of fine spray or the breath of fog. He was up-borne, open-armed. He was only thinking, My dear love comes.

What has taken place in this remarkable scene of climax? From the look of it, the Spaniard has been threatening Eugene's life by swinging him around at the edge of the cliff: a feminine voice (from one of a pair of passing lovers) cries out, "Oh, is he going to throw him over? . . . Aren't you ashamed of yourself, teasing a little fellow like that, scaring him?" Some fateful encounter has indeed taken place between the two men: half in play, half in dead earnest, each has momentarily seized the fate of the other, grappled with and closely confronted the other. But the Spaniard is the stronger. First when Eugene puts on the great warm black hat and later when he flies like a bird over the sea out from those strong hands, it is as though the stranger's life-force has flown out from the hat and hands into Eugene's blood, so that he briefly participates in the Spaniard's powerful, fearless mode of being, from which springs passion; and out of that could spring a new life, a new child. The episode forms a curious parallel to the climax of "Moon Lake." The hero of each book, through an action suggestive of the sexual act, brings to life one apparently dead: both Eugene and Easter are put literally into the posture of love by the unconscious "lovers" of their lives—those who have life to give from the glorious excess or "waste" of their own lives.

Eugene's story does not end happily. His change, his rebirth, have, after all, not been shared by his wife, nor has Eugene's experience miraculously provided him with the tongue of men and of angels to speak of the wonders of his vision. He returns home to find Emma exactly the same. Though not in tears (she has had a long day to recover and has found a fresh cause for self-solicitude since that morning episode: a slight burn where the hot grease had spattered on her hand), she is gossiping with a neighbor and feeding her face: petty, unimaginative, smugly opinionated, dominating as usual—far indeed from the passionate woman who had met Eugene in his ecstatic vision on the cliff. He hears the two women reduce his marvelous friend to a scurrilous Latin type who exhibits "bad taste" by laughing out loud with a woman in church. No comment is made to indicate Eugene's response, but one senses the deep misery and hopelessness inundating him again. His wife's nature has settled firmly into a mold basically hostile to spontaneity, happiness, or fulfillment; Eugene hasn't the chance to rebuild his marriage as has Randall, whose wife's gay and spontaneous nature is largely congenial to happiness.

The later history of Eugene is brief and poignant. Returning to Morgana, he dies of tuberculosis apparently soon afterwards. Passing the cemetery where Eugene is buried in the MacLain plot, Virgie Rainey remembers the story of this sadly strange son of King:

Eugene, for a long interval, had lived in another part of the world, learning while he was away that people don't have to be answered just because they want to know. His very wife was never known here, and he did not make it plain whether he had children somewhere now or had been childless. His wife did not even come to the funeral, although a telegram had been sent. A foreigner? "Why, she could even be a Dago and we wouldn't know it." His light, tubercular body seemed to hesitate on the street of Morgana, hold averted, anticipating questions. Sometimes he looked up in the town where he was young and said something strangely spiteful or ambiguous (he was never reconciled to his father, they said, was sarcastic to the old man—all he loved was Miss Snowdie and flowers) but he bothered no one. "He never did bother a soul," they said at his graveside that day, forgetting his childhood.

Eugene is one of those wanderers who, like Miss Eckhart, pluck the golden apples only in a rare, isolated moment or two during an entire lifetime. They remain essentially thwarted, crushed, victimized by the cruel and devious workings of fate.

VI

The final section of *The Golden Apples,* "The Wanderers," has many functions in the structure of the book as a whole. As an epilogue, it provides the denouement of several careers followed, lends perspective to the meaning and interrelations of these life histories, and gives a sense of mutability. It also provides a fully detailed portrait of the Morgana community by showing it engaged in a major tribal ritual, that of the funeral; furthermore, it recapitulates and makes concluding statements of the major themes of the book. But it is also, and perhaps chiefly, the story of Virgie Rainey, who, as a woman now past forty, is the most perceptive and emotionally mature of the wanderers and is getting a belated start (after an early abortive attempt) on her long search for the golden apples. The ending of the book is really, therefore, another beginning, and the sense of an epic cycle is achieved.

The initiating action of "The Wanderers" is the death, by heart attack, of old Mrs. Fate Rainey, narrator of the first section. For decades, from her selling post at the turn of the Mac-Lain Road, Katie Rainey has watched the passing and trafficking and has been a central and familiar community figure who records and represents the change as well as the constancy of Morgana life. To Virgie the old woman has been a bondage both dear and confining. After running away briefly at seventeen with her sailor, Bucky Moffitt, Virgie returns home, living out through the long years of her endless youth (her dark hair never loses its spring) a battle between affectionate loyalty and a sense of oppression. Katie Rainey has caused Virgie to impose on her own life a pattern inimical to her talents and desires: an office job in which her skillful pianist's fingers are rigidly set to typing, or turned to farm and domestic chores—milking the cows, dressing the quail, cooking and sewing.

The only rebellion of Virgie's mature years has been an affair or two discreetly conducted with some inferior man (the only kind available); the town knows this, and Mrs. Rainey is exposed to their twittering gossip, but dignity requires that she ignore their lack of "chivalry."

Her love for Virgie and a subliminal memory of her own youthful independence provoke the pity and understanding which prevent her from a terrible confrontation with her daughter; yet stubbornness keeps her always fretting after the girl, demanding that she appear when expected in order to perform the necessary chores according to schedule. Pride, affection, and a costly control have kept this difficult relationship going until it is finally broken by death. When Mrs. Rainey is struck by her final heart attack, Virgie is busy cutting out a dress from some plaid material. "There's nothing Virgie Rainey loves better than struggling against a real hard plaid," the old lady thinks with the first thrust of pain; and her last clear feeling before she staggers to the bed is a desire to be "down and covered up, in, of all things, Virgie's hard-to-match-up plaid." Discipline achieved against odds—this has been the source of Katie Rainey's pride in her daughter ("It's a blessed wonder to see the child mind"); and the obedience and affection which motivate it have been the warming mantle spread over the old woman in her declining years.

Soon after her death the whole community, white and Negro, descend on the Rainey house, and the funeral rites begin with the "laying out" of the corpse (beautifully performed, all agree, by old Snowdie), with housecleaning and the preparation of great quantities of food and drink, the cutting and arranging of flowers, and the gathering of the clan. Virgie displays none of the anticipated signs of hysteria or grief to the expectant

visitors; when she finally weeps briefly, it is out of a generalized
sense of loss at the old order's passing, which no one seems to
understand. She is busy but detached, watching and waiting
until, at the close of the first night, when all but Snowdie
(who stays to sit with the corpse) depart, they seem "to drag
some mythical gates and barriers away from her view." Then
she goes down to the river, takes off her clothes, and slips in.
A strong physical sense of union with nature suffuses her, for
"all was one warmth, air, water, and her own body . . . one
weight, one matter." Swimming, her body is soothed and sen-
sitized, and the sand, pieces of shell, grass, and mud which
touch at her skin seem "like suggestions and withdrawals of
some bondage that might have been dear, now dismembering
and losing itself." She experiences an emotional ablution, an
emptying, a sensation purely sensuous but strangely disembodied, a feeling of being on the edge of metamorphosis, "suspended in the Big Black River as she would know how to hang
suspended in felicity." Not in the tribal rites and clichés, but
only in this intensely personal ritual with its subtle, insinuating
mode of address to her mind and senses, does Virgie find clues
to the unspeakable meaning of the great change in her life.

And so through the funeral services the following afternoon,
though she is bereaved, the only experiences meaningful to
Virgie are the private or spontaneously shared ones. When an
orgy of weeping has been induced by the minister's remarks
and a child's singing of a sentimental hymn, Virgie watches
King MacLain steal back and forth from a table in the hall to
pick at the ham, and it is then that she sees him push out his
lip and make his hideous face at her, "like a silent yell." The
sound of his cracking a little bone in his teeth refreshes her.
Looking out the window and hearing the happy sounds of the
MacLain children playing, she experiences another moment of
alliance—she doesn't know whether with Ran or with King—
but it is a spontaneous, timeless moment of kinship and loyalty.
With or without benefit of friendship or intimacy, Virgie knows
that these are her people, her kind. They are all rebels—King,
his son, his impious, curious grandchildren, and Virgie herself
—all have the "pure wish to live," to be individual; they refuse
to be crushed or defeated by life or by death, or by the stul-
tifying effects of sentimental conformity or piety.

Later in the day, returning home from the cemetery, Virgie
has a sense of the "double coming-back." She remembers the

time of her return at seventeen when on the way from the train to her home she had looked about her "in a kind of glory." Then, as now, having gone through an experience of despair, she had felt the beauty of the golden earth meet some ineffable impulse of life and hope in herself, and the product was a resurgence of joy. "Virgie never saw it differently, never doubted that all the opposites on earth were close together, love close to hate, living to dying; but of them all, hope and despair were the closest blood—unrecognizable one from the other sometimes, making moments double upon themselves, and in the doubling double again, amending but never taking back."

The impulse of hope now drives Virgie away from her home and on to some unknown place and condition of the future. She gives away or packs up for storage all her mother's belongings, and sets out in her old car. Seven miles out from Morgana, the town of MacLain is the natural stopping-off place for Virgie to make her final reflections—the last dearly familiar place, drenched with the legends and memories of the wandering MacLain clan, several of whom are already buried in the cemetery (and King himself, surely, the next to go). Here, too, Miss Eckhart is buried. On the stile in front of the courthouse Virgie sits quietly as Mr. Mabry, her last lover, passes by unnoticing; she is "bereaved, hatless, unhidden now, in the rain" and finally, all alone. Then she remembers a picture Miss Eckhart had hanging on her wall, showing Perseus with the head of the Medusa. Only now does she begin to comprehend its meaning:

> The vaunting was what she remembered, that lifted arm.
> Cutting off the Medusa's head was the heroic act, perhaps, that made visible a horror in life, that was at once the horror in love, Virgie thought—the separateness. She might have seen heroism prophetically when she was young and afraid of Miss Eckhart. She might be able to see it now prophetically, but she was never a prophet. Because Virgie saw things in their time, like hearing them—and perhaps because she must believe in the Medusa equally with Perseus—she saw the stroke of the sword in three moments, not one. In the three was the damnation— no, only the secret, unhurting because not caring in itself— beyond the beauty and the sword's stroke and the terror lay their existence in time—far out and endless, a constellation which the heart could read over many a night.

What Virgie sees—or half-sees, since hers is a limited human and not a prophetic vision—is that every hero, as well as every heroic act, implies a victim, a slaying, and hence a source of horror and terror to the onlooker. The reiteration of the theme of love and separateness in this passage recalls the crucial scene from "A Still Moment." Audubon has performed a heroic act in slaying the white heron: heroic because his will and intelligence as artist and naturalist have asserted themselves over his natural feeling for the bird's beautiful life. Since he cannot paint from memory he must kill the bird to save its beauty for the eternal world of art. The bird becomes victim, and to Lorenzo, the witness, the effect is one of horror.

What clouds the symbolism in this analogy, to be sure, is that the bird is innocent, unaware, and lovely, whereas the Medusa appears to be evil and ugly. But even in the legend the Medusa was victim from the start: originally a beautiful Gorgon, she was transformed into a monster by an enraged and jealous Athene. Certainly in this use of the myth, and in Miss Welty's vision generally, evil is never pure and unambiguous, nor is heroism a simple matter of the triumph of good over evil. The underlying similarity is that both the white heron and the Medusa are victims—they are necessary to the heroic act. Whoever conquers does so to the cost of someone or something else, producing in the moment of destruction physical and metaphysical horror. To the merely human eye, from which the larger, eternal perspective is withheld, such acts of violence are horrible because they bring the death which is the final cause or essence of all separateness in life or in love. And so the protest is raised in any tender heart—that of a Lorenzo or Virgie—when an act of destruction, however heroic, is witnessed. The human way is to see actions and relationships "in their time," as music is heard, in a succession of moments; the human way is to feel out, or through, the whole painful process of tragedy and heroism. Just now, for Virgie, there is no "hurt," only the revelation of a "secret" or mystery, since the incident pictured is without immediacy; the implications of the heroic action have been transmuted and distanced to the world of art, where like a constellation loftily removed it may be eternally read, studied, contemplated.

If the human burden is tragedy (separateness), the human glory is the ability to absorb that tragedy, to project it in the forms of art, and then to give to others this knowledge turned to beauty. All this Beethoven had done for Miss Eckhart, and Miss Eckhart had done for Virgie:

> Miss Eckhart, whom Virgie had not, after all, hated—had come near to loving, for she had taken Miss Eckhart's hate, and then her love, extracted them, the thorn and then the over-flow—had hung the picture on the wall for herself. She had absorbed the hero and the victim and then, stoutly, could sit down to the piano with all Beethoven ahead of her. With her hate, with her love, and with the small gnawing feelings that ate them, she offered Virgie her Beethoven. She offered, offered, offered—and when Virgie was young, in the strange wisdom of youth that is accepting of more than is given, she had accepted *the* Beethoven, as with the dragon's blood. That was the gift she had touched with her fingers that had drifted and left her.
>
> In Virgie's reach of memory a melody softly lifted, lifted of itself. Every time Perseus struck off the Medusa's head, there was the beat of time, and the melody. Endless the Medusa, and Perseus endless.

In time, our present human life, the tragic pain and the triumph, the horror and the beauty, the despair and the joy, the frustration and the fulfillment, the separateness and the love, exist in an endless counterpoint: this is the experience of Virgie Rainey, and of every wanderer in *The Golden Apples*.

VII

Miss Welty's use of myth in *The Golden Apples* has already been suggested: explicitly, in her relating the amorous career of King to that of Zeus; less explicitly, in her presentation of the adventures of the boy-hero Loch, the odyssey of Eugene; the search for a father of Randall; most generally, in the quest of all the wanderers. Woven through the book we also find patterns of developing images and symbols which serve important structural functions: they relate and unify the individual careers presented in the book, they support and embody its themes, they are the means by which the texture of an event or feeling is conveyed, they invest the prose with the quality of poetry.

One cluster of these images grows out of the title and its use in the Yeats poem. Plucking the golden apples is the prelude to tasting and enjoying the fruit: fruit and things golden are generally associated with pleasure and fruition; frequently, though not always, they are associated with sexual and emotional fulfillment through love. The golden rays of the sun make earth fertile: King visits and impregnates Snowdie in a shower of gold; he leaves Mattie Will Sojourner in light "like golden smoke"; his familiar sign is the golden panama hat. Finally, his offspring are crowned with golden hair: the twins, Easter with her crest of "withstanding gold," and little Fan, King's grandchild, whose hair when she flies out in play is "a band of sunlight soft and level," or when at bedtime it ripples all around her face, is like "a little golden rain hat."

To young ones, for whom experience and fulfillment lie dimly and alluringly in the future, a golden harbinger may intimate the coming mystery in a moment of quiet reflection. Loch hears the distant songs of Cassie and her friends returning from their hayride. He looks out into the dark leaves of the tree, then sees beyond a low cloud lighted, looking like "a single low wing. The mystery he had felt like a golden and aimless bird had waited until now to fly over." In the camp at Moon Lake, the sound of Loch's golden horn playing taps is a "fairy sound, . . . a holding apart of the air," evoking the dreams and longings of the young girls in the tents; seeing the boy in the distance, Nina puts him into "his visionary place." To Virgie, however, who at seventeen is already initiated into both love and despair, golden light is a sign of returning joy and hope. When the fields glow in the "ripe afternoon" of her return home after running away, she feels like dancing, "knowing herself not really, in her essence, yet hurt; and thus happy."

References to ripening, or ripe, juicy, sweet fruit ("the golden apples of the sun") are usually associated with sexual anticipation or fulfillment. From his bedroom window Loch views not only the progress of the affair between Virgie Rainey and her sailor but the ripening of figs on the old rusty fig trees nearby. Loch is waiting for the day when the sailor will take the ripe figs. "When they cracked open their pink and golden flesh would show, their inside flowers, and golden bubbles of juice would hang, to touch your tongue to first." To Loch the fig tree is "a magic tree with golden fruit that shone in and among its branches like a cloud of lightning bugs," and he dreams of "the sweet golden juice to come." When Virgie Rainey comes in to Miss Eckhart's for her piano lessons she is often "peeling a ripe fig with her teeth." To the teeth of Mattie Will Sojourner, set in the small pointed ear of a MacLain twin, the ear has "the fuzz of a peach."

Because the time of fruition is usually brief and precious, ripe fruit may also be associated with the idea of time's fleeting. Once Nina thinks of ripe pears, "beautiful, symmetrical, clean pears with thin skins, with snow-white flesh so juicy and tender that to eat one baptized the whole face, and so delicate that while you urgently ate the first half, the second half was already beginning to turn brown. To all fruits, and especially to those fine pears, something happened—the process was so swift, you were never in time for them. It's not the flowers that are fleeting, Nina thought, it's the fruits—it's the time when things are ready that they don't stay."

Butterflies and humming birds appear with a cluster of associations related to those of the golden apples. Butterflies are again associated with delight, sexual pleasure, or exoticism; they are the sign of the lover, as Psyche, beloved of Cupid, appears with butterfly wings. Miss Eckhart gives to Virgie the gift of a butterfly pin to wear on her shoulder. In "Moon Lake" Nina sees the silhouette of two lovers, each on one end of a canoe floating on the bright water, and looking like "a dark butterfly with wings spread open and still." On the streets of San Francisco Eugene spies a butterfly tatooed on the inner side of the wrist of a romantic-looking young man with a black pompadour and taps on his shoes; later he sees a strangely beautiful butterfly woman, a Negro or Polynesian "marked as a butterfly is, over all her visible skin. Curves, scrolls, dark brown areas on light brown, were beautifully placed on her body, as if by design, with pools about the eyes, at the nape of her neck, at the wrist, and about her legs too, like fawn spots, visible through her stockings. She had the look of waiting in leafy shade, . . . of hiding and flaunting together."

The humming bird symbolism is more complicated. When "The Wanderers" was first published separately in *Harper's Bazaar*, it appeared under the title of "The Humming Birds." The basic analogy is this: as the small aerial wanderers suck sweetness from flowers, so their human counterparts try to suck sweetness from life. But in their swift darting, humming birds also suggest the mystery and elusiveness of joy; in their peculiar mode of hanging suspended while they suck, they suggest both physical suspension in space (swimming, floating, or flying) and the suspension in time (the sense of being outside time) which comes with the moment of ecstasy (the word means, literally, the state of being outside oneself).

The humming bird image is first introduced in Cassie's reflections as she sees one of them go down in a streak across her window:

He was a little emerald bobbin, suspended as always before the opening four-o'clocks. Metallic and misty together, tangible and intangible, splendid and fairy-like, the haze of his invisible wings mysterious, like the ring around the moon—had anyone ever tried to catch him? Not she. Let him be suspended there for a moment each year for a hundred years—incredibly thirsty, greedy for every drop in every four-o'clock trumpet in the yard, as though he had them numbered—then dart.

The humming bird image again appears in the memory of Eugene while he is sitting in the restaurant with the Spaniard. Through a process of association and synesthesia, Eugene is reminded by the sweet, exotic odor of the Spaniard's tobacco of the mimosa flowers which used to bloom outside the window when as a boy he played a favorite piece on a hot summer's day and the notes of music were transformed into drops of light "plopping one, two, three, four, through sky and trees to earth, to lie there in the pattern opposite to the shade of the tree. He could feel his forehead bead with drops and the pleasure run like dripping juice through each plodding finger, at such an hour, on such a day, in such a place. Mississippi. A humming bird, like a little fish, a little green fish in the hot air, had hung for a moment before his gaze, then jerked, vanishing, away."

Once again the humming bird appears, to Virgie. She is standing at the bedside of her mother, a moment after her death, when suddenly her vision turns to pure image and sensation. "Behind the bed the window was full of cloudy, pressing flowers and leaves in a heavy light, like a jar of figs in syrup held up. A humming bird darted, fed, darted. Every day he came. He had a ruby throat. The clock jangled faintly as cymbals struck under water, but did not strike; it couldn't. Yet a torrent of riches seemed to flow over the room, submerging it with what was over-sweet."

The suspension of the humming bird is related to those incidents in which a character is literally and symbolically suspended in a moment of felicity. Eugene spread out, flying over the sea like a bird from the Spaniard's hands, and Virgie spread out, floating like a fish in the Big Black River, experience moments of pure ecstasy. These moments carry with them a suggestion of change in a life pattern which registers as the pause before some actual physical metamorphosis; the state is dream- or trance-like, the sensations are at once disembodied and acutely sensuous; the postures, and in Eugene's case the thoughts, are those of the act of love. Floating is also related to felicity in other contexts: floating in a boat on Moon Lake is dream-like enchantment; mist floating on a river or lake in moonlight suspends the viewer in felicity.

Other patterns of symbolism in *The Golden Apples* have to do with freedom, confinement, and the need for discipline. If fulfillment is to be achieved, a person must be free. To the characters with family bonds and internal inhibitions, the state of being, or appearing to be, completely free, is glorious and enviable: thus Cassie envies Virgie; Nina envies Easter (in the "beatific state" of being "not answerable to a soul on earth"), Eugene envies the Spaniard ("There was no one he loved, to tell him anything, to lay down the law"). But even to the free ones, walls and barriers are unavoidable. Beating against a wall may signify the rebel's revolt against rules, as when Virgie as a child in school is angered because recess is to be held in the basement on account of rainy weather, and she announces that she is going "to butt her brains out against the wall." (The teacher says, "Beat them out, then," and she goes ahead and tries while the children watch admiringly.) To Eugene, the open, free look of San Francisco is deceptive; he could tell the Spaniard how the hills and clouds could bank up, one upon the other: "they were any man's walls still," and a man could feel closed in there as anywhere.

Walls are also symbolic of separateness, of the barriers between human beings. People may "wall up" against each other, feel so acutely their isolation, the privacy and uniqueness of their experience, the impossibility of being penetrated, that they might as well be dead to others. This kind of inwardly constructed wall is a type of the final cause and result of separateness, death itself. Returning from the cemetery, Virgie thinks about King MacLain's conquest of these and all other walls and barriers to fulfillment:

> Virgie had often felt herself at some moment callous over, go opaque; she had known it to happen to others; not only when her mother changed on the bed while she was fanning her. Virgie had felt a moment in her life after which nobody could

see through her, into her—felt it young. But Mr. King Mac-
Lain, an old man, had butted like a goat against the wall he
wouldn't agree to himself or recognize. What fortress indeed
would ever come down, except before hard little horns, a rush
and a stampede of the pure wish to live?

If the freedom necessary to fulfillment cannot be attained
without a struggle against the confinements and barriers of
life, neither can it come to meaningful expression without the
exercise of discipline. Music speaks of, and embodies, a type
of fulfillment, but it can be achieved only out of a costly control; it is passion made orderly, form imposed on the chaos
of feelings. Most of the wanderers are musicians of one sort
or another: even Loch has his golden horn, Eugene his favorite
piece of music, Easter her plan to be a singer. Miss Eckhart's
fierce attachment to her metronome indicates her recognition
of the need for control in the life and music of her students
as well as in her own life; when she becomes a living metronome at her lover's grave, it is her instinctive way of avoiding
an expression of uncontrolled grief or hysteria. The Spaniard
guitarist has his moments of looking as wild and fierce as a
bull, but playing his music, even the most tender and passionate
love songs, he only looms remotely. When he ends his recital
with a formal bow, it seems to Eugene "as though it had been
taken for granted by then that passion was the thing he had
in hand, love was his servant, and even despair was a little
tamed animal trotting about in plain view." Virgie too must
learn discipline if she is to achieve expression through love
or music. In one remarkable passage, images of confinement,
work, and the expression of will and sexual desire are combined
to show the kind of process she is undergoing during the years
of her "apprenticeship" at home:

Her fingers set, after coming back, set half-closed; the
strength in her hands she used up to type in the office but
most consciously to pull the udders of the succeeding cows, as
if she would hunt, hunt, hunt daily for the blindness that lay
inside the beast, inside where she could have a real and living
wall for beating on, a solid prison to get out of, the most real
stupidity of flesh, a mindless and careless and calling body,
to respond flesh for flesh, anguish for anguish. And if, as she
dreamed one winter night, a new piano she touched had turned,
after the one pristine moment, into a calling cow, it was by her
own desire.

Paradoxically, it is the art form most dependent on time, existing in a present sequence of moments, which has the greatest
power to put the listener outside his ordinary sense of present
time. Music enables him to summon the past and imaginatively
to perceive its meanings. Its effect in *The Golden Apples*
reminds one of the effect of the little phrase from the sonata
of Vinteuil in Proust's *Remembrance of Things Past;* in Miss
Welty's book, music provides insight into the meaning of
beauty, love, suffering, and loss, and it has the power to sus-
pend, compress, or protract time and experience. Music often
functions in this manner for the characters in *The Golden
Apples*. The *"Für Elise"* theme is a "greeting" to Loch, and takes
him back "to when his sister was so sweet, to a long time ago."
To Cassie the theme brings tumbling the lines from the Yeats
poem, and with them the gathering past which breaks like a
wave over her head. Listening to the Spaniard play the subtle
love songs of his native land, Eugene experiences "a deep lull
in his spirit that was as enfolding as love. . . . He felt a lapse
of all knowledge of Emma as his wife, and of comprehending
the future, in some visit to a vast present-time. The lapse must
have endured for a solid minute or two, . . . as positively there
and as defined at the edges as a spot or stain, and it affected
him like a secret."

If music suddenly evokes the timeless moment, time's own
passing creates the wisdom of attrition in those who have survived many deaths (their own and others') and have witnessed
decay and change. The small party assembled at Mrs. Rainey's
grave show this wisdom when a cornucopia of flowers spills
over and no one bothers to set it straight: "already, tomorrow's
rain pelted the grave with loudness . . . ; this was the past now."
And in the narrator's own withdrawal from the world of her
fiction in the final paragraph of her book, time is telescoped
by the swift evocation of prehistoric or mythical animal life,
even then mysterious, heroic, and beautiful, as it is now. An
ancient Negro woman sits down by Virgie for shelter from the
rain. At first a couple of stray familiar figures pass. "Then she
and the old beggar woman, the old black thief, were there alone
and together in the shelter of the big public tree, listening to
the magical percussion, the world beating in their ears. They
heard through falling rain the running of the horse and bear,
the stroke of the leopard, the dragon's crusty slither, and the
glimmer and the trumpet of the swan."

CHAPTER 8

The Bride of the Innisfallen:
from Innocence to Experience

I

THE FIRST IMPRESSION given by Miss Welty's last collection of stories, *The Bride of the Innisfallen* (1955), is that a number of departures have been made from the patterns of her earlier fiction. A major change is the predominant shift from her usual regional settings and southern characters. The action of four of the seven stories takes place outside Mississippi. "Circe," set on a legendary island and based on the Circe episode in *The Odyssey*, is Miss Welty's only explicit use of a Greek myth. The title story depicts a group of chiefly Irish people enroute from London to Cork; "Going to Naples," a group of Italian-Americans on a ship headed for Italy; the viewpoint, in both cases, is largely that of an outsider. "No Place for You, My Love" has a southern setting (the delta country south of New Orleans), but one unfamiliar to Miss Welty; furthermore, the two principal characters of this story are an open-faced, self-conscious young woman from the Middle West, and a sophisticated eastern businessman.

"Kin" is one of the three stories with a Mississippi setting, but its point of view is that of a girl who at the age of eight moved away from the state to the urban North and is making a return visit. "The Burning" is Miss Welty's first and only Civil War story. Only in "Ladies in Spring" do we return to something familiar: rural Mississippians in their own setting, in and near a tiny town named Royals.

Experiment, range, and variety are apparent in the stories, but the consistency of Miss Welty's vision is equally apparent in her continued focus on love and separateness, the human mysteries, the sense of exposure and need for protection, the comprehension of human experience through rare moments of genuine communication with another, or through private, unshared insight. Also apparent is the varied "weather of the mind" in her shifts from comedy to pathos, both among the stories and within the consciousness of her characters: as, for example, in the American girl from the title story who sees, at the end of her first day in Cork, that "all she had come here to know . . . was light and rain, light and rain, dark, light, and rain." The large, steady rhythms of nature, as well as its caprices, find parallels in the human mind and heart.

Joy is part of the freshness of strange places and persons encountered: they are remarkable, surprising, or funny. The stories abound in many kinds of delights. The beholder may have the innocent eye of the child, like Dewey in "Ladies in Spring," proud of his freshly caught fish, wondering about the strange, beautiful lady who flies like a doe through the woods, happy to be marching in the pouring rain in advance of a small procession toward town. It may be an adolescent discovering the delights of love, as Gabriella does when Aldo buries his face in her blouse. It may be a young adult like the American girl of "The Bride of the Innisfallen" who retains the child's vision, but has grown up enough to identify in herself the primal joy: "the kind you were born and began with."

The beholder may also be an experienced person to whom joy returns as nostalgia for something felt in youth, lost, revived in the memory by chance association or vicarious experience. To Dicey, in "Kin," the sight of the old stereoptican revives memories of Sunday afternoons spent with Uncle Felix, when both of them were lost in pleasurable dreaming about the "picture cities." This sense of kinship makes her immediately sensitive to the meaning of Uncle Felix's scribbled note, "River —Daisy—Midnight—Please": the delirious old man, seeing a pretty and beloved young girl who was "kin" to him, confuses her with an old love of his youth with whom he had once made a tryst. At the close of "No Place for You, My Love," the easterner remembers "for the first time in years when he was young and brash, a student in New York, and the shriek and horror and unholy smother of the subway had its original meaning for him as the lilt and expectation of love." So also the old people going to Naples; while sitting in the sun watching the amorous play of Gabriella and Aldo, they contemplate "the weakness and the mystery of the flesh" and feel "something of an old, pure loneliness come back to them—like a bird sent out over the waters long ago, when they were young. . . .

Only the long of memory, the brave and experienced of heart, could bear such a stirring, an awakening. . . ."

II

Dominant themes, feelings, and the continued shaping influence of place reveal the continuity of these stories with Miss Welty's fiction. But other changes are apparent than those resulting from the shift in locale and the use of the "outsider's" vantage point. The stories of this volume are noticeably lacking in plot, the strong, coherent shaping of external events. What is any story "about"? A great deal happens, and yet little that can be reduced to summary. The climaxes are internal and difficult to locate: they are likely to occur in a series of moments, or realizations, which do not usually effect a turning point in external action or behavior. Brilliant descriptions, pictures, moods, snatches of conversation, epigrammatic summations contribute to the whole, which tends to be a dominant impression rather than a clear rational design.

One critic sums up his response to this collection of stories by saying that "the impacts are like tiny beads of transient sensation patterned together by a delicate thread of reasoning."[1] The image used in this statement is more complimentary than was probably intended, since it calls attention to process and progression, as does the series of events and impressions which constitute a trip or voyage; and the total effect of a string of beads, as of these journeys (real or symbolic), is unified. But not, I believe, with the artless clarity of some of Miss Welty's other stories.

The difference emerges more clearly through comparison. "A Worn Path" and "The Wide Net" are both "process" stories. In each case a journey is taken for a specific purpose: Old Phoenix goes to fetch the "soothing medicine" for her grandson; William Wallace and his entourage drag the river to recover the body of Hazel. In each case episodes, stages, and diversions, engage the attention of characters and readers; the journey becomes a progression in which the final purpose is temporarily lost sight of (as when William Wallace dances with the fish in his belt, or Old Phoenix forgets why she made her trip). In each case the trip also takes on a ceremonial significance, and becomes a symbol for a whole life, in which processes and rituals carry us, unwitting, on to our goals and destinies.

"The Bride of the Innisfallen," "No Place for You, My Love," and "Going to Naples" are also stories of "process" or journey. But whose is each journey, why is it taken, what is its significance? In the title story the central character is not, as might be expected, the bride, but the American girl for whom the bride becomes a symbol. Contrasted with the motivations of Phoenix or William Wallace, her motivation for taking the journey is as obscure as her central "problem." She has an excess of hope and joy; it is like a burden on her heart because it cannot be communicated or acted upon. How often, in modern literature, is the excess of joy a "problem"? I can think of only one other obvious example, and that is in J. D. Salinger's character, Seymour Glass, a suicide, apparently, from a rather complicated overindulgence in ecstasy (and the only character who appears to have followed literally the injunction of Carl Sandburg: "Let joy kill you, keep away from the little deaths.") I do not say that this motivation is incomprehensible: it seems to me both credible and moving. But it is somewhat rarified and difficult for the reader to discover, especially outside the context of Miss Welty's work as a whole; and part of this difficulty is the lack of the immediate, tangible human relationships found in "A Worn Path" or "The Wide Net."

A similar vagueness surrounds the flight of the young woman in "No Place for You, My Love." We know only from the Easterner's point of view, that back home she must be involved in some hopeless love relationship (possibly with a married man), that there may recently have been a "scene," since she has on her temple a bruise which affects her "like an evil star," that her frantic need is for escape and the protection of distance and anonymity, and that her painful obsession is with exposure. But if the heroine's situation is vague, we know from Miss Welty's account in "How I Write" that it is intended to be; we also know that the point of view was neither the woman's nor her companion's but that of a mysterious third presence:

It was . . . fished alive from the surrounding scene, where as it carried the story along it revealed itself (I hoped) as more real, more essential, than the characters were or had any cause to be. In effect there'd come to be a sort of third character present—an identity, rather: the relationship between the two and between the two and the world. It was what grew up between them meeting as strangers, went on the trip with them. . . . I wanted to suggest that its being took shape as the strange, compulsive journey itself, was palpable as its climate and mood, the heat of the day. . . .

I wanted to make it seen and believed what was to me, in my story's grip, literally apparent—that secret and shadow are taken away in this country by the merciless light that prevails there, by the river that is like an exposed vein of ore, the road that descends as one with the heat—its nerve (these are all terms in the story), and that the heat is also a visual illusion, shimmering and dancing over the waste that stretches ahead. . . . I was writing of exposure, and the shock of the world; in the end I tried to make the story's inside outside and then throw away the shell.

Miss Welty accomplished what she set out to do, but it was a perilous undertaking. She took a human feeling—a panicky, raw-nerved sense of exposure—and invested an entire landscape and journey with that feeling; she rendered a strong emotional effect without supplying much information about its cause. The vivid impressionism of this method is strangely exciting, but the story is not as fully and solidly alive as is a story like "A Worn Path," in which there seems never to have been a shell to throw away because every part—plot, character, setting, theme—seems essential to every other part.

Experimentation in narrative technique is also evident in "The Burning." The characters in this story are clearly conceived, but monolithic: a pair of genteel maiden sisters, and an obedient young slave, Delilah. The point of view is difficult to locate, but the narrator is usually hovering in and around the consciousness of Delilah, recording what is said and done in a language subtly adjusted to the minds, mode of life, relationships, and idiom of the three women. With a few notable exceptions—particularly where the narrator is entering into and interpreting Delilah's hallucinations—the sentence structure and language are simple, and the description is sharply detailed, textural, impressionistic. Frequent gaps in the action have the effect of averted eyes; confusions and ambiguities are abundant.

The action which can be pieced together is sufficiently horrible. Two of Sherman's soldiers, with a white horse, invade the home of the two ladies; though it is not clear how the soldiers attack the women, it is implied that at least Miss Myra is raped, and all three women are put out; the house is looted by soldiers and Negroes, then burned with a child named Phinney in it. The three women, who witness the burning, then wander toward and through a devastated Jackson; Miss Theo murders her sister by hanging; then, with Delilah's help, she tries to hang herself but apparently succeeds only in breaking her neck and dies by inches in the grass. After a day or two Delilah returns to the blackened ruins of the house, finds and takes Phinney's bones, and is seen, finally, with a "Jubilee cup" set on her head, advancing across the Big Black River.

The effect of all these grim happenings is not what the facts would suggest. It is weirdly diffused, muted, diverted by the variety of irrelevant detail which swamps Delilah's consciousness and by the quaint, lady-like speech, behavior, and "props" of the two old maids. Only the slightest hint notifies the reader of some new horror: "the soldier . . . dropped on top of her" tells us Miss Myra is being raped; "when it came—but it was a bellowing like a bull, that came from inside—Delilah drew close" tells us that Phinney is being burned alive. Then the profuse details come flooding: pictures of the elegant interior of the house, "glimmering with precious, breakable things white ladies are never tired of"; or outdoors, of butterflies and insects and "black-eyed susans, wild to the pricking skin, with many heads nodding." Or there are bits of dainty, playful argument or assertion, which are madly inappropriate to the grim occasion, such as this one of Miss Theo, who is tying the noose for Miss Myra: "I learned as a child how to tie, from a picture book in Papa's library—not that I ever was called on. . . . I guess I was always something of a tomboy." Because the felt reactions often have no correlation with the events, the effect on the reader is ironic almost to the point of perversity.

There are two main reasons for this apparent perversity. The first is that the old style of southern gentlewoman behaves with faultless consistency, which means, in extreme circumstances (as in Faulkner's "A Rose for Miss Emily"), that she may behave insanely. The proud Miss Theo has the godlike strength which befits her name. Sufficiently warned of the coming destruction, she can't "understand" the message, pulls down the shutters, and goes on living as if nothing is going to happen; attacked, turned out, she retains her dignity and consummates her protest with suicide. Miss Myra persists in the only mode known to her: that of being a gentle, passive, protected child-lady. The second reason for the strange, perverse-seeming narrative technique is involved in the use of Delilah as the main center of consciousness in the story. Delilah is innocent and does not understand the meaning of the horror, cruelty, and catastrophe that she witnesses. Her world is shattered into fragments, but she cannot make a tragic shape out of the fragments. Like Little Lee Roy in "Keela, the Outcast Indian Maiden," she is incapable of the moral comprehension of her experience.

Delilah's nature accounts, then, for the fragmented, confusing effect of the narrative method, and it could also be used to justify the ambiguity surrounding Phinney's parentage. Delilah takes care of Phinney, but does not know who he is, and the debate of the sisters on the subject is unintelligible. The child is clearly illegitimate; but whether Negro or white, Miss Myra's by an old beau or brother Benton's by a Negro slave, it is impossible to determine. The major clue to his identity is Delilah's association of Phinney with a Negro child named Jonah—possibly her own son, "her Phinney," taken away from her for some unknown cause. But the mystery is never cleared up, and this unnecessary ambiguity remains a flaw in the narrative structure.

The major symbol in "The Burning" is an important container of the story's meaning. In the parlor is a large Venetian mirror, the ornate roof of which is supported by two black men (Moors), who stand on either side of it and appear almost to be looking into the glass themselves. When the soldiers and horse invade the house at the beginning of the story, the two ladies raise their eyes to the mirror and regard the intruders reflected there instead of turning to face them directly. While Miss Myra is attacked, Delilah's vision is turned away from the violence and fixed on the mirror; it reflects her, obediently holding the white horse, and the tranquil parlor interior with the "bare yawn" of the hall reaching behind. The elegant mirror is the symbol of a way of life: placid, decorative, sheltered, lived at a remove, out of touch with reality, and supported by slaves.

Returning to the ruins after the burning, Delilah finds the mirror. The black men are now "half-split away, flattened with fire, bearded, noseless as the moss that hung from swamp trees"; the glass is clouded "like the horse-trampled spring." Peering into it, Delilah has a hallucinatory vision in which the mirror's decoration (images of aristocratic Venetian life) are blended with images of "Jackson before Sherman came"; then, "under the flicker of the sun's licks, then under its whole blow and blare, like an unheard scream, like an act of mercy gone, as the wall-less light and July blaze struck through from the opened sky, the mirror felled her flat." And finally, in a phantasmagoria of destructive images, Delilah sees and feels her world violently shattered.

Elaborateness, subtlety, and sophistication are distinguishing marks of the stories in *The Bride of the Innisfallen*. These qualities are visible not only in choice and motivation of character, structure, and narrative technique, but also in style. The changes, though in no way absolute, become most apparent at their two extremes in Miss Welty's earliest and latest work, and may be illustrated by a comparison of the opening sentences of a few stories from *A Curtain of Green* and *The Bride of the Innisfallen*. Following are a few from the first volume:

> One morning in summertime, when all his sons and daughters were off picking plums and Little Lee Roy was all alone, sitting on the porch and only listening to the screech owls away down in the woods, he had a surprise. ["Keela, the Outcast Indian Maiden"]
>
> Old Mr. Marblehall never did anything, never got married until he was sixty. You can see him out taking a walk. ["Old Mr. Marblehall"]
>
> R. J. Bowman, who for fourteen years had traveled for a shoe company through Mississippi, drove his Ford along a rutted, dirt path. It was a long day! ["Death of a Traveling Salesman"]
>
> I was getting along fine with Mama, Papa-Daddy and Uncle Rondo until my sister Stella-Rondo just separated from her husband and came back home again. ["Why I Live at the P.O."]
>
> It was December—a bright frozen day in the early morning. Far out in the country there was an old Negro woman with her head tied in a red rag, coming along a path through the pinewoods. Her name was Phoenix Jackson. ["A Worn Path"]

And following are a few opening sentences from *The Bride of the Innisfallen*:

> They were strangers to each other, both fairly well strangers to the place, now seated side by side at luncheon—a party combined in a free-and-easy way when the friends he and she were with recognized each other across Galatoire's. ["No Place for You, My Love"]

There was something of the pavilion about one raincoat, the way—for some little time out there in the crowd—it stood flowing in its salmony-pink and yellow stripes down toward the wet floor of the platform, expanding as it went. ["The Bride of the Innisfallen"]

"Mingo?" I repeated, and for the first moment I didn't know what my aunt meant. The name sounded in my ears like *something* instead of *somewhere*. ["Kin"]

The pair moved through that gray landscape as though no one would see them—dressed alike in overalls and faded coats, one big, one little, one black-headed, one tow-headed, father and son. ["Ladies in Spring"]

Striking in the first set of opening sentences is directness of style. Characters, setting, time of day or season, the beginnings of situation or action are at once set before the reader purely and plainly. The sentences are short and simple; in even the longest of them—the one introducing Little Lee Roy—the parts are knitted together by the use of a simple series of participles.

By comparison, the style of the second set of opening sentences is oblique and sophisticated. Characters are introduced without their names (in two of the four stories they never get names). Questions are raised, and the reader knows instinctively that answers may not be immediately forthcoming. The pertinence of each opening to the central action is subtle rather than explicit. Sentence structure is relatively complicated: the most direct opening of the four, that of "Ladies in Spring," contains a delicately mystifying phrase, "as though no one would see them," and proceeds by the use of a small, rhetorically structured set of contrasts. "The Bride of the Innisfallen" opens with an attractively fancy, teasing metaphor: a gaily striped raincoat has "something of the pavilion" about it. The style is that of a storyteller who knows there are a thousand different ways of getting into a story rather than the one of simply beginning with persons, places, and things.

It is difficult to isolate the changes in Miss Welty's style without considering their relation to character, situation, and point of view. The sophistication of style in "No Place for You, My Love," for example, is fitted to the sophistication of the two main characters and their situation: two self-conscious modern people, briefly whirled together and then apart, whose relationship is determined by the nature of the environment they encounter together and by the heat and speed of their journey, as much as by their own natures. The self-consciousness of the relationship invades, or pervades, the style. Even the metaphors are affected, and some of them are difficult to interpret, as, for instance, the following, which appears toward the end of the story, just after the couple have returned to New Orleans and are about to leave each other: "Something that must have been with them all along suddenly, then, was not. In a moment, tall as panic, it rose, cried like a human, and dropped back." Without the help of Miss Welty's explanation in "How I Write," one might puzzle over that metaphor long and fruitlessly. She says the cry was that of "the fading relationship—personal, individual, psychic—admitted in order to be denied, a cry that the characters were first able (and prone) to listen to, and then able in part to ignore. The cry was authentic to my story and so I didn't care if it did seem a little odd: the end of a journey *can* set up a cry, the shallowest provocation to sympathy and love does hate to give up the ghost." The metaphor *is* odd, but it was born legitimately out of an odd story with an odd point of view.

It is, finally, the storyteller who reveals sophistication in the stories of *The Bride of the Innisfallen:* a writer who is far more aware of multiple choices, the varieties of form and technique possible to the creative imagination, than was the writer of *A Curtain of Green.* As an artist, Miss Welty seems to have gone through the kind of change she has so often described in her fiction: the passage from innocence to experience. What is lost in this process is simplicity, purity, lucidity, immediacy in relation to the materials of fiction, a natural and instinctive grace, an intuitive perception and realization of form, and relative ease and spontaneity of creation. The sophistication which is gained at the expense of the loss of innocence has a compensating value: the stories provide the delight which comes from the experience of an art beautifully and skillfully executed, varied, mature, experimental. And throughout, the power of feeling has never been lost.

Between and including the two extremes just described lies the abundance of Miss Welty's fiction. The development from innocence to sophistication as revealed in the forms and techniques of her fiction in no way follows a steady pattern; it is clearly visible *only* in its extremes. If experimentation in narrative technique is taken as a distinguishing tendency of the later stories, the experimentation of "Powerhouse" and "Asphodel" disprove that theory; if it is shifts in setting and type of character, "Kin" and "Ladies in Spring" disprove that theory. A wholly consistent pattern cannot be found in her work: its variety is, in fact, one of its happiest features. To borrow her own words, if one should attempt "the nicest, carefullest black-and-white tracing" of her development as a writer, a "breath of life" from one of her stories would "do for" it.

III

Yet one may attempt a tracing of her development: a progress from innocence to experience in Miss Welty's vision of life, which is the parallel or counterpart to the formal changes in her art. The materials for this fragile tracing are a few biographical facts, and inferences drawn from the stories themselves. Though the experiences projected in any story are not literally drawn from actual experiences in Miss Welty's life (she has explicitly stated that they are not), the stories speak of a life process which is peculiar to her artistic vision, though it is, in a broad sense, widely shared. The present connotations of the resonant and ambiguous terms "innocence" and "experience" should emerge in the following discussion: suffice it to say here that in Miss Welty's vision "innocence" is not associated with the lack of a knowledge of moral evil and sin, nor "experience" with the recognition and awareness of evil either through observation of or complicity in guilt.

A prominent fact about Miss Welty's childhood is that it was externally and internally secure, orderly, filled with love, protection, "prevention." Her parents were solidly upper-middle class, she lived in a solid brick two-story "English style" house on a respectable street, she enjoyed every advantage that affection, indulgence, and a mild discipline could bring to insure a child's happiness and content. There is no doubt that she lived her childhood fully and even managed to carry over into adulthood that primal sense of wonder, awe, delight—the innocent, naïve sight of the world as always fresh and new—which pervades her work.

What no amount of security could prevent, however, was her seeing that life was not everywhere secure and orderly—not permanently so, and not for everybody. There was no preventing those steadily focusing, wide-open child's eyes from also taking in the disorder within the order of nature, the human vulnerability, pain and suffering, the threats of chance and catastrophe, and the final fact of death. Given love itself, there is no preventing a child from reaching out, giving love to others, and hence of seeing where and how the others suffer. And thus very early the seeds of distrust—not of any particular person, but of life itself—were planted in that young, secure-seeming life; the stories tell how these seeds grew, silent and unseen, despite kind and careful nurturing. One passage from "A Memory" tells the story:

> When a person, or a happening, seemed to me not in keeping with my opinion, or even my hope or expectation, I was terrified by a vision of abandonment and wildness which tore my heart with a kind of sorrow. My father and mother, who believed that I saw nothing in the world which was not strictly coaxed into place like a vine on our garden trellis to be presented to my eyes, would have been badly concerned if they had guessed how frequently the weak and inferior and strangely turned examples of what was to come showed themselves to me.

She saw that it was not in the nature of vines to be neat and orderly; she guessed at the wildness and disorder which lies at the heart of life, the response to which must be pity and fear.

Her father was head of an insurance company—an institution set up by human beings to provide corporate security and "prevention." The company exists in apparent defiance of the facts; it is capable of reducing human misery materially, but it is completely impotent in the face of real human tragedy. She must have heard of these tragedies—sweeping ones like wars, floods, and tornadoes; and smaller, freakish ones, like a man's being crushed to death in his car by a falling tree.

During the violent storm portrayed in "The Winds," little Josie is fearful about Cornella:

> "I see Cornella. She's on the outside, Mamma, outside in the storm, and she's in the equinox."
>
> But her mother would not answer.
>
> "Josie, don't you understand—I want to keep us close together," said her father. She looked back at him. "Once in an equinoctial storm," he said cautiously over the sleeping Will, "a man's little girl was blown away from him into a haystack out in a field."
>
> "The wind will come after Cornella," said Josie.

That woeful prediction, that little girl's sweet, fearful wail of love, can be heard in a hundred transmutations throughout the fiction of Eudora Welty. If we think of the number of catastrophes and accidents (or near-accidents) recorded in her stories, then we may observe the tragic discovery of this child of security: there is no prevention.

A Curtain of Green records the shock of the world on the sensitive, innocent mind and heart. The potential or actual brutality is directly faced in such stories as "A Memory," "A Curtain of Green," "Flowers for Marjorie," and "Keela, the Outcast Indian Maiden." The underlying causes of this disorder are probed; the focus on nature is intent and relentless. What lies behind that wild "curtain of green"? We do not know, because the curtain is never drawn back: the revelation is of a mystery.

Another fact of existence felt from the inside by the young dreamer and noted from the outside by the observer, is that human beings are essentially alone and essentially lonely. Often there is no one to love, or no one to return love; more often, there is no adequate way to express or communicate love. Human beings are walled up in their own inescapable identity. The will to communicate leads only to the confrontation of opacity in the self, self-destruction, or the destruction of love in others. The tragedy or pathos of loneliness and separateness is also directly faced in those early stories: in the lives of the two salesmen, of Clytie, of old Mr. Marblehall, of Joel Mayes. Again underlying causes are probed. A few stories suggest that causes for loneliness may be partially economic and social: the salesmen are rootless because their jobs put them on the road; Howard is driven from home in Mississippi into his chain of nihilistic action because of the Depression. Social stratification is another potential cause of loneliness: Clytie and Jenny Lockhart, born into self-consciously "cultured," aristocratic homes, are not allowed to mix with the common folk of the village. But these are not the real answers to the question of separateness in Miss Welty's fiction.

There is another, tentative answer in a general complaint about humanity at large: "nobody cares." The words recur like a refrain in "Old Mr. Marblehall" and "The Purple Hat"; the refrain is also implied in such stories as "Death of a Traveling Salesman," "Clytie," "Petrified Man," and "June Recital." People are too caught up in their own concerns and complacencies to pay much attention. If they give any sympathy, it is likely to be the sort displayed by the small waiting-room crowd in

"The Key" when they first notice that among their company is a pair of deaf-mutes: "Shallow pity washed over the waiting room like a dirty wave foaming and creeping over a public beach."

But the vision which gazes relentlessly sees in addition to, or behind, these general causes of economic disorder, social stratification, or public indifference, a far more basic cause of loneliness. There is a *primal* loneliness which springs from the mystery of human life and which manifests itself in the mystery of personal identity. It flickers across every human face. It makes of every human being a stranger not only to others but to himself. The primal loneliness—the mystery of identity, the way it is met by the innocent, and the way it can hurt—is recorded in *The Wide Net*. Through the wide net of these stories flow the rivers of consciousness, the dreams of the dreamers, in their quests for identity and love. Three are children—Joel Mayes, Jenny Lockhart, Josie—who are seen in their initial awakening to these mysteries; others are adults who must relearn the mysteries, like William Wallace, or who fly in face of their torment, like Lorenzo, Dow, Murrell, and Audubon.

When the innocent mind first encounters the mysteries of the universe, observes and feels the separateness between human beings, the immediate response is "Something must be done." Because the stories tell us that Miss Welty knew, before she ever wrote them, the exact sense in which nothing *could* be done, it is, strictly speaking, inaccurate to call her early stories "innocent" in their implied view of the world. She knew both the absoluteness of the mysteries, and the ways in which something *could* be done. But what she is chiefly saying in the early stories is only "see and wonder." Her characters meet the mysteries head on through painful experience, probe and pursue, have a revelation of themselves in relation to the mysteries, and then often are stopped dead—literally so in "Death of a Traveling Salesman" and "Clytie"; psychically or internally so in other stories. In "A Curtain of Green" Mrs. Larkin submits herself to "unaccountability" in a deathlike exhaustion of mind and body. In "A Still Moment" Lorenzo Dow, Murrell, and Audubon pursue the meaning of their lives until they confront enigma; they will continue in the frenzied pursuit of their goals but with a fresh knowledge of their helplessness.

After those first two volumes of stories (*A Curtain of Green* and *The Wide Net*) Miss Welty does not continue in this frontal attack on the enigma of the universe. The fruits of experience are apparent in an implied resignation; the positive fruits of that resignation are visible in a new set of attitudes toward personal identity and human relationships. And "something can be done": hints of what that is are already supplied in several of the early stories. But particularly in the character of George Fairchild in *Delta Wedding*, she shows us someone doing it.

The new attitude is that human isolation and loneliness are not tragic, but right and necessary. It is good to be "apart"— to know and feel one's own mystery and that of others. This knowledge evokes gentleness, respect for dignity and privacy. It develops poise and encourages freedom; it provides protection for inner development, delight in the perception of human variety and individuality, and a boundless potential for love and insight. The attitude is, like that of George, "divinely careless," fearless; abandoned, but without recklessness; ready and eager for experience, but not insatiably greedy for it; open and receptive to pleasure, but steady in the endurance of pain. The process of growing toward an awareness of these values and of putting them into actions and relationships "in the world" is the experiential process of the main characters in the novel.

This attitude reflects the most basic human wisdom—there might have been nothing more for experience to say after *Delta Wedding*. But there was, of course, a new way to say it. In *The Golden Apples* Miss Welty returned to her first and essentially most congenial form, that of the short story of indeterminate length, which provided her great liberty for a variety of experiments in narrative method. But everything else is extended, broadened. The focus widens from that of *Delta Wedding* to include the relationships not only of persons in a family, but families in a town ("Main Families in Morgana, Mississippi," the author announces at the beginning of her volume, then lists the characters in their family groups). The time span covers forty years instead of a few days—we are shown the complete history of a generation and parts of a cycle of three generations. But even beyond that, the perspective reaches back to myth and out to infinity. Morgana itself, as well as the individual lives of its characters, is seen in time from out of time, and perhaps it would be true to say that the presiding character is fate.

In *The Golden Apples* a new tone of voice can be heard

around and through the consciousness of the characters. It reflects on the human odyssey. It speaks of aspiration and defeat, joy and sorrow, birth and death; it tells of all the larger, eternal rhythms of life which are reflected by the rising and setting of the constellations and planets, and which are visible in the legends of ancient Greeks and Celts as well as in the lives of these small-town Mississippians who become legends both to each other and to us. Occasionally we hear in that voice the accents of the seer who looks out with a compassion and penetration so deep as to be passionless; who sees, as from an immeasurable distance, "human beings terribly at large, roaming on the face of the earth, . . . human beings, roaming, like lost beasts"; the seer who absorbs both the hero and the victim, and then offers them to us in her art.

With *The Golden Apples,* the progress from innocence to experience is complete. In the tracing of this pattern, however, Miss Welty's comedy has not been mentioned. Although this element has always been present in her fiction, parallel shifts and changes can also be noted. Pure humor is less evident in *A Curtain of Green* than in any subsequent volume; the comedy of that first volume tends to be caustic, satirical, ironic. The shock of the world comes in a variety of forms, some of them human; and tolerance of human faults is a quality notably lacking in the innocent mind. Disgust and contempt are the initial responses to human vulgarity, perversity, and cruelty; and these are the dominant feelings evoked in relation to the "common" types presented in "A Memory" and "Petrified Man." To take some measure of the change in Miss Welty's comic and satiric tone, we need only contrast the whole Peacock tribe of *The Ponder Heart* with those anonymous bathers in "A Memory" or with the denizens of the beauty parlor in "Petrified Man." The Peacocks are both purely vulgar and purely funny in their vulgarity; their antics at the trial are pictured with obvious relish rather than distaste. Somewhere along the way disgust and scorn drop out of Miss Welty's comedy, never to reappear.

Miss Welty has discovered that along with the primal loneliness, there is in each person a primal joy. She has retained that joy from her childhood and projected it in her fiction. Her high spirits erupted fully in *The Robber Bridegroom.* Just before it was published she said of that book, "It is about the Natchez Trace, and planters' beautiful daughters and Indians and bayonets and so on are in it—and a lifetime of fairy-tale reading. Everything in it is something I've liked as long as I can remember and have just now put down."[2] The book bears the stamp of an innocence not only individual but national; as Alfred Kazin has pointed out, it "captures what many have failed to capture through bibliography alone, the lost fabulous innocence of our departed frontier."[3]

When Miss Welty heard that *The Robber Bridegroom* was to be published, she had a few misgivings. She feared it was "a wrong length"—guessed no one would pay much attention to it. But she had enjoyed doing it. Some years later, after the publication of *The Bride of the Innisfallen,* she said, "I tried some stories laid in locations new and strange to me (result of a Guggenheim that let me go to Europe), and tackled with some pleasure the problem the stories set me of writing from the outside, where my honest viewpoint had to look in from."[4] These two comments are indicative of a relationship between Miss Welty's view of life as expressed in her stories, and her performance as an artist. Fully conscious of the hazards of existence, she has constantly taken risks, and they are apparent in the development of her art. The genuine freshness and surprise which can come only out of a writer's experimentation is what she aspires to, and most admires in other writers. The novelist who has "the grace of daring," who astonishes with his variety, who shows no sign of repeating himself, who "has stood for experiment and must continue to stand for this," is, for her, "the most interesting and vital imagination in English fiction in our time"—and that novelist is Henry Green.[5]

Her advice to young writers has always included some such word as this: "Write according to the way you are seeing and learning, and take chances; go out on a limb and dare as much as you can."[6] Again and again the reader may see her crawling out on that limb, like Loch Morrison in "June Recital," creeping out to the shimmering bridge of the tree, pulled by the dark magnet of the unknown. And occasionally, to one's stricken view, comes the sight of her blithely sawing off the limb she has ventured out on. Protection and security have played a large part in her philosophical view of life, but very little in her artistic practice. She has plunged with interest and zest into each new subject and problem of form. The reward for us is that joy, adventure, and the deep allurement of mystery fill her pages.

CHAPTER 9

The Achievement of Eudora Welty

I

O N THE BASIS of an informal investigation into the state of public knowledge about Eudora Welty's fiction (gathered simply from responses elicited by the mention of her name among people who read), it would appear that even the most visible facts about the total nature and variety of her work are not widely known. The analogy which could be made—appropriate only in its central thrust—is that of the old Indian legend about the three blind men, each of whom approached a different part of the elephant, and so pronounced it to be very like a rope, or a wall, or a tree trunk, depending on whether he had seized on the tail, the great side, or the trunk of the beast. "She's a fine social satirist," states one who has encountered "Petrified Man"; "nostalgic Southern romance," says another from a dimly remembered reading of *Delta Wedding;* "very funny, though trivial," says a third, fresh from *The Ponder Heart;* "Southern Gothic," says a fourth who has read "Clytie" or "Keela, the Outcast Indian Maiden." The reason for this variety of response is that Miss Welty's genre is the story (long or short), that most readers have encountered only one or two of these stories, usually in a magazine or an anthology, and that the stories are exceptionally varied.

But these partial and spontaneous views often have a kind of limited accuracy, which is more than can be said for some of the authoritative statements of literary historians and critics. The following example of such a summation is taken from a highly esteemed history of American literature:

> The same difficulty in finding a middle ground between journalistic fluency and psychological complexity became increasingly evident in fiction and drama after 1947. The Mississippi

Delta School that took its inspiration directly from Faulkner
and secondarily from Kafka, Proust, Joyce, and ultimately from
James and Hawthorne, had already found by 1940, in Carson
McCullers, a supreme artist of the lonely heart, and in Robert
Penn Warren, a novelist of weight and stature, capable of mak-
ing much inner brooding comprehensible to the outer mind.
Similar introspective and symbolic studies of abnormal psychic
states attracted Eudora Welty, Truman Capote, and Frederick
Buechner.[1]

Despite its Olympian tone, this statement is muddled. The
names summoned to illustrate the new development in fiction
are arbitrarily chosen. An entire school springs out of the fertile
Delta mud. Where but from the specific region named could
this "school" have received its title?—and yet, besides Faulkner,
the Mississippi Delta fostered none of the writers mentioned,
with the possible exception of Truman Capote, who was born
in New Orleans. (Miss Welty does not come from the Delta
and uses it as a setting only rarely. Carson McCullers comes
from Georgia, Robert Penn Warren from Kentucky and Tennessee, Frederick Buechner from the metropolitan northeast.)
The "school"—at least a school of those members—never
existed; and it could scarcely, then, have taken its inspiration
directly from Faulkner or anyone else; nor could it have "found,"
full-blown, its supreme introspective artists in Carson McCullers and the weighty Robert Penn Warren, by a line of descent
which leaps across the ocean and back, ultimately, to James
and Hawthorne (whose ultimate inspiration doubtless came
from the introspective Jonathan Edwards and the New England
Puritans, whose ultimate inspiration presumably came from—
their Creator?). The individual writers do most certainly exist,
but from the evidence of their writing, not one of them seems
to have taken his inspiration directly from Faulkner; and though
broad parallels may be found in their fiction, the writers could
not be said to constitute a school. Miss Welty is found in
rather strange company, but it is stranger still to find, as the
single generalization made about her work, that she is attracted
to studies of "abnormal psychic states." All this is as incomprehensible to my "inner brooding" as to my "outer mind."
In isolating such a passage from a monumental work, I am
guilty of the same fault of which these critics have been accused
—limited vision, or taking a part for the whole. But it seems clear
that since the truth about any single writer is highly complex,

the truth about any group of writers, any literary trend or movement, is proportionately more complex; and generalizations ought to be made either with a discernment based on knowledge, or most tentatively and cautiously. This is especially true when it comes to contemporary writing, and it is still more true of southern writing. I do not wonder at a recent complaint of Flannery O'Connor: "Most readers these days must be sufficiently sick of hearing about Southern writers and Southern writing. . . . No one has ever made plain just what the Southern school is or which writers belong to it."[2]

Furthermore, since the dispersion of the Nashville Fugitives and Agrarians, there has been no southern group of writers close enough geographically, or even cohesive enough in their attitudes and preoccupations—still less in artistic performance—to be called a literary school. My guess is that a reader who has paid close attention to the work of any one of a dozen good southern writers will have been more impressed by differences than similarities, and will flinch at the generalizations made about them less out of loyal support for a favorite than out of a regard for the truth about a literary situation of rich and bewildering complexity.

As clearly as Eudora Welty is a highly original, complex, and varied writer, however, she is also southern, American, contemporary—and one among many writers with whom she has much in common. Like them, she is subject to many similar cultural influences and to several indirect literary influences. Difficult as it is to make true statements about *her* work in all its variety and then to place it in that larger complexity, it is not too soon for an attempt at generalization, nor for a tentative reckoning up of comparative achievement.

II

In the leading essay of the collection called *Southern Renascence* (1953), Robert Heilman shows a remarkable strength for making large summations which are nonetheless valid and just, and then supporting them with finely perceptive illustrations. His essay is entitled "The Southern Temper"; his choice of the word "temper" indicates his caution, and the opening paragraph shows his awareness of the complexity of his subject:

> The Southern temper is marked by the coincidence of a sense of the concrete, a sense of the elemental, a sense of the

ornamental, a sense of the representative, and a sense of totality. No one of these endowments is unshared; but their concurrency is not frequent. This concurrency is *a* condition of
major art and mature thought. The endowments, like most
endowments, are not possessed in entire freedom, without
price. . . . To live with an endowment runs risks, and even
the concurrency of several endowments does not guarantee a
funding of the counter-deficiency which may accompany the
possession of any single one.[3]

Heilman's discussion may serve as a useful base of reference
in an attempt to see the work of any single writer in terms of
the whole southern literary movement. Not only are the terms
of his essay large enough to support a number of interesting
comparisons of southern fiction, poetry, drama, and criticism,
but he faces honestly the basic paradox involved in any process
of evaluation: namely, that a certain set of gifts or powers
necessarily involves a corresponding set of limitations, or de-
fects. It is, furthermore, one of the few essays on southern literature I have seen which deals in categories both meaningful
and commodious enough to include Miss Welty's fiction along
with that of many other southern writers, and each brief generalization he makes about her work is just and pertinent.
    In illustrating "the elemental" in southern fiction, Heilman
speaks, for example, of "a certain mystery of being inseparable
from the closest factuality in Elizabeth Madox Roberts and
Welty"; in showing how the "sense of the concrete" interacts
fruitfully with the "sense of the representative," he notes that
"in Welty's work we see Everyman as salesman." He supports
his generalization about the southern sense of totality—which
he describes as "a sense of time, of the extent of human need
and possibility, of world and spirit"—with a number of general
illustrations, including an illuminating statement about Miss
Welty's fiction:

The sense of totality . . . appears in Faulkner's style; in the
critical focussing on the organic whole; in the anti-nominalism
which has been most explicitly formulated by Richard Weaver;
in Tate's emphasis on mythic or non-scientific values; in the
conjunction, in numerous pieces of fiction, of violence and spiritual awareness—a conjunction disturbing to readers who are
used to taking one part of the whole at a time; in the penumbra
of mystery—a mystery to be accepted, not solved—always bor-
dering the clean light of Welty's characters and scenes; in the

nostalgia, so frequent in Porter, for the reality felt behind the stage of action; in the questioning of nostrum and panaceas which can exist only by treating a part of human truth as if it were the whole; in suspecting our inclination to separate the present from all the rest of time, to exhaust all devotion in the religion of humanity, and to consider scientific inquiry as the only avenue to truth.[4]

There is no doubt that Miss Welty shares this general "Southern temper."

If we look more closely at the fiction produced by southern writers, we shall find a cause for much of the similarity so basic as to be self-evident, but often overlooked for the simple reason that many readers and critics of southern fiction have never lived in the South. The materials of this body of fiction are regional, and they are based on what sociologists, for example Howard Odum in *An American Epoch,* have called a powerful folk society and culture in a period of transition. The physical and cultural environment are similar: from the work of many authors we become familiar with the red clay farms, the cotton fields, the hills and forests, the primitive farm houses, the small hamlets with their post offices, general stores, courthouses, banks, churches, all of which serve as communal gathering spots. We become familiar with the porches where small groups collect on summer afternoons and evenings to tell and retell legends out of the local past, events out of the present. And we know the sound of their voices speaking.

Furthermore, these southern communities consist of a wide variety of classes and types of people who are both plainly and subtly stratified within and among their larger or smaller groupings—whites and Negroes, farmers and townsfolk, professional and business people, "cultured" and "common," landowners and sharecroppers, Methodists and Baptists. Yet all live in the greatest intimacy, with much factual and intuitive knowledge about each other, with a widely shared core of attitudes and beliefs. The southern writer is party to all this, mixing and sharing in the life of the southern community, which is not particularly conscious of or impressed by his being a writer. In a sense the southern writer of fiction has only to see and record, to listen and write "by ear."

But of course this is not what happens, or great fiction would not now be coming out of the South. To use Henry James's famous metaphor, the southern (or Mississippi) scene is only that small piece of the large human scene upon which several writers look from various windows or apertures of the "house of fiction." Every one of these windows "has been pierced . . . in its vast front, by the need of the individual vision and by the pressure of the individual will." At each window "stands a figure with a pair of eyes, or at least with a field glass, which forms, again and again, for observation, a unique instrument, insuring to the person making use of it an impression distinct from every other."5 The individual creative mind, personality, experience, selects and molds the "common clay," and so produces an original body of fiction.

III

One characteristic of Miss Welty's individual vision of the South is that it indicates no strong shaping idea of its meaning and history. It has been suggested earlier that this may be, in part, the result of her not having received the southern birth-right by ancestry; perhaps as a result she does not feel person-ally and passionately involved in the burden of southern his-tory. This is evident, first of all, in the way she has largely skipped over the Civil War period and has settled for her "historical" works on the frontier period, which is part of the common American heritage. In *The Robber Bridegroom* the native influences are those of frontier tall-tales and folk legends —but these are also freely mixed with the tradition of the Euro-pean folk and fairy tale, in a spirit of light and playful inno-cence. In "First Love" and "A Still Moment" the historical times and settings are used as backgrounds to intensely private search-ings—not into the significance of that historical period and its relevance to the present but into the meaning of love and indi-vidual destiny. *Delta Wedding* appears to set the stage for explicit social and historical comment, but none emerges.

Miss Welty is obviously not untouched by southern history; she is aware of its stages in the passing of time. But her work does not show a deep involvement in any of the peculiarly southern preoccupations: the race problem; the complicity in guilt resulting from slavery; the suffering and tragic knowledge of defeat produced by the Civil War and the dissolution of the aristocratic way of life; the beneficent role of the land as a force in the social economy, a mode of life threatened both from within and without by industrialization and commercialism. Furthermore, if the distinguishing marks of the conservative are lacking in her fiction, so are the signs of liberal rebellion or dedication, or an awareness of current political history, even in the subjects of her fiction. (They are present, on the other hand, in those beautiful stories of Katherine Anne Porter, "Flowering Judas," "Old Mortality," and "The Leaning Tower.")

This curious lack of a social or political attitude has obvious advantages and disadvantages. One advantage is that it has enabled Miss Welty to let her vision fall freely on a wide variety of persons—traveling salesmen and farm folk, Negro entertainers and southern ladies, immigrant music teachers and Baptist preachers—with an equitable and detached sympathy and without dominating them by her outlook and theories. She is free, therefore, from the hazards of opinion which fluctuate with the social and economic problems which create them. But she misses the sweep and drive, the hypnotic power over the mind and imagination, of the writer who, like Faulkner or Robert Penn Warren, shows the individual in relation to the large social forces which affect and determine his struggle.

Perhaps a strong historic sense is a necessary component of a great tragic vision in the classical sense of the term: it is certain, at least, that Miss Welty has neither. But then neither is well suited to the genre of the short story, a genre instinctively chosen by Miss Welty as the right medium for what she has to say. Tragedy in Miss Welty's stories is most often the result of an external catastrophe which brings the individual up against the enigma of the universe. It is not seen as the result of personal, social, or even cosmic evil. We may search the pages of Miss Welty's fiction, but never find a clear villain, or even a hero with a tragic flaw. Evil is never a vile well gushing out of any individual heart, visible as pride, lust, murder, pure hatred, vicious rapacity; nor is it seen as the gradual and insidious process of becoming enmeshed in corporate social evil. If anything, it is impersonal—the general hostility of life to man's fulfillment; or it is a temporary weakness, a confusion, a blunder, and always forgivable. Miss Welty has no preoccupation with sin; she does not share even the unorthodox kind of southern orthodoxy, variations of which may be found in the work of Faulkner, Warren, and Ransom.

Her ethical outlook is unconscious and implicit, relaxed and tolerant, though stable. Her characters are never roundly judged or emphatically "placed" morally; they are often delighted in (there is obvious relish in much of her description), but they are never sympathized with to a point of sentimental indulgence. They are usually just *seen*, inside and out, with that relentlessly clear vision, which records but does not judge, and which seems, at times, so closely to relate experiences of joy and sorrow, that they become almost identical. In "The Wide Net" the philosophical Doc says, "The excursion is the same when you go looking for your sorrow as when you go looking for your joy." When Jenny is being raped by the river men in the closing episode of "At the Landing," she cries out in protest, and the sound of her cry blending with the rude laugh of the men "could easily have been heard as rejoicing, going out over the river in the dark night": human terror and pain, lust and triumph, are mingled in that sound. In many of her stories Miss Welty shows how interrelated are the worlds of dream and reality, but she does not imply that either world is better than the other—more "sound," or moral, or real: it is simply a fact that human beings live in both worlds, and that strict lines cannot and need not always be drawn between the two.

Given any definition of that slippery critical term "Southern Gothic," we shall not find Miss Welty's fiction particularly representative of what the term implies. Traditional Gothic elements—violence, horror, the use of the grotesque, the supernatural, the decadent—are present in some of her stories, but not their emphases. In "Clytie" we find a decadent southern aristocratic household, physical and psychological horror in the heroine's reactions, and a powerful, grotesque image at the conclusion: but the focus of the story is on Clytie's inner life, her confused and lonely search for love, her attempts to recover her original, laughing self. Feelings of guilt and horror are the psychological materials of "Keela, the Outcast Indian Maiden"; but the horror is felt to be past rather than present, and therefore subdued in its effects: the victim is happily unaware of being victimized; the guilty man is essentially innocent. War, rape, suicide are the factual materials of "The Burning," but the narrator's focus is turned away from the horror of these events to the uncomprehending mind and sensibility of the chief witness, Delilah.

In Miss Welty's fiction there are relatively fewer grotesque types of persons and fewer images of human perversion or brutality than in the work of Truman Capote, Carson McCullers, and Flannery O'Connor; and one encounters nowhere in her stories anything so purely horrible as the ending of Erskine Caldwell's "Kneel to the Rising Sun," Faulkner's "A Rose for Miss Emily," or Tennessee Williams' "Desire and the Black Masseur." Few of her characters live with "ghosts in the mind"; her presentation of loneliness, unlike that of Carson McCullers, is counterbalanced by her view of the beneficent effects of human separateness; the sexual love presented is healthy and pleasurable. The continual resurgence of the comic spirit, the rapid shifts in tone and feeling, would give her work a capricious and uneasy residence in the more gloomy chambers of that mysterious house of fiction, southern Gothic.

Her spirit would be more familiar, however, in the chamber where the grotesque or pathetic is allied with the comic. Like Faulkner's, her comedy is frequently born out of a total situation which includes either dominant or subordinate elements of pathos and satire. The essential ingredients of Faulkner's "Spotted Horses," for example, are to be found in one of the crucial scenes of Miss Welty's "June Recital." In Faulkner's story a major element is broad comedy of situation and character coming out of the mayhem produced by the frenzied horses and, in turn, the varied practical responses of Mrs. Littlejohn, Ratliff, and Tull; the second element is a satiric vision of the devilish greed and cruelty of Flem Snopes and his clan, which is fitted to the corresponding foolishness and gullibility of the farmers; the third element is grim pathos, which springs from the painful situation of the Armstids: Henry's insane fury and Mrs. Armstid's strangely hopeless passivity.

All of these elements are present, though in different proportions, in the scene from "June Recital" in which Old Man Moody, the town marshall, and his fishing companion, Mr. Fatty Bowles, come to the abandoned MacLain house just as Miss Eckhart lights her fire. Comedy is inherent in the general mixup which follows: the blundering way in which the two men put out the fire; King's sudden appearance; Loch's confusion of King for Mr. Voigt and the metronome for a time-bomb; the meeting both of Old Man Moody and his party and of Virgie Rainey and her sailor by the woman's "Rook" party which comes pouring down the street. The element of pathos is found in Miss Eckhart's bitter and lonely existence, her state of being reduced from a person of great pride and dignity to a "crazy old woman" who must be taken to Jackson; the element of satire, though mild in comparison with that in

"Spotted Horses," springs from a view of the town's habit of "placing" persons and events seen—not being surprised, not caring. The combination of these elements in both stories produces an effect of irony which is characteristic of much southern humor, including that of Robert Penn Warren, Erskine Caldwell, and Flannery O'Connor.

To the extent that Miss Welty has a literary debt to Faulkner, it seems to be chiefly technical and formal. His work may have suggested to her that the Natchez Trace could be another Yoknapatawpha County, or Morgana another Jefferson. He may also have been one of the writers who made her aware of how many ways there are to tell a story, get inside a human mind, and perceive a given set of events or experiences. And occasionally, in the later stories, the sound of the Faulknerian rhetoric is heard in her prose:

> Florabel, with no last name, was a slave. . . . Herself was an unknown, like a queen, somebody she had heard called, even cried for. As a slave she was the earth's most detached visitor. The world had not touched her—only possessed and hurt her, like a man; taken away from her, like a man; turned another way from her and left her, like a man. Her vision was clear. She saw what was there and had not sought it, did not seek it yet. . . . Many commands had been given her, some even held over from before she was born; delayed and miscarried and interrupted, they could yet be fulfilled, though it was safer for one once a slave to hear things a second time, a third, fourth, hundredth, thousandth, if they were to be carried out to the letter. In that noon quiet after conflict there might have been only the two triumphant, the mirror which was a symbol in the world and Florabel who was standing there; it was the rest that had died of it.[6]

Although this particular passage from "The Burning" never got into the revised version of the story which appeared in *The Bride of the Innisfallen,* one or two passages similar to it were included. This is not Miss Welty's kind of perspective or rhetoric, and such echoes of Faulkner are rarely found in her work.

IV

Since one of Miss Welty's special achievements has been her projection of the hidden inner life, there is another large group of modern short story writers and novelists to whom she has an equal if not greater general debt than to Faulkner and other southern writers. James, Proust, Joyce, Dorothy Richardson, and Virginia Woolf all extended the range of fiction by developing new methods of catching and conveying the inward atmosphere, the subtle nuances of human thought and feeling.[7] These novelists worked by means of a deep penetration into the minds of their characters, who were often thinly disguised versions of themselves: persons, at least, very like themselves in general intelligence, sensibility, and experience. The inner life was variously rendered through strict control of point of view, the use of the internal monologue or "stream-of-consciousness" style, and the free use of metaphor and symbol adapted to the consciousness explored. And because these writers were, in their several ways, faithful to the essential nature of the hidden inner life, they disclosed the quantity and texture of the reverie and dream life which transpires there, the random associations, the private meanings put on objects in the outside world. They showed time as it is actually experienced— radically compressed or protracted, or meaningless either as a concept or a sensation; the past as caught in the present, the moments of stasis, the passages of flux.

Miss Welty's fiction shows tendencies in all these directions. She also works by means of a deep, intuitive penetration of the minds and feelings of her characters—a process which began, we might guess from her portrayal of certain types of children, very early in her life. In "The Winds" Josie thinks, "there, outside, was all that was wild and beloved and estranged, and all that would beckon and leave her, and all that was beautiful. She wanted to follow, and by some metamorphosis she would take them in—all—everyone." And Nina, in "Moon Lake," reflects that "it's only interesting, only worthy, to try for the fiercest secrets. To slip into them all—to change. To change for a moment into Gertrude, into Mrs. Gruenwald, into Twosie—into a boy. To *have been* an orphan."

The characters Miss Welty "slips into" are not, generally, of her own level of intelligence and education, though they often possess her own kind of sensibility. They are most often simple folk, children, young girls, housewives, and uneducated middle-class Mississippi people. She seems to know, to an astounding degree, how it feels to be a Livvie or a Ruby Fisher, and she has never forgotten how it feels to be a child. She endows her simple characters with an emotional and psychological depth and complexity which seems to be independent of rational intelligence. Their mode of apprehension is wordless intuition; the sum of their knowledge is the most elemental human wisdom.

Miss Welty does not employ the stream-of-consciousness style, though in "The Winds" she approaches it in conveying the content of Josie's dreams during the storm. She usually begins her stories with exposition and the close description of an observer: then, so much being already known from the outside, we scarcely notice when she "slips into" the mind, or as quietly slips out again, in an easy and natural blend of scene and summary, interior monologue and dialogue, "objective" and "subjective" description, fact and fantasy. The transitions are unobtrusive because diction, sentence structure, and metaphors are usually (though not always) of a piece with the rich simplicity of the characters. Metaphors are abundant and homely; folk expressions are freely used. The following passages illustrate Miss Welty's way of using metaphor and presenting the reverie and "free association" of her characters, the breath and texture of simple minds: "Happiness, Albert knew, is something that appears to you suddenly, that is meant for you, a thing which you reach for and pick up and hide at your breast, a shiny thing that reminds you of something alive and leaping." " 'Did you ever see so many cosmetics in your life?' cried Miss Baby Marie. 'No'm,' Livvie tried to say, but the cat had her tongue. . . . 'Try this!' she said. And in her hand was unclenched a golden lipstick which popped open like magic." The fragrance of the lipstick reminds Livvie of chinaberry flowers, and that odor carries her far back and away "in the air through the spring" to a purple cloud from which she views, with a "half-drowsy smile," a chinaberry tree from home, "dark and smooth and neatly leaved, neat as a guinea hen in the dooryard," with her mama sitting near, her heavy apron loaded with figs, and her papa fishing by the pond, its water transparent, "the little clear fishes swimming up to the brim."

The puzzle is why such primitive characters as Livvie and Albert are sufficiently interesting to command our attention. Henry James might have been astonished to encounter these relatively limited "vessels of consciousness."[8] Albert and Ellie Morgan, Ruby Fisher, Livvie, Old Mr. Marblehall, Phoenix, Clytie, are scarcely "acute," "finely and richly responsible"; as types of persons, we might ordinarily class them among "the stupid, the coarse and the blind," for whom, James says, our sympathy and curiosity "care comparatively little." Yet Miss Welty has managed to make us care for her characters. She moves surely into the deeper rhythms of their natures and moods. Her characters give us the double impression of being both absolutely clear, thoroughly seen and understood, and yet mysteriously unknowable—with the "clean light" shining *around* them as well as flowing from within them. Seeing everything, the narrator knows nothing, but quietly lures us into the pure dazzlement of her own wonder. The world of her fiction is a community of interest and sensibility in which the deaf and dumb, the child, the old country Negro, and the traveling sales-man are equally and infinitely precious as "vessels of conscious-ness" because of their unique and their common humanity.

The flashes of insight which come to the heroine of Dorothy Richardson's novels, Virginia Woolf's preoccupation with "the moment of importance," Joyce's "sudden spiritual manifesta-tions" or "epiphanies"—all are closely related to the various moments of revelation which appear in Miss Welty's fiction. In *Short Stories* she says, "When [plot] is identifiable in every motion and progression of its own with the motions and pro-gressions of simple revelation, then it's at its highest use." The plots of her own stories constantly move toward revelations which function importantly in the total structure of each story, each revelation bringing a new stage of awareness. "First Love" and "At the Landing" are both built on a steady progression of these revelations. "Death of a Traveling Salesman" contains two: one which comes before Bowman sees that the farm woman is young, when he feels strongly his loneliness and the need to communicate his love; the second which comes as an ironic realization after his perception that the mystery in the home is only that simple thing, a fruitful marriage, which "any-one could have had." "A Still Moment" works slowly up to a climax of two sets of revelations: one, in the minds of each of the three men when they all view the white heron at rest after its slow spiral flight; the other, immediately after Audubon's shot, in response to the death of the bird.

V

Three other important writers with whom Miss Welty shares an affinity are Chekhov, Katherine Mansfield, and Elizabeth Bowen. The resemblance to Chekhov is a basic spiritual kinship marked by the lack of an "attitude," the view of the world as an enigma, quiet skepticism, a pervasive tolerance and compassion, an eye for the ludicrous and the pathetic, and a tragicomic vision. It is perhaps this sympathy in outlook which makes Miss Welty's primitive characters seem like authentic American versions of Chekhov's Russian peasants.

Quite apart from confluence of spirit, which is more a matter of temperament than influence, Miss Welty has a general debt to Chekhov for his contributions to the form of the short story, as had Katherine Mansfield, in turn, before her. Both Chekhov and Katherine Mansfield developed individual techniques for conveying psychological subtlety. Sylvia Berkman has summarized the characteristic attitude of each writer toward his material:

> Neither one is greatly interested in event as event, or even in the primary emotion inhering in an event. Though Chekhov often deals with violent subject matter . . . his concern is never with action in itself but with the emotional repercussions of action on the characters involved. The modulation thus is always subdued; when the sensation is dealt with it is presented, as it were, in another room. . . . Miss Mansfield does not often write of violence, but, like Chekhov, she usually presents her material not for the overt meaning of the happenings but to make a tangential point, slanting the elements of the central situation to extract an oblique theme.[9]

This analysis constitutes an exact description of what happens in many of Miss Welty's stories. In "At the Landing" and "First Love," for example, the violence of such external events as storm, flood, rape, conspiracy, trial, and flight is entirely subdued: the important action takes place quietly in "another room"—inside the mind and heart of the young girl and boy. In *Delta Wedding* and "The Wanderers" elements of the material presented—an elaborate wedding and a funeral—are slanted to extract an oblique theme.

Since the central meaning is to be conveyed by indirection, all of these writers have developed their own methods of shaping their material with minute care. They invest with maximum significance each detail, each small piece of dialogue, narration, or description; and they endow each metaphor with an emotional resonance comparable to that of poetic metaphor. This

care and subtlety in formal construction, this lyrical and poetic
richness and psychological complexity, ask for corresponding
sympathetic qualities in the reader, as does the fiction of James,
Joyce, Virginia Woolf, and Katherine Anne Porter. All of these
writers have prepared the way for Miss Welty's writing and
also for our reading with pleasure and discernment her particular kind of fiction.

The work of Elizabeth Bowen stands in the tradition of fiction just sketched, but it bears a special relationship to Miss
Welty's not only because of a remarkably similar artistic credo
or statement of intent, but also because in a few of Miss Welty's
later stories there appears something like a shaping influence.
In a recent (1959) introduction to a collection of her stories
chosen by herself, Miss Bowen summarized her attitudes and
intentions and described the basic characteristics of her work
in the genre of the short story. She expresses her conviction
that art should not be "self-expression" and that a story should
"detach itself from the author's ego"; she acknowledges, however, that the short story is linked with poetry, and is therefore
lyrical and passionate, the "unique susceptibility" of the poet
or short story writer *being* the experience, and therefore never
absent from his work.[10] These opinions may be compared with
some of Miss Welty's on the craft of fiction: her distaste for
the bad novel of "confession," which is inclined to be "self-
absorbed, self-indulgent, too often self-pitying" ("Place in Fiction"); her belief that a writer's stories "take on their quality,
carry their signature, because of one characteristic lyrical
impulse of his mind" ("How I Write"); her conviction that
"in the end, our technique is sensitivity" (*Short Stories*).

Miss Bowen also notes that for her, "on the whole, places
more often than persons have sparked off stories," and she
then describes how "an intensified, all but spell-binding behold-
ing" of a particular place has produced an atmosphere or mood
in which characters and events naturally find their place. She
mentions also the importance of fantasy in her fiction, both as
"fabric of the actual plot, or governor of the behaviour of the
characters."[11] The parallels with Miss Welty's views are here
sufficiently clear.

Jocelyn Brooke, a critic of Miss Bowen's fiction, has found its
distinguishing traits to be a "pictorial quality" which suggests
the work of French Impressionist painters, and "an abnormally
acute apprehension of the visible world." She mentions that Miss

Bowen intended in her youth to be a painter. Miss Bowen's fiction, she says, is not chiefly notable either for plot or character delineation, but for its creative achievement in presenting the *"relationship between the individual and his environment."* Her work is a "landscape with figures," a landscape which includes both nature and "the whole social scene, together with its deeper implications."[12] Miss Bowen herself, in the aforementioned introduction, says she does not feel that the short story "can be, or should be, used for the analysis or development of character"—this is the task of the novelist. The short story should strive for a "central, single effect."[13]

The parallels and contrasts are instructive. Miss Welty too began with a youthful intention to be a painter, and her fiction is also notable for its pictorial quality. Unlike Miss Bowen, however, she has used the short story rather than the novel as her chief medium. Miss Welty might well agree with Miss Bowen's view of the role of character in the short story. She recently wrote that "in stories, characters are only one brief element, on a par with place, the feeling of the place and time, etc. They exist already developed, by necessity, to *be* the instrument of awareness. In a novel, of course, this is all different— the characters must live, grow, become their identities under our eyes. . . ."[14]

In several of Miss Welty's best stories, however, characters are not "on a par" with any other element, but are unquestionably the most memorable and compelling part of the story. Though she uses a wide variety of methods in presenting her characters, two prominent modes of character portrayal may be distinguished in her fiction. The first kind is a vivid presentation, usually from the point of view of an observing narrator or some other character in the story, of a non-developing, fabulous, mythic person: fascinating, exotic, and overwhelming, like Powerhouse and the big Spanish guitarist; richly poetic, like Old Phoenix; strong-willed, passionate, and blighted, like Miss Eckhart. The second kind of character is presented from the inside, and is often shown in the process of developing, of being "educated" into life, as, for example, are Jenny Lockhart and Joel Mayes, Virgie Rainey, and several of the characters in *Delta Wedding*. Both types of characters are given a large measure of their life and credibility because of their being so securely fastened to their places, but they themselves remain most vividly in the memory.

The Bride of the Innisfallen, however, includes less of either of these two types of character portrayal than do the earlier stories. The vivid apprehension of place, atmosphere, mood is predominant; characters form a part of the rich surface texture, and plot and theme are subordinate. This descriptive impressionism, together with the increasing complexity of style and a more sophisticated kind of awareness and sensibility, makes one feel the influence of Elizabeth Bowen's kind of story. It is as though a certain set of tendencies in Miss Welty's fiction, undeniably her own and present in her fiction from the start, had now become dominant in these stories.

There is no valid reason for setting arbitrary limits to the form of the short story, especially at this stage of its development, when the "rules" for the genre have so often been broken —and often with happy results. A short story can become anything the writer chooses to make of it: there is no *a priori* reason why it should not be as close to a poem, or a piece of music, or choreography, or an Impressionist painting (or a series of such paintings) as words can make it, and achieve a comparable effect of interest and beauty. But I believe Miss Welty's greatest contribution to the genre has so far been made in those stories in which the traditional elements of fiction— plot, character, setting, theme—are most freely and spontaneously blended, in which no single element appears to be manipulated, radically out-balancing the others. She seems to be able to achieve this balance most effectively when she is, in every sense, closest to home. "Home" refers not only to the Mississippi setting (though perhaps mostly to that), but also to the kinds of characters with whom she is "at home" in her fiction, whether from the inside or the outside, and to the kinds of social custom and environment she has observed closely enough to have understood. "At home," she has both her distance and involvement: more than enough knowledge of her material to make the story convincing; the objectivity to shape it; and the feeling and sensibility to give it the unmistakable lyric impulse which identifies it as her own unique product.

VI

It seems true of Miss Welty, as of many original artists, that a peculiar artistic virtue may, if slightly misplaced, overemphasized, or reduced from its highest uses, turn into a particular flaw or weakness. Miss Welty has a great power to reveal the atmosphere of place, and a great power to reveal mystery, when the *reality itself* is mystery. But with a slight shift in emphasis, mystery may become either ambiguity or obscurity—a fact not faced, a secret kept, a mystery (in the popular sense) never cleared up. There are times when Miss Welty does not mediate clearly enough between the reader and the actuality of persons and events presented.

"The Purple Hat" is a story in which Miss Welty pushes to a dangerous point both her fascination with place (in this case the New Orleans "Palace of Pleasure") and her cultivation of fantasy. One reviewer found the story "so confused that a reader tires finally of wondering where the fantastic leaves off and reality begins," but he adds that this confusion "seems to represent merely the unsuccessful application of the very methods by which Miss Welty achieves her finest stories."[15] The reader is asked to "give over" to the mood of strange fascination, but the abundance of sharply drawn realistic details makes it impossible to accept the story as pure fantasy. Its meaning remains a puzzle.

Another of Miss Welty's powers is her intuitive knowledge of the mysteries of the inner life. And yet her knowledge about her own characters very often resembles our knowledge of people in real life: it is filled with mysterious gaps. The paradox is that as creator of her characters she has every right to full knowledge of the facts of their lives, their relationships and motives; but often she chooses not to know—or at least not to be forthright—as though a writer's pressing for or even assuming knowledge were as much a violation of human privacy as it would be in real life. In "No Place for You, My Love," the "exposed" young woman reflects, "How did it leave us— the old, safe, slow way people used to know of learning how one another feels, and the privilege that went with it of shying away if it seemed best?" There is a good deal of "shying away" from both fact and motivation in *The Bride of the Innisfallen.*

Lack of factual explicitness may be seen in "The Burning." What do the soldiers actually do to Miss Myra and Miss Theo? What is implied by Delilah's being "dragged down on the grass" outside the house? Who is Phinney? This kind of obscurity about facts can become a source of annoyance to the reader who hunts for "clues"—and we are taught by Miss Welty's fiction to read closely because so much of the meaning is conveyed by subtle intimations and hints. This is the kind of mystery that does not reveal, but rather obfuscates. In *The Golden Apples,* however, obscurity is often put to better use. We do not know how many of the children of Morgana have been fathered by King MacLain, but the mystery here is enhancing because it adds to the heroic or legendary dimension of these altogether human characters.

Sometimes Miss Welty shies away from the clear presentation of a character's motivation. An example of this is to be found in "The Whole World Knows." Because Randall MacLain soliloquizes, we should be able to perceive the reasons for his behavior—just as we know the motivations of the self-revealing heroine of "Why I Live at the P. O." But as Snowdie says, "Son, you're walking in a dream." Randall is totally confused. It takes a good deal of intuitive "sleuthing" to determine what "ails" Randall, or what ails the American wife in "The Bride of the Innisfallen," or to determine what kind of relationship has come into existence by the chance encounter and journey of the couple in "No Place for You, My Love."

And these demands made on the reader's sensibility apply not only to the understanding of motivations and relationships, but often to the smallest gestures, words, and metaphors. As early as 1944, Robert Penn Warren observed in the first two volumes of her stories Miss Welty's tendency to "squeeze meaning from the item which, in ordinary realistic fiction, would be passed over with a casual glance. . . . She wants us to get that smallest gesture, to participate in her vision of things as intensely meaningful."[16] By now readers have seen stories in which that sensibility has been enormously compounded; they have seen her attempt to convey virtually ineffable psychic glimmerings in the smallest gestures and by the use of the most dazzling and elusive metaphors.

As an artist, in her most sensitive area Miss Welty is, naturally, most vulnerable: that is, most susceptible to attack. In real life, there is sometimes a hair's-breadth—dizzying to contemplate because of the importance of giving things their right value—between what is deeply portentous, though ever so slight and small, and what is simply trivial, inconsequential. And so it is with some of the fleeting, elusive feelings, motives, gestures, relationships presented in Miss Welty's fiction. They are presented to us with the strong suggestion that they are meaningful; usually, as in life, it is only our impatience, blindness,

and insensitivity which make them appear meaningless. Sometimes, however, Miss Welty has not convinced us of the importance of each small impression; she has not shown that either
individually, or taken together, these impressions may reveal
to us a genuine, or significant, human mystery. The reader's
reaction will depend on the kind and quality of his attention.
Miss Welty does not rely greatly on her own or her reader's
logical and rational powers. She uses, and must be met with,
an active creative imagination, the free exercise of intuition,
rapid shifts in mood, the ability to perceive by way of metaphor
and symbol, and the power to feel with interest, concern, and
love.

It will by now be clear that Miss Welty's creative imagination is wholly, and in the best sense, feminine. To use Robert
Heilman's terms once again, this is an "endowment," and endowments "are not possessed in entire freedom, without price."
From the woman's or child's point of view she sees beautifully
and convincingly. But she has not often entered into a male
consciousness with assurance, though she has done so, I think,
in the two salesman stories (possibly because she had learned
from observation and experience how it feels to be heartsick
and tired on the road). The portraits of George and Battle
Fairchild and Troy Flavin in *Delta Wedding* are all the more
convincing for being done from the outside. "The Whole World
Knows" seems to me the least effective story in *The Golden
Apples* not, finally, because of its obscurity, but because it is
unconvincing as the soliloquy of Randall MacLain. It is a piece
of narrative patchwork, the only authentic parts of which are
straight dialogue, the passages given over to Miss Perdita
Mayo's rambling advice, and snatches of the town gossip. Even
granting the weakened and confused state of Randall, he never
sounds like a man speaking or thinking: he begins to *look*
like one, however, in "The Wanderers," where he is observed by
a character whose consciousness Miss Welty knew thoroughly,
Virgie Rainey. One suspects that in telling Randall's story Miss
Welty was "going out on a limb"—and was lured to do so by
an untried point of view, a new technical device. This may well
have been the case also with "June Recital," but the narrative
technique of that story seems to me a triumph and that of "The
Whole World Knows" a failure.

In her use of myth and symbolism, however, Miss Welty has
been consistently effective. Symbols and myths are always

inherent in the materials of her stories: characters, names, and actions are not manipulated or denatured to underscore their deeper meanings, but all are subtly extended, infused with something greater than their surface values. In a symbol, as Carlyle said, "there is concealment and yet revelation"; the use of the symbol is therefore natural to Miss Welty's kind of vision, because it serves to deepen and enhance the mysteries she seeks to convey. By her use of myth she suggests what is permanent in the human race—in character types, rituals, and heroic action. In her fiction the less obvious uses of myth and symbol seem to have the greatest power to provide depth and beauty. King MacLain as Zeus, particularly in "Sir Rabbit," is less convincing as a mythical type of person than is Old Phoenix, whose bright coloring, fabulous old age, and ritual act of sacrifice, quietly suggest the self-immolation and resurrection of the ancient bird whose name she bears so naturally.

A summary of Miss Welty's achievement would be incomplete without further mention of how her two initial artistic interests—that of painting and photography—have shaped her writing. The eye of the painter is especially evident in her descriptive writing, which indicates a close scrutiny of the details of the natural world—chinaberry, fig, plum, mimosa trees, roses and four-o'clocks, butterflies, humming birds, mourning doves, June bugs, slow deep rivers with their watersnakes and twisted roots, and the "curtain of green" with its thickly interlaced, impenetrable patterns of leaves—all this detail, together with a rapturous feeling for light, color, texture, atmosphere. In "A Sketching Trip" Miss Welty presents a young painter who had always, from childhood, loved the textures of the natural world and rejoiced in putting out her hands to touch this world. But she had never been able to show her joy in painting, nor render the "pulse of life," that "tender surface underneath which flowed and trembled and pressed life itself. It was as if this pulse became the green of leaves, the roundness of fruit, the rise and fall of a hill, when she began to paint, and could have become—anything."[17] Miss Welty turned that pulse of life into words—nor did she stop with the natural world. She applied the same close and loving scrutiny to human faces, forms, gestures. Atmosphere in the outside world was translated directly into human feeling, and her characters retain something of the mystery of nature's voiceless beauty.

In an article on "Literature and the Lens," Miss Welty made

some interesting observations about the parallels between the "lowly" art of photography and the higher arts of painting and literature. She described how, after she had taken a snapshot of Royal Street one day in New Orleans, three old ladies had started to mutter in vague protest. Why, she asked, is the act of taking a picture always suspect?

> Perhaps it goes back to atavistic beliefs that to carry off an image of something, or its picture, means you want to steal its soul. In Mexico a woman forbade me to photograph her baby because he had not yet been christened, and an eccentric old lady in Louisiana threatened to shoot me with her gun if I dared photograph a beautiful statue in her garden. It is clear that the fascination of a photograph of anything is that it imprisons a moment in time—and is that really different from stealing its spirit, its soul? Perhaps one does right to protest.
>
> Yet this must be, in a sense, the purpose of nearly everything we do—certainly in the arts, painting and writing, we steal spirits and souls if we can, and in love and devotion, what do we do but pray: Keep this as it is, hold this moment safe? So in the lowly photograph we can do this to anything—a little boy walking fast in a shuttered street—with a little machine and the slightest motion of the finger. Photography is crude in itself, but the act of photography is kin to something better. . . .[18]

The moment crystallized in time and forever removed out of time, the still moment, the quiet center, the instant of revelation, the elusive gesture captured—these are all moments in Miss Welty's fiction when a picture is taken, and she has caught for permanent safe-keeping a precious scene or person, an act, a thought, a feeling.

The power of the painter—and of the eyes behind the lens—is the power to focus, to bring the gaze that looks outward to a steady point where the subject is. In *Place in Fiction* Miss Welty defines the attributes of focus as "awareness, discernment, order, clarity, insight—they are like the attributes of love. The act of focusing itself has beauty and meaning; it is the act that, continued in, turns into meditation, into poetry." Miss Welty herself has this power of focusing, and to this fundamental artistic act she brings a pure and benevolent mind, a loving temper, an open sensibility, an impressive gift with language.

She has also the kind of love for her characters which John Bagley has described as "a delight in their independent existence as *other people,* an attitude toward them which is analogous to our feelings towards those we love in life; and an intense interest in their personalities combined with a sort of detached solicitude, a respect for their freedom."[19] The logical consequence of the artist's love, his feeling for the freedom and independence of his creation, is the sense of "joy in Nature," "lightness of touch," buoyancy and humor. Because her stories are celebrations, springing from the lyrical impulse to praise or wonder, it is not difficult to see why Miss Welty has always enjoyed writing, and hopes for readers who will come to any story fresh, prepared for pleasure, "with a storehouse of hope and interest."

We cannot (happily) predict what kind of new stories Miss Welty will write, nor which of them, new or old, will be most often read or best remembered; nor can we foresee what permanent place she will occupy in American letters. Her reputation will inevitably be tied up with the future of the genre, and the relative value placed upon it. The short story has gradually rid itself of the stigma of "popularity" received from its close association with an ephemeral medium of publication, the magazine, which has been and continues to be given over to the rapid consumption of larger or smaller interest groups. Serious readers of fiction have come to a full appreciation of the formal advantages of the genre: its capacity for compression, and thus, for being fully understood and possessed as a unity in which the relation of each part to the whole may be perceived and held in the mind, as in a painting or lyric. Only with these smaller art forms can we have that rare delight of seeing a thing round and complete, and feeling, "this is a gem, this is perfection." A few of Miss Welty's stories offer exactly that rare delight: among them would be included "A Worn Path," "Livvie," "The Death of a Traveling Salesman," "A Curtain of Green," and "The Wide Net."

Miss Welty has also extended the range and potential of the story by the variety of her experiments in length, subject matter, theme, form, and feeling. Only when the totality of her work is known does one begin to see the whole as possibly greater than the sum of its parts. All she has hoped is to give us each story bright and new, like a surprise. She has wished no more than that we should see each particular story solitary— as a "little world in space, just as we can isolate one star in the sky by a concentrated vision." But after we have gazed for a long time at each of these little solitary worlds, some of them brighter, some dimmer, we begin to perceive the outlines of a new constellation of great depth and beauty, created by her vision, put out in the timeless world of art—"far out and endless, a constellation which the heart may read over many a night."

Notes and References

Chapter One

1. Most of the material in this chapter Miss Welty generously supplied the present writer during two interviews (March 14 and 15, 1961) and later by correspondence. I have also borrowed from information Miss Welty has given other interviewers, especially Robert Van Gelder (*New York Times Book Review*, June 14, 1942) and Katherine Hinds Smythe, who has kindly given me permission to use material from her unpublished master's thesis, "The Life and Works of Eudora Welty" (Duke University, 1954). References will be cited for direct quotations from printed sources only.

2. Robert Van Gelder, "An Interview with Eudora Welty," *Writers and Writing* (New York, 1946), p. 287.

3. *Ibid.*, p. 289.

4. Bernard Kalb, "The Author," *Saturday Review*, XXXVIII (April 9, 1955), 18.

5. Van Gelder, p. 290.

6. *Harper's Bazaar*, No. 2786 (February, 1944), p. 156.

7. This essay, originally given as an address at Cambridge University in 1955, was first published in *South Atlantic Quarterly*, LV (January, 1956), 57-72. In 1957 it was separately issued by House of Books in 300 copies, 20 pages, unnumbered. I have omitted all page references in my quotation from Miss Welty's essays and stories, because the relative brevity of her works has seemed to obviate the need, and the variety of forms of publication and editions has seemed only to complicate the use of exact page references.

8. "Eudora Welty," *Wilson Library Bulletin*, XVI (February, 1942), 410.

9. Van Gelder, p. 288.

10. *Virginia Quarterly Review*, XXXI (Spring, 1955), 240-51. Reprinted in Brooks and Warren, *Understanding Fiction* (New York, 1959), pp. 545-53.

11. Quotations from Miss Welty's work in this present volume are taken from versions of the stories appearing in collected editions, which in many cases are considerably revised from earlier versions appearing in magazines.

12. Van Gelder, p. 288.

13. Among the writers she has most freely praised are Faulkner, Chekhov, Virginia Woolf, Katherine Mansfield, James, Lawrence (with some reservations), and most recently and enthusiastically,

Henry Green, whose work has "intensity greater," she believes, "than that of any other writer of imaginative fiction today." (*Texas Quarterly*, IV [Autumn, 1961], 246.)

Chapter Two

1. *Short Stories* was originally an address on "The Reading and Writing of Short Stories" delivered by Miss Welty at the University of Washington in 1947. A shorter version was published in the *Atlantic Monthly*, CLXXXIII (February and March, 1949), 54-58, 46-49, and the full text by Harcourt, Brace in 1950.

2. The first two quotations cited are from *Short Stories*, the last three from "How I Write."

Chapter Three

1. William C. Seitz, *Claude Monet, Seasons and Moments*, published by the Museum of Modern Art (New York, March, 1960), pp. 8-9.

2. "The Love and Separateness in Miss Welty," *Kenyon Review*, VI (Spring, 1944), 254.

3. *Ibid.*

Chapter Four

1. E. B. White and Katherine S. White, *A Subtreasury of American Humor* (New York, 1941), pp. xvii, xviii.

2. Donald A. Ringe has suggested a further meaning of the word "pike," colloquial in New Orleans, the original home of Mrs. Pike. Apparently derived from "peek," the word means "to pry, to look with curiosity, to be nosy." *Explicator*, XVIII, No. 5 (February, 1960), Item 32.

3. Wylie Sypher, "The Meaning of Comedy," *Comedy* (New York, 1956), p. 235.

4. Review of *A Curtain of Green*, *Time*, XXXVIII (November 24, 1941), 111.

5. R. Van Gelder, "An Interview with Eudora Welty," *Writers and Writing*, p. 290.

6. W. Sypher, pp. 193, 194, 195.

7. "In Yoknapatawpha," *Hudson Review*, I (Winter, 1949), 597. A review of *Intruder in the Dust*.

Chapter Five

1. Mark Schorer, *The Story* (New York, 1950), pp. 354-55.

2. Robert Penn Warren, "Love and Separateness in Miss Welty," p. 247.

3. "The Abode of Summer," *Harper's Bazaar*, No. 2887 (June, 1952), p. 115.

Chapter Six

1. This point has been demonstrated by John Hardy, *"Delta Wedding* as Region and Symbol," *Sewanee Review,* LX (Summer, 1952), 398-401.

2. To the present writer in an interview on March 15, 1961.

Chapter Eight

1. Walter Elder, "That Region," *Kenyon Review,* XVII (Autumn, 1955), 661.

2. R. Van Gelder, "An Interview with Eudora Welty," *Writers and Writing,* p. 288.

3. "An Enchanted World in America," *New York Herald Tribune Book Review,* October 25, 1942, p. 19.

4. Bernard Kalb, "The Author," *Saturday Review,* XXXVIII (April 9, 1955), 18.

5. "Henry Green. A Novelist of the Imagination," *Texas Quarterly,* IV (Autumn, 1961), 246-47.

6. "The Teaching and Study of Writing," *Western Review,* XIV (Spring, 1950), 168. Cf. also *Place in Fiction:* "Writers must always write best of what they know. . . . But not for safety's sake. . . . In fact, when we think in terms of the spirit, which are the terms of writing, is there a conception more stupefying than that of security? . . . No art ever came out of not risking your neck. And risk—experiment—is a considerable part of the joy of doing. . . ."

Chapter Nine

1. Robert E. Spiller, *et al.,* "Postscript at Mid-Century," *Literary History of the United States* (New York, 1953), p. 1401.

2. Granville Hicks (ed.), *The Living Novel* (New York, 1957), p. 159.

3. Louis D. Rubin, Jr., and Robert D. Jacobs (eds.), *Southern Renascence* (Baltimore, 1953), p. 3.

4. *Ibid.,* p. 10.

5. Henry James, *The Art of the Novel,* edited by Richard Blackmur (New York, 1934), p. 46.

6. This passage appeared in the original version of the story, *Harper's Bazaar,* No. 2872 (March, 1951), p. 238. The slave's name was changed from Florabel to Delilah in the second version.

7. See Leon Edel, *The Psychological Novel, 1900-1950* (New York, 1955), for a discussion of this development in fiction.

8. James, *The Art of the Novel,* pp. 62, 63.

9. Sylvia Berkman, *Katherine Mansfield* (New Haven, 1951), p. 154.

10. Elizabeth Bowen, *Stories* (New York, 1959), p. vii.

11. *Ibid.*, pp. viii, ix.

12. Jocelyn Brooke, *Elizabeth Bowen* (London, 1952), pp. 7, 8.

13. Elizabeth Bowen, pp. viii, ix.

14. In a letter to the present writer, February 8, 1960.

15. Eugene Armfield, *New York Times Book Review,* September 26, 1943, p. 3.

16. Robert Penn Warren, "Love and Separateness in Miss Welty," p. 258.

17. *Atlantic Monthly,* CLXXV (June, 1945), 62.

18. *Vogue,* CIV (August 1, 1944), 102-3.

19. John Bagley, *The Characters of Love* (New York, 1960), pp. 7-8.

Selected Bibliography

WORKS OF EUDORA WELTY

I. *Fiction. (Stories collected in each volume are listed in chronological order of publication. A number in parentheses at the conclusion of an entry indicates number of appearances of that story in anthologies):*

A *Curtain of Green and Other Stories.* New York: Doubleday, Doran and Co., 1941.

"Death of a Traveling Salesman," *Manuscript,* III (June, 1936), 21-29. (5)

"A Piece of News," *Southern Review,* III (Summer, 1937), 80-84. (4)

"Flowers for Marjorie," *Prairie Schooner,* XI (Summer, 1937), 111-20. (1)

"A Memory," *Southern Review,* III (Fall, 1937), 317-22. (1)

"Lily Daw and the Three Ladies," *Prairie Schooner,* XI (Winter, 1937), 266-75. (2)

"Old Mr. Marblehall," *Southern Review,* III (Spring, 1938), 707-13 (under title "Old Mr. Grenada"). (2)

"The Whistle," *Prairie Schooner,* XII (Fall, 1938), 210-15. (1)

"A Curtain of Green," *Southern Review,* IV (Autumn, 1938), 292-98.

"Petrified Man," *Southern Review,* IV (Spring, 1939), 682-95. (14)

"The Hitch-Hikers," *Southern Review,* V (Fall, 1939), 293-307. (4)

"Keela, the Outcast Indian Maiden," *New Directions in Prose and Poetry, 1940.* James Laughlin, ed. Norfolk, Conn., 1940, pp. 109-17. (3)

"A Worn Path," *Atlantic Monthly,* CLXVII (February, 1941), 215-19. (12).

"Why I Live at the P. O.," *Atlantic Monthly,* CLXVII (April, 1941), 443-50. (10)

"Powerhouse," *Atlantic Monthly,* CLXVII (June, 1941), 707-13. (6)

"A Visit of Charity," *Decision,* I (June, 1941), 17-21. (7)

"Clytie," *Southern Review,* VII (Summer, 1941), 52-64. (1)

"The Key," *Harper's Bazaar,* No. 2754 (August, 1941), pp. 71, 132-34.

The Robber Bridegroom. New York: Doubleday, Doran and Co., 1942.

The Wide Net and Other Stories. New York: Harcourt, Brace and
Co., 1943.

"The Purple Hat," *Harper's Bazaar,* No. 2758 (November, 1941),
68-69, 115.

"First Love," *Harper's Bazaar,* No. 2761 (February, 1942), pp. 52-
53, 110-18. (1)

"A Still Moment," *American Prefaces,* VII (Spring, 1942), 226-
40. (7)

"The Wide Net," *Harpers Magazine,* CLXXXIV (May, 1942),
582-94. (3)

"The Winds," *Harper's Bazaar,* No. 2768 (August, 1942), pp.
92-93, 121-25. (2)

"Asphodel," *Yale Review,* XXXII (Autumn, 1942), 146-57. (1)

"Livvie," *Atlantic Monthly,* CLXX (November, 1942), 57-64 (under title "Livvie is Back"). (9)

"At the Landing," *Tomorrow,* II (April, 1943), 15-25.

Delta Wedding. New York: Harcourt, Brace and Co., 1946.

The Golden Apples. New York: Harcourt, Brace and Co., 1949.

"The Whole World Knows," *Harper's Bazaar,* No. 2823 (March,
1947), pp. 198-99, 332-38. (1)

"June Recital," *Harper's Bazaar,* No. 2829 (September, 1947),
pp. 216-17, 286-307, 311-20 (under title "Golden Apples").

"Shower of Gold," *Atlantic Monthly,* CLXXXI (May, 1948), 37-
42. (4)

Music from Spain. Published in a limited edition, Greenville, Miss.:
The Levee Press, 1948.

"Sir Rabbit," *Hudson Review,* II (Spring, 1949), 24-36.

"The Wanderers," *Harper's Bazaar,* No. 2847 (March, 1949), pp.
195-96, 227-34, 246-52 (under title "The Hummingbirds").

"Moon Lake," *Sewanee Review,* LVII (Summer, 1949), 464-508.

The Ponder Heart. New York: Harcourt, Brace and Co., 1954. Originally published in *The New Yorker,* XXIX (December 5,
1953), 47-138.

The Bride of the Innisfallen. New York: Harcourt, Brace and Co.,
1955.

"Circe," *Accent,* X (Autumn, 1949), 3-10 (under title "Put Me
in the Sky!"). (1)

"The Burning," *Harper's Bazaar,* No. 2872 (March, 1951), pp. 184,
238-47.

"The Bride of the Innisfallen," *The New Yorker,* XXVII (December 1, 1951), 53-84.

"No Place for You, My Love," *The New Yorker,* XXVIII (September 20, 1952), 37-44. (1)

"Kin," *The New Yorker*, XXVIII (November 15, 1952), 39-67.
"Ladies in Spring," *Sewanee Review*, LXII (Winter, 1954), 101-16 (under title "Spring").
"Going to Naples," *Harper's Bazaar*, No. 2912 (July, 1954), pp. 54-58, 100-3, 108-13. (1)

II. *A selected list of uncollected stories, narrative sketches, essays, and reviews:*

"The Doll," *The Tanager*, Grinnell College, Grinnell, Iowa, XI (June, 1936), 11-14.
"Hello and Goodbye," *Atlantic Monthly*, CLXXX (July, 1947), 37-40.
"Henry Green. A Novelist of the Imagination," *Texas Quarterly*, IV (Autumn, 1961), 246-56.
"How I Write," *Virginia Quarterly*, XXXI (Spring, 1955), 240-51. Reprinted in Brooks and Warren, *Understanding Fiction*, 2nd ed., 1959, pp. 545-53.
"Ida M'Toy," *Accent*, II (Summer, 1942), 214-22.
"In Yoknapatawpha," *Hudson Review*, I (Winter, 1949), 596-98. Review of Faulkner's *Intruder in the Dust*.
"José de Creeft," *Magazine of Art*, XXXVII (February, 1944), 42-47.
"Literature and the Lens," *Vogue*, CIV (August 1, 1944), 102-3.
"Pageant of Birds," *New Republic*, CIX (October 25, 1943), 565-67.
Place in Fiction. New York: House of Books, Ltd., 1957 (300 copies). Originally published in *South Atlantic Quarterly*, LV (January, 1956), 57-72.
"Retreat," *River*, I (March, 1937), 10-12.
Short Stories. New York: Harcourt, Brace and Co., 1950. A shorter version was published in *Atlantic Monthly*, CLXXXIII (February and March, 1949), 54-58, 46-49, under title "The Reading and Writing of Short Stories."
"A Sketching Trip," *Atlantic Monthly*, CLXXV (June, 1945), 62-70.
"Some Notes on River Country," *Harper's Bazaar*, No. 2786 (February, 1944), pp. 86-87, 150-56.

STUDIES OF EUDORA WELTY

I. *Bibliography:*

GROSS, SEYMOUR L. "Eudora Welty: A Bibliography of Criticism and Comment." *Sec.'s News Sheet*, Bibliographical Society, Univ. of Virginia, No. 45, April, 1960, pp. 1-32. An indispensable tool, containing an extensive list of critical essays and biographical articles, textbook explications of individual stories, and reviews of all Miss Welty's works, listed chronologically.

JORDAN, LEONA. "Eudora Welty: Selected Criticism," *Bulletin of Bibliography*, XXIII (January-April, 1960), 14-15. A short list of critical articles.

SYMTHE, KATHERINE H. "Eudora Welty: A Checklist," *Bulletin of Bibliography*, XXI (January-April, 1956), 207-8. Stories, books, and articles by Eudora Welty through July, 1954.

THURSTON, JARVIS, *et al. Short Fiction Criticism*. Denver: Alan Swallow, 1960, pp. 197-200. A valuable checklist of textbook interpretations and critical articles on twenty-five of Miss Welty's stories.

II. *A selected list of studies and reviews which treat at least one or more volumes of Miss Welty's fiction (explications of a single story only are not included):*

DANIEL, ROBERT. "The World of Eudora Welty," *Hopkins Review*, VI (Winter, 1953), 49-58. Reprinted in *Southern Renascence*, Louis D. Rubin, Jr. and Robert D. Jacobs, eds. Baltimore: The Johns Hopkins Press, 1953, pp. 306-15. A general résumé of Welty's work, dividing stories into four groups according to their characteristic settings; critical summary of *The Golden Apples*, interesting comparisons with Faulkner.

FOLSOM, GORDON R. "Form and Substance in Eudora Welty," Ph.D. dissertation, Univ. of Wisconsin, 1960. Available on Univ. Microfilm 60-3195. Excellent analysis of Welty's fiction in relation to southern regionalist theory and contemporary southern writing.

GLENN, EUNICE. "Fantasy in the Fiction of Eudora Welty," *A Southern Vanguard*, Allen Tate, ed. New York: Prentice-Hall, 1947, pp. 78-91. Reprinted in *Critiques and Essays on Modern Fiction, 1920-1951*, John Aldridge, ed. New York: The Ronald Press Company, 1952, pp. 506-17. Shows relationship of surface reality and fantasy in Welty's fiction; contains an interesting though somewhat forced analogy between Hawthorne and Welty's use of allegory and symbolism.

GRIFFITH, ALBERT J. "Eudora Welty's Fiction," Ph.D. dissertation, Univ. of Texas, 1959. Available on Univ. Microfilm 59-4719. A good over-all study of Welty's fiction, stressing her use of "place," modes of characterization, mastery of moods, characteristic themes, and style.

HARDY, JOHN E. "*Delta Wedding* as Region and Symbol," *Sewanee Review*, LX (Summer, 1952), 397-417. An excellent critical analysis of the symbolic structure of the novel, based on the thesis that it is a "version of pastoral."

HEILMAN, ROBERT B. "The Southern Temper," *Hopkins Review,*
VI (Fall, 1952), 5-15. Reprinted in *Southern Renascence,* pp.
3-13. A general summary of the outlook of southern writers,
useful as background.

HICKS, GRANVILLE. "Eudora Welty," *College English,* XIV (November, 1952), 69-76. Also in *The English Journal,* XLI (November, 1952), 461-68. A valuable introduction to characteristic
themes and techniques of Welty's fiction, showing her use of
objective and subjective narration, her versatility, the universality inherent in her regionalism.

JONES, WILLIAM M. "Name and Symbol in the Prose of Eudora
Welty," *Southern Folklore Quarterly,* XXII (December, 1958),
173-85. A rather heavy-handed treatment of mythical sources
and parallels in Welty's fiction—several far-fetched—assuming
she began with mythical materials and then found ways to
"modernize and southernize" them.

MORRIS, HARRY C. "Eudora Welty's Use of Mythology," *Shenandoah,*
VI (Spring, 1955), 34-40. Shows progress of Welty's use of
myth culminating in *The Golden Apples,* and places her work
in the tradition of Pound, Joyce, Eliot, and Yeats.

PORTER, KATHERINE ANNE. "Introduction" to *A Curtain of Green,*
1941. Reprinted as Introduction to Modern Library edition of
Selected Stories of Eudora Welty (New York: Random House,
1954), pp. xi-xxiii, and in *The Days Before* (New York: Harcourt, Brace and Co., 1952), pp. 101-8. A sympathetic introduction to Welty's life and a critical appraisal of *A Curtain
of Green.*

RANSOM, JOHN CROWE. "Delta Fiction," *Kenyon Review,* VIII (Summer, 1946), 503-7. A warm appreciation of *Delta Wedding,*
but a gentle rebuke for its failure to exhibit "political sense."

RUBIN, LOUIS D., JR. "Two Ladies of the South," *Sewanee Review,*
LXIII (Autumn, 1955), 671-81. An interesting treatment of
the use of time in *The Bride.*

TRILLING, DIANA. "Fiction in Review," *Nation,* CLXII (May 11,
1946), 578. A negative review of *Delta Wedding* for its nostalgic treatment of southern culture; an attack on its value-scheme and style.

WARREN, ROBERT PENN. "The Love and the Separateness in Miss
Welty," *Kenyon Review,* VI (Spring, 1944), 246-59. Reprinted
in Warren's *Selected Essays* (New York: Random House, 1958),
156-69. The best of the essays on *A Curtain of Green* and
The Wide Net, showing basic themes and techniques of Welty's
early fiction; also a considered refutation of Diana Trilling's
charges against *The Wide Net* for its self-conscious virtuosity
(*Nation,* October 2, 1942, pp. 386-87).

Index